CW00410166

TITANIC AND THE
CALIFORNIAN

TITANIC AND THE CALIFORNIAN

THOMAS B. WILLIAMS

Edited and revised by
Rob Kamps

TEMPUS

Frontispiece:

Above: One of the last photographs of the Titanic ever taken as she prepared to steam out of Cork Harbour and into the history books. Courtesy of *Cork Examiner.*

Below: The Californian pictured in 1902. Courtesy of Peabody Museum of Salem.

First published 2007

Tempus Publishing Limited
The Mill, Brimscombe Port,
Stroud, Gloucestershire, GL5 2QG
www.tempus-publishing.com

© Thomas B. Williams. Edited and revised by Rob Kamps 2007

The right of Thomas B. Williams, Edited and revised by Rob Kamps
to be identified as the Authors
of this work has been asserted in accordance with the
Copyrights, Designs and Patents Act 1988.

All rights reserved. No part of this book may be reprinted
or reproduced or utilised in any form or by any electronic,
mechanical or other means, now known or hereafter invented,
including photocopying and recording, or in any information
storage or retrieval system, without the permission in writing
from the Publishers.

British Library Cataloguing in Publication Data.
A catalogue record for this book is available from the British Library.

ISBN 978 0 7524 4278 5

Typesetting and origination by Tempus Publishing Limited
Printed in Great Britain

Contents

Dedication

Not many men can count themselves lucky enough to enjoy the love and respect of two wonderful women in their lives. It is therefore with great love in my heart that I dedicate this book to my late wife Mary, who passed away before this work was completed, and to my current darling wife Marie, my best friend and soulmate, who has always had faith in my passion for writing. Thank you both for putting up with me!

This book also honours most respectfully the memory of all those men, women and children who lost their lives in the freezing waters of the North Atlantic when the White Star Liner RMS *Titanic* slipped beneath the waves on that fateful night of 14 April 1912. It is also dedicated to all those people who, over the intervening years, have carried on a relentless fight to clear the good name of an officer and a gentleman – the late Captain Stanley Lord – Master of the SS *Californian* and yet another victim of the *Titanic* tragedy.

Foreword

'The purpose of this book is to get to the facts' states its author Tom Williams, and he has certainly made a determined and fascinating effort to do so.

Titanic and the Californian is an in-depth investigation into what went wrong on that fateful night of 14 April 1912. It goes behind the headlines and delves into the contemporary reports to study the many contentious issues surrounding one of the greatest maritime tragedies the world has known.

Tom Williams re-examines the entire situation with the eye of a lawyer who might have been present at the time, and he arrives at some thought-provoking conclusions. He finds Captain Stanley Lord of the Californian innocent of any crime and proves his case beyond the slightest shadow of a doubt. Being a fervent believer in the integrity of Captain Lord, I am personally delighted about this and am most impressed at how he has set out to prove his case most meticulously. It is an issue of which I feel strongly about and that, I suspect, is why Tom Williams invited me to write this foreword. Indeed, I dedicated a book on the tragedy to the memory of the captain, whom I too believe to have been a man maligned.

No pun is intended when I say that this book delves much deeper into the events of that momentous night than it was possible for me to do in my own slim paperback, which focused primarily on the characters and personalities aboard both vessels. One astounding and important point made by the author is that the RMS Titanic was, in fact, unseaworthy and should never have been allowed to be put to sea in the condition she was in! But this fact – like so many others – was covered up in order to keep certain aristocratic and political noses clean.

To back up his claim, Tom Williams has produced some vital and remarkable evidence, hitherto hidden from the general public. His thorough and relentless research over a number of years has finally put him in a position to unearth the truth surrounding the tragedy. What is the truth? Sorry, but to reveal it at this stage would be to spoil the reader's enjoyment of the book. Suffice it to say that his intensive research and attention to detail produced evidence sufficiently impressive for the 'Powers That Be' to reopen the hornets' nest after a lapse of almost eighty years. The (then) Secretary of State was finally put in a position to give his blessing for a reappraisal of the entire case surrounding Captain Lord.

And it was particularly kind of Tom Williams to give me first bite of the journalistic cherry in order for my own paper to have a world exclusive.

Predictably, when the story broke, Titanic buffs the world over were wild with excitement. They – like the Press – recognised a hot potato when they saw one. However, over a decade onwards, the buffs are still divided between Lordites (those who believe Captain Lord was guilty of no crime) and anti-Lordites (those who insist on perpetuating the myth that Lord's ship was nearer to the scene of the tragedy than it actually was). Even after the findings of the Marine Accident Investigation Branch (MAIB) were finally made public, the antis refused to see sense. It is to be hoped that Tom Williams' book will act as an eye-opener and change their views.

In any event, it has been established that the Titanic and the Californian were not the only two vessels involved that fateful night. Tom Williams has shown that there were up to seven ships in the general area – some of them unidentified.

Indeed, the captain of one of the ships made a written statement shortly after the disaster which would have effectively cleared Captain Lord of any wrongdoing, had anyone in authority taken notice. Odd, is it not, how that statement mysteriously 'disappeared' and, though it did in fact reappear from time to time, no one obviously attached enough importance to it to take action. What we now know of course – but did not know then – is that it was all part of the plan to throw blame on Captain Lord and thus divert attention from the truly guilty. Enter one ready-made scapegoat!

As a direct result of the remarkable amount of research conducted by this probing writer, all sorts of other snippets of information are revealed. Who among us for instance, knew of the Lusitania's involvement in the case and the proliferation of suspect and dirty deeds among the high and mighty?

Tom Williams has done his work well. What he has produced reads like a first-rate detective story. And on that point I speak authoritatively. As a professional book reviewer, I am called upon to read over 100 books per month. Most are read in the speedy style we reviewers cultivate, but a few – a rare few – are read and enjoyed from cover to cover. This book is one such.

I devoured it in a single sitting, staying up all night to do so. I came away being reminded of two other real-life mysteries, narrated with equal gusto. One was about Jack the Ripper, the Victorian murderer whose identity has always been something of a mystery. The other was about the death of Marilyn Monroe, who died under questionable circumstances. Conspiracy theories surrounded these cases, just as they do the Titanic.

Scandal in high places of course is nothing new and, when it occurs, there is inevitably a scapegoat. Poor Captain Lord; an honourable, but self-effacing man, he was never given the opportunity to defend himself in public, preferring to maintain his dignity and treat the character assassination with the contempt it deserved. He knew that he was innocent, and so did anyone with any sense. What else mattered?

So now, at long last, the good captain has been exonerated of any implication in the deaths of all those unfortunate people. In almost every sense of the word, Captain Lord, too, was just as much an innocent victim of the tragedy as those who perished. Now however, justice has finally been done. How entirely laudable that this new and enthusiastic author has made such a determined effort to get the facts in order to clear an innocent man's name – albeit posthumously.

Tom Williams' fascinating and remarkable book deserves to take its place, not only in the annals of maritime documentation, but prominently displayed in bookshops and libraries internationally.

RMS Titanic did not sink, he insists, but was sunk. Read the book. Not only is it guaranteed to upturn all those old prejudices and myths, but it must surely shed a powerful beam of light on the events of that cold, dark night in the North Atlantic; a night which resulted in the loss of over 1,500 human lives and the reputation of an honest and honourable man.

Sadly, those lives are lost forever, until that final day when the sea shall give up her dead, but fortunately, thanks to Tom Williams, the good name and character of the late captain has finally been restored.

Thomas B. Williams has paved the way. The time has now come for a public apology.

Monica O'Hara
Merseyside, 2007

Preface

Down through the centuries the sea and ships have conjured up many thoughts of adventure and excitement to the mind of man. Perhaps because of its vastness and unpredictability, a certain amount of respect and mystery has always attached itself to this great section of our planet which we call the sea.

Few ships have ever made such an impact on the mind and imagination of mankind as the White Star liner RMS Titanic. This colossus of a ship, more than a sixth of a mile long and as tall as an eleven-storey building, was launched in Belfast on 31 May 1911. As yet without her four gigantic funnels or her massive superstructure, the Titanic was a ship already blooded. As she rolled down the slipway on that memorable day almost a century ago, assisted by no less than twenty-three tons of oil, soft soap and tallow, some of the shorings gave way, pinning an unfortunate workman beneath the giant hull and killing him instantly. The tragedy received little attention in the popular press, being overshadowed by the fascinating story of man's spectacular feat of engineering. Those who did remark on the tragedy declared it to be a bad omen and said it boded some sinister evil to befall the ship. Little did they realise how accurate their predictions were to be.

Curiously enough, although thousands of people had gathered to watch the launching of the world's largest ship, no official ceremony or naming of the Titanic ever took place. She was simply run into the waters of Belfast Lough, and that was that. A shipyard worker at the time is quoted as saying, 'They just builds'er and shoves'er in.'

There were, of course, many reports of premonitions of disaster regarding the Titanic, ranging from the ludicrous to the unexplainable. Perhaps one of the most profound and thought-provoking of these is Morgan Robertson's story, Futility. However, it is not the intention of this book to delve into the supernatural aspects of the tragedy of the Titanic. Suffice it to say that when the Titanic steamed out to the wide Atlantic on her maiden voyage, fate had already taken a hand. The premonitions and the predictions were about to be fulfilled in a frightening manner and the lives of thousands of people were about to be affected for all time. One of those people whose life the Titanic was to touch was a quiet family man who was not even onboard the ship. In fact, when the tragedy struck he was many miles away. Yet consequences, and the aftermath of the disaster, were destined to catapult him into the headlines of the media where he would find himself branded as a coward and a drunken murderer. This unassuming man would see his reputation in shreds, his good character in ruins, and his very name spoken of with derision. Cruel fate would ordain that he would be castigated and maligned for the rest of his life. Forever after, his name was to be inextricably linked to that of the Titanic. He was to become as famous as Captain Edward J. Smith, the Master of the Titanic. His name? Captain Stanley Lord, Master of the SS Californian.

In the media of 1912, such as it was, sensationalists of the writing fraternity immediately pounced on the story of Captain Lord and, in many instances, padded out their stories with various embellishments. By and large, it mattered not to these people that the allegations made against Captain Lord were nothing more than just that, allegations. Neither, apparently, did it matter that the reputation of this man was being sacrificed to public opinion. It was, in effect, an early example of 'trial by media' and, as quite often happens in such cases, the media won. This of course gives rise to the observation that if something appeared in print, people were inclined to believe it. People, it must be said, do not appear to have changed much in this respect. Nowadays, however, unfortunates who find themselves maligned in any way by the media have recourse to actions to defend themselves. Such was not the case with Stanley Lord. Everybody will no doubt be aware of the procedure which follows a road traffic accident. The police and ambulance arrive, and, after performing their respective duties, depart. A pick-up truck from some garage will then arrive and tow away the vehicles involved in the accident. Finally, the road is swept up by the local council and life gradually reverts back to normal. Eventually, as time progresses, the incident becomes but a dim, distant memory in the minds of the locals and, in time, that too slips away and is finally forgotten. It is forgotten by everyone, except by those who were directly involved in the accident. Although the wrecks have all been cleared away and the legal process dealt with, the consequences of the accident will go on and on – particularly if serious injury or death has occurred. So it was with Stanley Lord. The consequences refuse to go away.

Without doubt there are still very many people for whom the consequences relating to the Titanic tragedy will go on and on, handed down from one generation to the other. The better-known survivors immediately spring to mind, so do the relatives of those who lost their lives on that cold night out in the North Atlantic. For the vast majority of those who either survived or lost their lives on that fateful 15 April, someone, somewhere, remembers them, albeit those relatives now probably boast of the fact rather than bemoan it. Sadly, it is now recognised as the 'in' thing to have had a connection with the Titanic. While this may appear on the surface to be rather unkind, it is, however, a facet of human nature. Granted, not everybody is inclined to puff up their feathers and boast of having a connection with the Titanic. There are those who undoubtedly still have a very deep feeling of lasting sadness and frustration over the affair. Perhaps it is only these people who can fully appreciate what Captain Lord – and his family – felt in this respect. It is a sad commentary of our times that over the years, and right up to his death in 1962, Captain Lord (and since then, his son) had to suffer the good name of his family being sullied and maligned in a veritable collection of newspapers, magazines, film and television programmes. It must be said that all of those people were not unscrupulous writers out to make money. They were, by and large, sincere people who relied upon the 'evidence' as it pertained at the time. There were, however, other writers of a more dubious nature who used the name of Stanley Lord as one would a common criminal. These people were not interested in the truth. They were only interested in a story – any story – as long as it sold the shabby pages of the gutter press and made them some money. After all, the truth can often be boring. Fiction is much more acceptable and the gate can always be left open for future embellishments.

In retrospect, we can see that human nature has changed very little over the intervening years. Perhaps it will never change. Then, as now, whenever a tragedy of substantial proportion occurs, it is almost second nature to immediately point the finger of blame – as long as the finger is pointed at someone else! In this case the unfortunate person at whom the finger of blame and hate was pointed was Captain Lord. There is perhaps no situation more painful for any person, or indeed so emotive, than to be blamed for something he or she did not do. In such a devastating situation, the emotion and sense of helplessness is increased and magnified ten-fold when nobody believes you. The situation is made all the more traumatic and exasperating when it has the unwanted effect of interfering with your life and the lives of your family, and you find yourself utterly unable to do anything to resolve the situation. This, then, was the unenviable predicament in which Stanley Lord found himself after the Titanic disaster. It was, sadly, destined to become a long drawn-out emotional situation which was to follow him to the grave. It can only be to the captain's credit, not to mention his stalwart character, that, in spite of being so castigated and losing his job, he simply refused to let the situation wear him down. Where a lesser man might have taken many courses of action to evade the public attention, Captain Lord simply got on with his life as befitting a man with a clear conscience.

This is a book which is not interested in sensationalism or idle speculation and conjecture. It is a book which attempts to put the facts before the reader and, it is hoped, set the record straight once and for all. It is a matter of sincere regret that this can only be done now, so long after the captain's death. Nevertheless it is still vitally important that the facts of the case be made public and that the truth, both from the point of view of posterity and justice, be made known, and that the slur which has attached itself to the name of Captain Stanley Lord for far too long be removed. In essence, this book is written not only for the foregoing reasons, but to show the world that Justice is finally being done, and being seen to be done, and that decency still prevails in this mad world.

Acknowledgements

I wish to express my sincere and deep appreciation to my good friend and colleague Rob Kamps of Maastricht, in the Netherlands, for his unstinting and devoted attention to the editing and revision of this book and also for his literary skills in preparing the book for publication. Many, many thanks, Rob!

I must also acknowledge my deep and sincere appreciation to fellow writer Monica Harding O'Hara. Monica is more than deserving of all my appreciation, not only for her dogged insistence that Captain Lord was an innocent man and as much a victim of the Titanic tragedy as those poor unfortunates who lost their lives on that great ship, but also for kindly agreeing to write the foreword to this book. Indeed, it is as a direct result of Monica's convictions that this book came to be written and that the evidence unearthed during research was instrumental in bringing about a reappraisal of the evidence surrounding Captain Lord.

I must likewise offer a very special word of thanks and appreciation to Mr Stanley Tutton Lord, Captain Lord's son, now also deceased, for bearing with me in what must have been for him an opening of old wounds.

In England, my sincere thanks go to Mr John Booth of White Star Publications, formerly Titanic Signals Archive, co-author (with Sean Coughlan) of *Titanic: Signals of Disaster*, for his permission to reproduce his Olympic Message Book in full. I'd like to also thank the author Mr Geoff Whitfield of Merseyside; author Mr Brian Ticehurst of Southampton; Mr Howard G. Mortimer from the Department of Leisure and Tourism in Liverpool; Mr Gordon J. Read of Merseyside, who is Curator of Archives, National Museum and Galleries; author Mr Richard Garrett of Tunbridge Wells in Kent; author/journalist Mr Derek Whale (deceased) of Liverpool; Mr Alastair Porsyth, who is a maritime researcher in Southampton City;

Messrs Lloyds of Lime Street in London and the Public Record Office in Kew. I must also record my grateful appreciation to my late friend and mentor, Mr Leslie Harrison (RIP). The invaluable assistance of this noble man will always be remembered.

A special word of thanks to the staff and officers of the Marine Accident Investigation Branch, Guildhall Library in Aldermanbury, London. Also thanks to the Department of Transport which put up with my incessant representations on behalf of Captain Lord. In particular, I wish to extend my appreciation to Chief Inspector Captain P.B. Marriott; Deputy Chief Inspector Captain J. de Coverly; Commissioned Inspector Captain T.W. Barnett and also to the British Secretary of State (then Mr Cecil Parkinson, MP) for reopening the case.

In Northern Ireland my thanks go to Mr Michael McCaughan, author and curator of the Ulster Folk & Transport Museum in County Down, and to Messrs Harland and Wolff of Belfast.

In the Republic of Ireland grateful thanks to Patricia Grimes of the Irish Titanic Historical Society, the historical librarian Mr David O'Brien of the Cork County Library; Dr John de Courcy (1911–2006) from the Maritime Institute of Ireland; Dr R.B. Swain from the Department of Applied Psychology at University College in Cork. Although Dr Swain was able to offer little in the way of concrete assistance with my research, he did manage to bring a smile to my lips and therefore merits a mention for psychology successfully applied. Thanks as well to journalist Mr Colm Connolly of Radio Telefis Eireann; the staff of the American embassy in Dublin; the Cork Examiner Newspaper Group on Patrick Street in Cork; photographer Mr Bob Rock of Youghal, County Cork; and printer and stationer Mr Billy Field of Youghal, County Cork.

In America, my thanks go to Messrs Charles Haas and Jack Eaton of the Titanic International Society Org.; Mr Ed and Mrs Karen Kamuda of the Titanic Historical Society Inc.; and Mr Jon Hollis of Whitman, Massachusetts. Jon, a worldwide authority on shipping in general, and the Titanic in particular, has become a valued friend. Thanks also to the Peabody Museum of Salem, Massachusetts, and author Mr Joseph A. Carvalho of Winchester, Massachusetts. Joe too has become a good friend and his letters are always looked forward to with great interest.

In Sweden, my sincere thanks to Mr Claes-Goran Wetterholm, author, lecturer and noted authority on Titanic and Lusitania.

In Spain, special appreciation to Mr Pete Elverhøi of the former Den Nordiske Titanic Foreningen.

In conclusion, I must offer my deepest gratitude and appreciation to all those kind people who took the time and trouble to respond to my various advertisements for information and who kindly offered me all their assistance. They are, unfortunately, much too numerous to mention here. Suffice it to say that the intentions of these good people were more than instrumental in bringing about justice for Captain Lord and his memory. I salute you.

Finally, if there are any people or organisations whom I have inadvertently forgotten to include in my list of acknowledgements, I sincerely offer my apologies and deepest thanks.

Thomas B. Williams

Youghal and Portaferry, 2007

About the Author

Thomas B. Williams was born in the seafaring town of Youghal, County Cork in 1946. Williams was always highly interested in the sea and its mysteries. He has published many articles and stories of a maritime nature, and this – his first major work – is a passionate crusade to clear the name of an innocent man.

Quite a few obstacles and disappointments were to be put in his way before this book saw the light of day. Sadly, in October of 1991 his young wife passed away from breast cancer, leaving him to rear five young children. For the next decade he put his writing on the back burner and concentrated on raising his family. Then fate took a hand in his life. He met and married a lovely lady from Northern Ireland who had also lost her partner to this dreadful disease. Today, more than a decade after he thought his world had ended, Thomas is living happily with his new wife in Portaferry, County Down, and is determined to make up for all the lost years of writing. He is currently working on a book about emigration during the famine times and hopes to include some of the local history of Portaferry and its environs during that time.

The author,
Thomas B. Williams.

Editor

Mr Rob Kamps, translator and researcher, became convinced of Captain Lord's innocence when he was first intrigued by the subject in 1974 while reading Peter Padfield's *The Titanic and the Californian* and gladly accepted the invitation to update and revise Thomas B. Williams' almost forgotten manuscript. In addition, Kamps completed a detailed article with author Eric Longo, 'Mauretania, Last Voyages, Demolition and Remaining Artefacts', of that great liner's demise seven decades ago.

Kamps wishes to express his gratitude to Mr Williams and to Master Mariner Mr Leslie Harrison (1912–1997), author of *A Titanic Myth* and general secretary of the Mercantile Marine Service Association from 1956 until 1975, to whom Captain Lord turned for help in 1958 after reading about his portrayal in the movie *A Night to Remember*. Mr Harrison became thus the prime mover in the campaign on Lord's behalf, and as such had all the facts pertaining to the case at his fingertips. Harrison was a truly great and gifted person, modest, scrupulously honest and dedicated to his cause. At present he is maligned, like the man he defended, by individuals who oppose him and allege that he suppressed evidence that would otherwise have damaged Lord's case. However, in a libel suit against the publishers of a rogue book of highly dubious origin and content, on the basis of which these people still think they can build a solid case, the high court judge ruled in 1995 that Mr Harrison 'has always been motivated by a desire to uncover the truth'. The truth also is that all his critics are self-appointed experts laying down the law about technical matters on which they are not, in the least, qualified to speak. Unlike any of them, Mr Harrison was technically qualified as a Master Mariner, appointed navigation instructor to RAF-pilots during the Second World War, which proved that his superiors had absolute faith in him. Harrison proved rightfully the Californian could not have possibly saved any additional lives. This rogue book was withdrawn from sale as a result of the court's decision. The publisher offered Mr Harrison a formal apology for the false statements it contained about him and agreed to pay him a substantial sum of damages in compensation.

Kamps also wishes to thank Ms Diana Bristow of Florida, USA, author of *Titanic R.I.P. Can Dead Men Tell Tales* (1989) and *Sinking the Myths* (1995). The latter book also provides insight into the political and social structures of the Edwardian era and explores a cover-up. It is the most comprehensive account of the Titanic disaster and its aftermath so far.

Gratitude is also due to the late Mr Dave Carr, an antiquarian book dealer in Merseyside, for his suggestions.

Many thanks as well to Mr Charles P. Chafee of Pennsylvania, USA, author of *The Californian Question* (1989), which is a re-assessment after Titanic's 1985 discovery and numerous other articles in Captain Lord's favour. Mr Chafee has carried out experiments on the distance audibility of fireworks. He has also studied appropriate manuals at the time concerning the precise Board of Trade-certified distress signals.

Mr Kamps also sends special thanks to the following people for their support and comments: Mr Tim P. Cooper, a railway and paddle steamer historian and long-time friend in the UK who proofread the final draft of the manuscript, Mr Jean Frèrejean of the Netherlands who scanned the original manuscript and relentlessly assisted in tackling numerous problems. The layout of the book is entirely his work. Thanks also to Mr Eric Longo of New York, USA, who is a landscape painter, a 1939 New York World's Fair researcher and an avid collector of original photographs of the first Cunard Mauretania. Thanks are also due to Mr Peter Padfield of the UK, author of *The Titanic and the Californian* (1965), to Dr Alan Ruffman, president of Geomarine Associates Ltd in Halifax, Nova Scotia, Canada, to Mr Paul Slish of Buffalo, New York, USA, who also proofread and offered technical assistance, and to Mrs Muriel and her late husband Mr Jim Fairweather of the UK, who knew Stanley T. Lord personally for over thirty years.

List of Illustrations
and Letters

Photographs

Notes on Technical Terms

Distances shown in the charts included may be calculated by allowing one nautical mile to each minute of latitude. The directional bearing from one ship to another remains the same regardless of what direction either ship's bow is pointing or heading. Titanic's estimated rate of speed at the time of the collision was twenty-two knots, equal to approximately 25mph.

Bells and Watches Onboard Ship

Time is kept by a bell, struck every half-hour. To divide the work fairly, the crew is divided into two watches – starboard (right side, looking forward) and the port side (left). The day commences at noon, and is divided thus:

WATCH BELLS   (in half-hours)

Afternoon	Noon to 4.00 p.m. (1 to 8)
First dog	4.00 p.m. to 6.00 p.m. (1,2,3,4)
Second dog (last)	6.00 p.m. to 8.00 p.m. (1,2,3,8)
First Night	8.00 p.m. to Midnight (1 to 8)
Middle	Midnight to 4.00 a.m. (1 to 8)
Morning	4.00 a.m. to 8.00 a.m. (1 to 8)
Forenoon	8.00 a.m. to noon (1 to 8)

This makes seven watches which the crew keeps alternately, so that the watch which is on duty in the forenoon one day has the afternoon the next day. The men who have only four hours' rest one night have eight hours the next night. This is the reason for having dog watches, which are made by dividing the hours between 4.00p.m. and 8.00p.m. into two short watches.

Ten cables (6,080ft) is equal to one nautical mile. One nautical mile is equal to 2,026 2/3 yards. Sixty nautical miles are equal to one degree, or 69.09 statute miles.

ONE

The Unsinkable Lifeboat

When one of the largest and most opulent liners the world has ever seen sinks with an appalling loss of life after colliding with an iceberg, some might call the tragedy an 'Act of God'. Others might say it was the direct result of irresponsible seamanship, coupled with defective manufacturing and a complete lack of foresight.

We shall not dwell too long on the events of the night and morning of 14/15 April 1912. Suffice it to say that we know that the pride of the White Star Line, RMS Titanic struck an iceberg in the North Atlantic while on her maiden voyage and subsequently sank with the loss of over 1,500 souls. Neither would it serve any useful purpose to re-hash the same old story all over again – that has been done far too often and far too inaccurately. Within these pages we are concerned with a tragedy of equal importance to the loss of the Titanic, the tragedy of Captain Stanley Lord. While both tragedies are inextricably linked, that of Captain Lord is one that has existed for far too long.

Thanks to modern technology we now know that the once sumptuous liner is lying in two main sections over two miles down on the floor of the Atlantic, with her expensive innards strewn across a wide expanse of the seabed, which also marks the resting place of over 1,000 men, women and children. At the outset, it is perhaps best to realise that, all things being equal, this magnificent ship should not have sunk. Her destruction was one of those 'one in a million' probabilities. Nevertheless it would be quite incorrect to say that the iceberg was solely responsible for the disaster. The iceberg, if anything, was but a contributing factor in the affair – a major factor, it must be admitted. There were of course many other contributing factors on that sorrowful night – the speed of the ship, the ignored warnings, the lack of any realistic lifeboat drill. Even the actual design of the ship itself contributed to her loss. It would be so easy to point the finger of blame at the Titanic's captain, Edward J. Smith, and say that he was negligent in the handling of his ship. He was later found to be guilty of recklessness. It must be pointed out that Captain Smith in fact did not quite do everything a captain should have done under the circumstances. However, it would also be both cruel and unfair to condemn a man who, losing his life as he did, was not in a position to defend his actions. The question of the captain's guilt or negligence must rest with the reader.

In order to ascertain the truth of the affair of the Titanic and the Californian involvement, it is necessary to take a long hard look at the cold facts surrounding the case. In order to do this in as fair a manner as possible, it is vital that we do not allow our emotions to become swayed by either sentiment or feelings of pity. In stripping the case of all its veneer and polish, we must accept several facts. Firstly, Captain Edward John Smith was the master of the Titanic and, as such, had a duty and moral responsibility to bring his ship safely to port and safeguard the lives and property of those under his care. This, for reasons which have become apparent, he failed to do. Secondly, he had obviously slipped into a state of shock when faced with the inescapable fact that his latest command, with the largest vessel in the world, was about to founder with terrific loss of life. He is reported to have done everything possible under the circumstances to protect the lives entrusted to his care when the end was a foregone conclusion. He continued to assist passengers and crew in the freezing water, eventually losing his own life. However, as a result of losing overall control, probably due to his mental state, he did fail to see that the lifeboats, already hopelessly insufficient in number, were filled to capacity. Several factors are major mitigating circumstances in Captain Smith's favour, and it would be totally wrong to condemn someone who was faced with such extreme conditions and his own impending death. It is therefore not the brief of this writer to stand in judgement of this unfortunate man.

The irony of the Titanic affair is such that if a certificate of seaworthiness were to be applied for in present-day standards, it would invariably be refused. The fact is, it should also have been refused in 1912. By virtue of the design of her bulkheads, which did not run high enough, the Titanic was in fact utterly unseaworthy and, despite the fact that the Board of Trade and the owners were fully aware of this, the ship was still allowed to be put to sea. Many reasons have been put forward for this decision, and while they may be construed as speculation, there is a ring of truth about them. Firstly, the White Star Line was loath to have any further delays and keen to put

Captain E.J. Smith, Master of
the RMS Titanic and Olympic.

their magnificent new ship into competition with their archrival Cunard and, secondly, the British government was also anxious to show off its ship-building prowess to the world. It was also suggested that the owners were not keen on disappointing the rich passengers, who represented the cream of affluent society. Whatever the reasons, the Titanic sailed off on what was destined to be a voyage of disaster.

As we shall be referring frequently to both American and British investigations into the tragedy, as well as taking a look at other 'evidence' put forward by those who, for one reason or another, found it necessary to blame Captain Lord for the loss of 1,500 lives, we will also take a brief look at the code of law and define the word 'evidence'. It would be well to bear in mind that Captain Lord was never tried in any court of law. Neither was he officially charged with any crime. Lord merely appeared as a witness in the case and had very little legal representation to argue his plight.

However, once the formal investigation had refused him an appeal, Lord's legal advisors found their hands effectively tied and there was little they could do to alter the decision of the court. The way, in effect, was closed to Captain Lord to attempt to clear his name. It was the Board of Trade which carried out the inquiry into the disaster, albeit a public inquiry, which, in effect, meant that the Board of Trade was actually investigating the Board of Trade. As they naturally already had questions at hand, it was but a simple job to suit the answers to them. This they did admirably. This rather suspicious action has been labelled as an effort to keep certain aristocratic noses clean and, to all intents and purposes, it worked quite well.

Although the Board of Trade was responsible, among other things, for the lack of sufficient lifeboats on the Titanic and, as we have seen, responsible for putting up the British inquiry, they were to state in the course of the investigation that if Captain Lord had come to the assistance of the Titanic, he might have been able to save 'most if not all of the lives which were lost'. Apparently it did not occur to them to say that if the Board of Trade had provided the ship with sufficient lifeboats, they might have saved many, if not all of the lives which were lost. This of course was a classic case of the 'reversed proof technique', and it worked out 100 per cent for the Board of Trade. Fortunately for them, the ship had sunk on an even keel. Had it listed heavily, only fifty per cent of the boats (ten) could have been used, increasing the death toll even more. Considering these pertinent points, it is hardly surprising that everyone connected with the affair came out of the inquiry unharmed, everyone except Stanley Lord.

Common Law

Common law denotes law which is the same for all members of society and is based on custom and usage as distinct from legislation. One of its maxims is that the king/state must recognise law which created the king/state. Common law is distinguished from statute law, which is enacted by Parliament and from civil law, which emphasises the power of the State.

Criminal Law

As distinct from law which deals with the private wrongs of individuals, (civil law), criminal law is concerned with acts which are contrary to peace, order and the well-being of society. It is an attempt by the State to preserve public order by making guilty persons liable to punishment in order to curb any tendency towards private vengeance. Criminal law recognises blame-worthy intention as a necessary component to a criminal offence. Before a person can be convicted of a crime, two things have to be proved. Firstly, an act forbidden by criminal law has resulted from an individual's conduct and, secondly, this conduct was accompanied by blameworthy intention. Criminal law requires that both of these must be proved beyond reasonable doubt.

Evidence

Evidence consists of statements made by witnesses in court about criminal matters, and includes relevant documents and exhibits. The purpose of evidence is to prove or disprove particular matters relating to a crime to the satisfaction of a jury. Evidence falls into two categories (classes): direct and circumstantial. Direct evidence is provided by an eye-witness who has seen a crime committed. Circumstantial evidence involves relevant facts from which inferences may be drawn that a crime was committed – the operative word being 'fact', as opposed to hearsay, gossip, speculation or rumour. This is necessary to protect the interests of the accused person. Remember, a person is deemed to be innocent until 'proven guilty beyond all reasonable doubt'. Consequently, certain forms of testimony are regarded as inadmissible. In court, the examination and cross-examination of witnesses forms the heart of the criminal trial. The witness relates what he saw or heard with his own senses. The judge ensures that the rules of evidence are maintained and directs the court as to the admissibility of any contentious testimony.

Captain Lord did not have the benefit of any of the foregoing. Neither was he tried under 'Section 6' of the Maritime Convention Act (1911), which carried the penalty of up to two years in prison, with or without hard labour.

In summing up this section, we see that Captain Lord, in effect, was not only castigated, but publicly condemned without benefit of trial. Not only was he thus condemned, but condemned on a charge which was never actually specified to him, and, by a tribunal before which he only appeared as a witness. To add to this obvious injustice, Lord was denied effective legal representation and opportunity to defend himself and present evidence on his own behalf, as was his democratic and constitutional right. To finally ensure that the captain would have no further grounds for charges of libel or slander, he was refused any legal fees or expenses and the right to appeal the findings of the inquiry. At one stage in the process, Captain Lord found it very difficult to raise the necessary fare to travel to London in connection with the case. This then was the 'justice' which prevailed in 1912, and, it must be said, has continued to prevail in Captain Lord's case ever since.

To give just a brief idea of the importance – or rather, lack of importance – which the Board of Trade and the marine department placed on the plight of Captain Lord, I append, verbatim, a brief letter from Sir Walter J. Howell, of the marine dept, to the president of the Board of Trade, Mr Buxton, on 18 August:

Dear Mr. Buxton,

In reply to your inquiry whether I think a copy of this letter from Captain Lord should be sent to Lord Mersey, I am of the opinion that it would be better not. Lord Mersey and his court have delivered their judgement and there is an end of the matter so far as they are concerned. I think if you communicate anything now, whether from Captain Lord or anyone else concerned, it might be misunderstood and would create a bad precedent.

I hope you are having fine weather and a real rest after your very busy time at the Board of Trade. I am having a delightful time here and am thoroughly enjoying it, but I hope you will not hesitate to write to, or send for, me, if I can be of any service to you.

I am,

Yours very faithfully,
Walter J. Howell

At the time the above letter was written, Captain Lord wrote on paper his own version of the events and sent it to the marine department asking that it be forwarded to Lord Mersey, who presided over the inquiry. The off-hand manner in which his request was treated speaks multitudes. Was it a case of the 'fish being on the line' and the 'anglers' loath to lose him? In any event, the matter was left alone.

It would be unwise, and probably boring, to become bogged down in a whole lot of legal red tape and misguided bureaucracy which has surrounded this case for so long and would serve no useful purpose, other than confuse the reader. It will be much more profitable if the case is approached with a clear mind and an outlook unswayed by emotions. We shall therefore simply take the facts of the case as they present themselves, examine them, and arrive at a conclusion. To lay the groundwork for such an appraisal, it will be necessary to return to the Titanic itself and look at its construction.

It is necessary to forget for a moment all the hype which surrounded this massive floating palace and take a look instead at the nuts and bolts of the ship, as it were. There can be absolutely no doubt that Titanic was a beautiful ship and utterly deserving of all the praise which was heaped on her. She was indeed everything her owners claimed her to be. The 'unsinkable' myth came into the public arena as a result of a journalistic comment in the maritime press. Neither Harland & Wolff nor White Star ever made this claim. One of the major flaws in the construction of the Titanic, which was a main contributing factor to her loss, was the engine and boiler room bulkheads. Initially, these bulkheads were designed and installed in such a manner as to allow several compartments to be flooded without endangering the ship. Unfortunately, the bulkheads were not completely watertight in that they did not reach up to the upper decks (D deck and Saloon deck) as was originally planned by David Archer, the ship's principal surveyor. As the bulkheads stopped short of the overhead ceilings, there was a gap of several feet over which water could pour over in the event of a serious collision. This omission meant that as soon as water would reach the top of one bulkhead, it would immediately spill over into the next. This situation would continue, in domino fashion, until all the compartments were full of water. This of course was exactly what happened on the night of the tragedy and is verified by the fact that the Titanic went down by the head.

Although the ship was reputed for decades to have suffered a gash in her side, measuring about 300ft, naval architect Edward Wilding calculated in 1912 that the overall damage to her hull amounted to 12sq.ft. This was confirmed to be 12.60sq.ft based on a 1995 computer analysis during an expedition to the wreck site. However, if the ship had suffered a 300ft gash, it is probable that she would have actually turned turtle, as all of her lower compartments would have filled up much more rapidly. It is therefore much more likely that the ice only managed to penetrate some of the forward plates all the way through, and went on to merely tear and punch the outer skin on the Titanic for the remainder of the gash (Titanic actually had two hulls, one inside the other). This would be a logical assumption when we consider that the right forward section of the ship would have taken the main force of the impact – estimated at one million foot tons – and the side only a superficial or glancing blow as the momentum of the collision pushed the ship away from the iceberg. New insights into the ship's breakup have led to the tentative conclusion that her bottom suffered damage during the collision as well.

At the subsequent British investigation, Mr David Archer, in his testimony, confirmed that the bulkheads did not reach as high as originally intended. He stated that he 'accepted this condition' after being shown a builder's calculation that even if the first and second compartments, and the firemen's passage, were to be simultaneously flooded, the Titanic would only sink 2ft 6in. by the head. After Archer had done some calculations of his own, he came to the conclusion that if the ship were to be down 2ft 6in. by the head, the tops of the 'unfinished' bulkheads between the fourth and fifth watertight compartments would then be no less than 15ft 6in. above the waterline. On the basis of this theory – which may have been fine on paper – he reached the conclusion that to increase further the height of the bulkheads would be an exercise in futility. He therefore passed the ship as being fit for sea and duly issued his declaration of seaworthiness.

Had the basis for tragedy been laid? There can be no doubt that Mr Archer had confidence in his calculations and that he could not possibly have envisaged the horrific results of his decision. In retrospect, it is a sobering thought to think that those extra feet of steel might have made the difference between life and death for so many unfortunates. In point of fact, the only mitigating circumstances which can be forwarded in support of the 'unfinished' bulkheads is that they played a part in slowing the advance of the seas rushing in after the impact. Surely bulkheads that ran higher and had no doors might have considerably impeded the ingress of water. Undoubtedly, the collision caused infinitely greater damage than her designers had accounted for. It is ironic to think that while so much money was spent on building and fitting out this sumptuous liner, an extra few thousand pounds could have slowed down her sinking, probably giving her enough time to transfer passengers and crew to other vessels that had rushed to the scene later that morning.

Yet another bone of contention over the years has been the lack of sufficient lifeboats, and, in spite of the legalities prevailing in 1912, it has long been a serious indictment for the owners of the Titanic. Clearly, if sufficient lifeboats had been available, then every single life would have probably been saved. Nevertheless, it is necessary to point out that the White Star Line was within its legal right in the matter of the lifeboats, despite the fact that they had reneged on former promises to equip the ship with substantially more boats. Even more thought-provoking is the fact that the Titanic was fitted with the latest Welin davits, which were capable of taking not just one, but three, or even four lifeboats each and launching them with perfect safety in a matter of minutes. Despite this, the White Star Line decided that 'one lifeboat per davit would be sufficient'. The ship had a total of sixteen davits, eight on each side. Why then should they bother with stacks of unnecessary lifeboats, cluttering up the decks?

Even before the Titanic was launched, the question of lifeboats was very much a sore point and cause of considerable argument. Apart from the inescapable fact that the number of lifeboats installed on the ship complied with the legal requirements of the day – indeed, they exceeded the legal requirements – it was widely held that the company had a moral responsibility to provide lifeboat accommodation for every single person on board. All requests and demands fell on apparently deaf ears and the Titanic eventually was put to sea with just sixteen lifeboats and four collapsible boats, some of which were welded to the deck by paint and completely inaccessible to passengers. The law, in 1912, stated that the ship was only obliged to supply lifeboat accommodation for just over 700 people. This might seem somewhat absurd, as indeed it was, when we consider that the Titanic was legally certified to carry no less than 3,547 passengers and crew while still only offering lifeboat space to a mere 1,178 people. Simple arithmetic shows that if there was only enough lifeboat space for just 1,178 people, it clearly follows that out of the total number of people on board, more than 1,000 people would have no other choice but to remain on board in the event of an accident which necessitated that the ship be abandoned. This is precisely what transpired after the impact. Even more devastating is the fact that some of the lifeboats left the ship with less than their full complement. The result of course was that an excess of 1,500 people perished in the freezing sea. The terrifying reality of this appalling loss of life is that, had the White Star Line and the Board of Trade applied themselves more diligently to the matter of safety, not one person onboard the Titanic need have died. Had the ship sailed with a full complement, one can only imagine how far more appalling the disaster would have been.

The moral issue of the lifeboats was seen some years earlier by the designer of the Axel Welin davits. In a letter to the John Bull magazine in December 1910, Welin stated that the davits which he had designed for both the Olympic and the Titanic were each capable of taking up to four lifeboats – even though at that stage he had no idea of how many life-boats were to be installed on the two sister ships. In February 1911, Horatio Bottomley, MP, who owned John Bull magazine and made full use of it for political purposes, asked the Board of Trade's president the following perti-nent questions:

> Would the President state the number of lifeboats necessary to be attached to passenger vessels, the date of the last regulations made by the Board in refer-ence to the number of lifeboats and whether having regard to the increased tonnage of modern ships he will consider the desirability of revising such regulations?

This was indeed a very pertinent question and showed the foresight and concern of a member of the House. The reply from the board, when it eventually came, seemed promising:

> These regulations were last revised in 1894 (eighteen years previously). The question of their future revision is engaging the serious attention of the Board of Trade and I have decided to refer the matter to the Mercantile Shipping and Advisory Committee for consideration and advice.

In actual fact, the president of the Board of Trade had already been made aware of the situation regarding the question of the lifeboats. Axel Welin had sent a blueprint of his double-acting davits to the board almost one year earlier. He had in fact incorporated his davits into one of the Titanic's plans and emphasised that by utilising his davits to their full potential, the ship would have a total of no less than sixty-four lifeboats, substantially more than would ever be required. Had Welin's proposals been adopted, it meant that the Titanic would have had lifeboat space for 3,840 people. Sadly, the plans and proposal fell on deaf ears. The company was adamant that they were within their legal rights, which of course they were.

Axel Welin, however, would appear to have been a stubborn man. He con-tinued his insistence that more lifeboats should be carried by the Olympic and Titanic. Whether this persistence stemmed from concern for the poten-tial passengers or whether he simply wished to extract a larger order from the company is unclear and a moot point. Both Welin and his colleague, Alexander Carlisle, who had previously worked for Harland & Wolff as a designer of the Olympic and Titanic, continued to press their case for extra lifeboats.

Carlisle himself believed that no less than forty-eight lifeboats should be installed but, because of his position as an employee of Welin's, he did not think it was his place to ask publicly for any set number of lifeboats. Nevertheless, he too had seen the gaping need for additional boats to be installed and, like his employer, was of the opinion that everybody on board the ship should have been guaranteed a seat in a lifeboat.

All would appear to have been going reasonably well when, just a week after Welin's proposals to the Board of Trade, he received a memo which stated: 'Titanic and Olympic are each to be fitted with thirty-two lifeboats which are to be carried under 16 sets of double-acting davits, eight on either side.' Welin was content with the figure. Although he had not managed to convince the board to install his original suggestion of sixty-four lifeboats, he consoled himself with the thought that the board had gone halfway in meeting his proposals and were providing enough boats to allow space for 1,920 people. Bearing in mind that the ship would also carry several collapsible boats, he declared himself satisfied with the arrangement.

It was July 1910 when the bombshell fell. The builders had submitted a print to the Board of Trade showing the number and arrangements of lifeboats to be carried – eight on each side! This was just a fraction of what had been promised by the board. Nevertheless, the Board of Trade promptly 'forgot' their promise to Welin and immediately accepted the reduced numbers, noting that they were still more than within their legal obligation. It was, obviously, a far cry from the original sixty-four boats suggested by Welin, and just half the number he had been promised a mere few months previously. It was destined to be but yet another retrograde step in the construction of the Titanic, one which would be counted in human lives.

Because of the appalling disaster following a short five-day commercial life, the Titanic has managed to capture the imagination of the world like no other ship before or since. The White Star Line readily agreed that the ship was not designed and built for great speed, but for weight of displacement and passenger and cargo accommodation. The main object of the White Star Line was of course, as we have seen, to compete with the rival lines, in particular Cunard. Ironically, one of the first ships to reach the scene of the disaster was the Cunard Carpathia ship. Even by the standards of present-day shipping, the Olympic and Titanic were ships of awesome proportions, but they were already outstripped in 1912 by the German Imperator class in dimensions, tonnage, sheer opulence and comfort. The fact that both ships were allowed to be put to sea with such glaring inadequacies must be taken into consideration when examining the circumstances surrounding Titanic's loss. If we liken the Titanic and the iceberg to two vehicles crashing into each other on an open road, we would have to concede that the ship was guilty of some percentage of contributory negligence, however large or slim. The ship's master was, after all, warned of icebergs in the vicinity. Taking all these facts into consideration, one can only conclude that the ship's owners and the Board of Trade must stand censured for the appalling loss of life. This is an inescapable fact and is made all the more harrowing when we consider that there was plenty of time available to have taken all the passengers and crew off the stricken ship, if there had been lifeboat accommodation for everybody on board. We must also remind ourselves of the fact that the ship might not conceivably have sunk in two hours and forty minutes if the bulkheads had been completed, as originally intended. Indeed, it was as a direct result of Welin's davits working so efficiently that all the lifeboats got away from the ship, albeit some less than full. In point of fact, several dozen more lifeboats could have been launched from the davits, if they had been available, in the time between the impact and the ship actually sinking. The fact that the Titanic carried more lifeboats than she was legally required does not detract from the inescapable fact that she did not carry sufficient boats to ensure the safety of all on board. Nevertheless, each time the question of the lifeboats was raised at both the British and American investigations, the same stock-in-trade answer was given: 'The Titanic carried more lifeboats than that required by either British or American law.'

At the later British inquiry into the loss of the Titanic, the question of the lifeboats produced what is tantamount to an official cover-up. Alexander Carlisle had stated in the Daily Mail of 18 April, that in his opinion, the Board of Trade's lifeboat's regulations were archaic, while admitting at the same time that the actual number of lifeboats, which he himself considered to be less than adequate, did exceed the number required by law. He went on to say that his original plan had provided for more than forty lifeboats for the Titanic. This statement was corroborated by Welin. However, as Carlisle's statement was considered to be potentially damaging to the company, notwithstanding their legal correctness, both Bruce Ismay, the managing director and effective owner of the Titanic, and his partner, Harold Sanderson, promptly denied having seen Carlisle's plans. Obviously taking their cue from this denial and not wishing to be left 'holding the baby', the Board of Trade attempted to discredit Carlisle's evidence by ignoring it in their final report to the inquiry. The fact that both the White Star Line and the Board of Trade took this evasive action clearly shows that they were not too keen to bring the wrath of public opinion down upon their heads and, ultimately, the entire question of the lifeboats was allowed to drop into obscurity. It was to be but yet another of the debatable inconsistencies which were to eventually pave the way for the systematic shredding of Captain Lord's character.

Many people would see the figure of Captain Edward J. Smith as a major contributing factor in the disaster and, while he may have been somewhat complacent in his attitude to the warnings of ice in the region, this situation was nothing out of the ordinary to the captain. He had made countless crossings of the Atlantic during his long career and always successfully negotiated problems with field ice and icebergs on many occasions.

Considering that it was an exceptionally clear night, we can well understand Captain Smith's reluctance to reduce the ship's speed. Certainly he took a gamble. Every captain who crossed the Atlantic took the same gamble, but for Smith on this occasion, it did not pay off. Nevertheless, the inescapable fact remains that Captain Smith did allow his ship to travel at what was later considered to be an 'excessive speed' in an area he knew to be dangerous. Later, during the British inquiry, Smith was to be posthumously, and mildly, rebuked for his action.

The name of Captain Edward John Smith has perhaps become as famous as the great ship he commanded and, understandably perhaps, many popular misconceptions have grown around him. So very little is actually known of the actions of Captain Smith after the tragedy that it would be futile to attempt to write anything concrete concerning his actions in the water. The idea has been put forward, on several occasions, that Smith, in the final moments before the Titanic took her death plunge, stood on the ship's bridge, in the great and utterly foolish tradition of the sea, and went down bravely with his ship. This type of myth is best left where it belongs – on the cinema screen or between the pages of some minor work of fiction. If we are realistic about Captain Smith's final moments, we must accept the fact that he was a normal human being with the self-same instincts for survival as anyone else. It is only natural that he would strive for the continuance of his life. Bearing this human characteristic in mind, we can rest assured that Smith somehow found himself swimming in the ocean with other victims. The impression must not be taken that Smith, fearful for his own life, abandoned his ship and left more than 1,500 people still clinging to the rails.

Captain Smith had gone about his duty in the time-honoured tradition of the sea. After he had detailed passengers and crew to their respective stations

and, when the end was both inevitable and imminent, he relieved his crew of
their duty, thanked them for their assistance, and advised them to save themselves. How Smith himself came to be in the water is something of a mystery.
It is highly unlikely that he would voluntarily leave the ship while so many
people still clung to the rails. Such an action would have been quite out of
character for this man. One uncorroborated report stated that the captain was
washed off the ship by a huge wave. This may not be as unlikely as it sounds.
However, as it was one of the calmest nights in memory, the question must be
asked, 'Where did this huge wave come from?' This is an interesting question
and one that is not as inane as it might first appear. Although it was an unusually clear, calm night, with the surface of the sea as smooth as a mirror, it must
be borne in mind that as the huge ship sank, a certain amount of pressure and
turbulence was caused which did in fact lead to several large waves forming
around the ship and the immediate area. Likewise, prior to the actual sinking,
one of the giant funnels crashed into the water, on top of people swimming
about, and this too could have caused a sizeable wave. In any event, Captain
Smith found himself, willing or not, in the sea. It is also well to bear in mind
that as the ship took her final plunge, hundreds of people were washed off
the ship. Who is to say that Captain Smith was not among those? The only
thing that is clear is that Smith did not go down with the ship. There are far
too many eye-witness reports to support this scenario. Several people later
recalled seeing the captain swimming, and no less than two sources of irrefutable evidence state that Smith, while in the water, was still attempting to
get people into the few lifeboats that were in the immediate vicinity. One of
those sources recalls attempting to pull the captain himself into a boat, but
Smith refused, swam away, and was never seen again. Taking everything into
consideration, this is probably exactly what Captain Smith, or any responsible
captain, would do. It is highly likely that the extreme cold of the sea, coupled
with his age and state of shock, had a tremendous effect on Smith. We can
only assume that, like the other unfortunates in the water that morning, he
succumbed to the elements and drowned. His body was never recovered.

It has often been suggested that Captain Smith, realising that he would
have to return to face a public inquiry, or that he would have to live with
the awful memory of the disaster for the rest of his life, chose suicide as an
alternative. While this aspect can never be proven, a couple of pertinent
questions need to be asked. If it was the intention of Captain Smith to
commit suicide, why then was he swimming about? Surely, if he did wish
to end it all, he would have carried out the deed in privacy. And, would a

person intent on self-destruction, with access to a loaded revolver, choose such an agonising death as drowning? Hardly. We must therefore return to the only logical conclusion – Captain Smith merely succumbed to the cold and exhaustion, and sank without trace.

Captain Smith was approaching sixty-three years of age when the Titanic sank and had spent his previous forty-three years at sea in many capacities. Prior to taking command of the world's largest ship, a position which was given to him as a gesture of appreciation and to mark his impending retirement after the voyage by the White Star Line, Smith was previously master of the Titanic's sister ship, the Olympic and had indeed brought many of his officers with him when he transferred to the Titanic. Reams of literature have been written about Captain Smith in the intervening years, some of it accurate, yet some quite implausible. To quote from any of these sources would be to invite speculation, so it is best to shy away from such.

Yet another myth concerning Smith must be dispelled. The allegation has been made on several occasions that, in an effort to impress his passengers and employers, Captain Smith attempted to make the crossing of the Atlantic in record time. There is absolutely no evidence for this. In fact, this myth is doubtful for two reasons. Firstly, the amount of coal available to the White Star Line was limited, due to a coal strike. Because of this, the Titanic had to sail with substantially less than her allocation of coal. Consequently the stock of coal would have to be rationed and used sparingly. Certainly there would be no question of piling on extra coal to run the ship at any great speed for long periods. Secondly, Smith was under specific instructions from the owners, as indeed were all White Star commanders, not to sacrifice safety for speed. These instructions were in fact quoted quite often at the sittings of the American Senate Committee:

INSTRUCTIONS TO COMMANDERS

Commanders must distinctly understand that the issue of regulations does not in any way relieve them from responsibility for the safe and efficient navigation of their respective vessels, and they are also enjoined to remember that they must run no risks which might by any possibility result in accident to their ships. It is to be hoped that they will ever bear in mind that the safety of the lives and property entrusted to their care is the ruling principle that should govern them in the navigation of their vessels, and that no supposed gain in expedition or saving of time on the voyage is to be purchased at the risk of accident.

> Commanders are reminded that the steamers are to a great extent unin-
> sured and that their own livelihood, as well as the company's success, depends
> upon immunity from accident; no precaution which ensures safe navigation
> is to be considered excessive …

The foregoing instructions are, quite obviously, clear and to the point.
Whether Captain Smith adhered strictly to these regulations or not is plain
conjecture. Bearing in mind that these instructions were looked upon by
most captains as a basic set of company rules which they were to adhere to
for obvious legal reasons, it does not follow that they were adhered to at all
times. More often than not, ship masters followed their own instincts and
experience and used their discretion in the matter of speed. If, for any reason, a commander found himself behind schedule, he would usually try to
make up for the lost time by short or prolonged bursts of speed. In this frequent instance 'familiarity bred contempt' when we consider the fantastic
odds of one single ship running into a huge iceberg in an area as vast as the
North Atlantic. Although the odds are probably much higher, experts have
reckoned them to be exactly one million to one. Well aware that the odds
were so vast, captains frequently took the risk of running their ships at top
speed and generally arrived at their destination unscathed. However, there
is a first time for everything, and it seemed that fate had chosen the Titanic.
This very point was amply illustrated in a letter to the London Times by Mr
Lawrence Beesley, a survivor of the disaster, just a few days after reaching
port:

> Sir,
> As one of the few surviving Englishmen from the steamship Titanic, which
> sank in mid-Atlantic on Monday morning last, I am asking you to lay before
> your readers a few facts concerning the disaster, in the hope that something
> may be done in the near future to ensure the safety of that portion of the trav-
> elling public who use the Atlantic highway for business or pleasure. I wish to
> dissociate myself entirely from any report that would seek to fix the respon-
> sibility on any person or persons or body of people, and by calling attention
> to matters of fact the authenticity of which is, I think, beyond question and
> can be established in any Court of Inquiry, to allow your readers to draw their
> own conclusions as to the responsibility for the collision.
> First, that it was known to those in charge of the Titanic that we were in
> the iceberg region; that the atmospheric and temperature conditions sug-

gested the near presence of icebergs; that a wireless message was received from a ship ahead of us warning us that they had been seen in the vicinity of which latitude and longitude were given. Second, that at the time of the collision the Titanic was running at a high rate of speed. Third, that the accommodation for saving passengers and crew was totally inadequate, being sufficient only for a total of about 950. This gave, with the highest possible complement of 3,400, a less than one in three chance of being saved in the case of accident. Fourth, that the number landed in the Carpathia, approximately 700, is a high percentage of the possible 950, and bears excellent testimony to the courage, resource, and devotion to duty of the officers and crew of the vessel; many instances of their nobility and personal self-sacrifice are within our possession, and we know that they did all they could do with the means at their disposal. Fifth, that the practice of running mail and passenger vessels through fog and iceberg regions at a high speed is a common one; they are timed to run almost as an express train is run, and they cannot, therefore, slow down more than a few knots in time of possible danger. I have neither knowledge or experience to say what remedies I consider should be applied; but, perhaps the following suggestions may serve as a help; First, that no vessel should be allowed to leave a British port without sufficient boat and other accommodation to allow each passenger and member of the crew a seat; and that at the time of booking this fact should be pointed out to a passenger, and the number of the seat in the particular boat allotted to him then. Second, that as soon as is practicable after sailing each passenger should go through boat drill in company with the crew assigned to his boat. Third, that each passenger boat engaged in the Transatlantic service should be instructed to slow down to a few knots when in the iceberg region, and should be fitted with an effective searchlight.

Yours faithfully,

Lawrence Beesley

The fact that major shipping companies adopted many of Mr Beesley's suggestions following the Titanic tragedy speaks for itself – a case of closing the stable door after the horse had bolted.

As stated in the above letter, most of the passengers were aware that the ship had received several warnings of icebergs. They also were aware that the ship was travelling at an excessive speed despite these warnings – the operative word being 'excessive' as distinct from 'top speed'. Also, the entire area where the Titanic found herself was deemed to be hazardous during that particular time of year. This is a fact well known to all captains, lest the impression be given that the ship ran into a single solitary iceberg. In fact, the ice field itself was estimated to measure more than seventy miles long and some 12 miles wide, and the entire area was dotted with numerous icebergs of varying sizes. It was, quite obviously, folly to run a ship at any great speed in these dangerous conditions, more so in darkness when visibility would be at a minimum. Indeed, the enormity of the ice field was remarked upon by the surviving officers of the Titanic at the subsequent hearings when they collectively stated that they had never before seen such dangerous ice floes and threatening icebergs. Their remarks were echoed when the crew of the Carpathia also stated that they saw 'an unbroken field of ice stretching as far as the eye could see'. It was to be into this death trap that the RMS Titanic would plough at enormous speed.

It has been both admitted and proven beyond all reasonable doubt that the Titanic was travelling at a high rate of speed when she collided with the iceberg, but burning questions arise. How fast was she moving? Was she – against all rules – running at close to top speed? Was she, albeit unlikely, attempting a record crossing? While the answer to the latter question is probably no, it is evident that Captain Smith had intended to make the crossing as quickly as possible for the simple reason that he was several hours behind schedule. This point is amply illustrated by looking at the mileage the Titanic covered prior to the disaster. From 12.00 noon on Thursday to 12.00 noon on Friday she covered a distance of 396 miles; relatively slow when we consider that she was sailing in comparatively safe waters. However, we see that she soon began to systematically increase her speed. During the following twenty-four hours, Friday to Saturday, she ran 519 miles. The distance was further increased the following day when the ship covered 546 miles, which is very close to her projected top speed. We see therefore that the speed and distance of the Titanic was being increased each day. By early Sunday morning, the ship was well within the danger zone and yet, apparently, no effort was made to decrease speed. It must therefore be naturally assumed that when she collided with the iceberg, the Titanic was travelling at a highly dangerous speed.

A discussion between a purser and some of the passengers lends weight to the argument that the ship was in fact systematically increasing her speed as each day passed and, if not actually attempting a record crossing, then certainly attempting to make up for the disappointing performance on Thursday and Friday. The purser remarked that as the Titanic had only covered 519 miles the second day, she would not now dock in New York until Wednesday morning instead of Tuesday night as originally thought. Later, however, the same purser declared himself to be satisfied with the 546 miles the ship had covered between Saturday and Sunday, and said that they might now dock in New York on Tuesday night after all. He went on to say, 'They are not pushing her this trip and don't intend to make any fast running. I don't suppose that we will do much more than 546 miles now. It's not bad for a day's running for the first trip.' The inference drawn from this conversation is that the ship was still capable of even more speed. This in turn leads us to the conclusion that although she may have been travelling at an excessively high speed prior to the impact, she was certainly not travelling at her top rate of speed. Against this, we do not know if it was the intention of Captain Smith to continue to increase speed each day until he attained his top rate of speed. The answer to this question will never be known. We must also bear in mind that the foregoing conversation was carried on by a purser, as while he held a responsible position on board the ship, he would hardly be likely to have been privy to any navigational plans the captain had in mind. At best, it is likely that the purser was merely repeating snatches of conversation he had possibly overheard between the ship's officers, and then expressing his own opinion on the matter.

Certainly Bruce Ismay, who was on board as a normal passenger, would not have had any say in the matter of navigation or speed. This was the sole prerogative of the captain and it rested with him to either increase or decrease the speed of the ship as he saw fit. As we have seen, Smith was obviously lulled into a false sense of security simply because he had made the crossing dozens of times without mishap. Notwithstanding, there remains one inescapable point – Smith was the ultimate person responsible for setting the speed of the ship and allowed the Titanic to run at a speed which was later found to be 'excessive', in view of the fact that he was in known dangerous waters and had been warned of the danger several times. His action cannot be completely justified, even if we were to accept this tragedy as a 'one in a million' probability.

If we therefore accept, as we must, the apparent culpability of Captain Smith, we must also accept the fact that he was a contributing factor to the loss of the Titanic. If we were to attempt to justify or rationalise his actions, we can only use the words of the British inquiry's president and admonish him for being 'overconfident' and 'reckless'. The fact that he took a gamble and lost does not enter into judgement for the simple reason that he should not have taken any gambles.

Understandably, public opinion and anger was at a boiling point. How could such a catastrophe happen? Had not the world been told that the Titanic was unsinkable? How could the largest ship in the world be sunk by a mere lump of ice? Why was there such devastating loss of life? The questions went on and on, and eventually changed to demands for a culprit. Somebody had to be at fault, but who? Captain Smith had only been mildly rebuked and no charges were ever brought against the White Star Line or the Board of Trade. There can be absolutely no doubt that if there had been an 'independent public inquiry' then things may well have turned out differently. The inquiry was hastily convened by the Board of Trade and they were hardly likely to condemn themselves. As it transpired, both the White Star Line and the Board of Trade came out of the investigation relatively unscathed. While the board was quick to exonerate the owners and themselves of any blame for the tragedy, they were also acutely aware that somebody, somewhere, would have to answer for the appalling loss of life, but who? Always ready for an interesting story, the media came up with the answer in scapegoating Captain Stanley Lord. As Lord had already been severely castigated by the inquiry, it was but a simple job to develop and blow this case out of proportion, as happens all too frequently.

Before we leave the question about the actual loss of the Titanic, it is essential and necessary that we take a brief look at another anomaly, which may well have had a vital bearing on the entire incident. Harold S. Bride and John George Phillips were, respectively, Junior and Senior Marconi operators on the Titanic. While there is no doubt that both men were exceptionally brave by remaining at their posts while the ship was sinking, the accusation could be made that their inadvertent actions, or lack thereof, were contributing factors. Contrary to popular belief, the wireless operators on the Titanic were not in fact employees of the White Star Line. In this context, it would be totally inaccurate to refer to them as ship's officers. Bearing this in mind, it would follow then that they were not under any orders to run to the ship's bridge with every message as quickly as they received it. Nevertheless, as both men had previous shipboard experience, they must have realised the importance of the ice warnings, which they received from several ships in the vicinity. In spite of this, it would seem that the warnings took a back seat to the paying messages which, apparently, were of much more importance to the coffers of the Marconi Company.

Yet another indiscretion of the Titanic's wireless operators was their apparent curt treatment of the attempted ice warning from the German ship, Frankfurt. At the time, it was common knowledge that Mr Marconi, for some reason best known to himself, actually forbade his operators to converse with rival German companies. This would of course account for the now famous 'YAAF' ('you are a fool') message sent from the Titanic to the Frankfurt. The fact that the Frankfurt was merely responding to Titanic's frantic calls for assistance makes one wonder at the logic of the retort and one would naturally assume that, in this ship sinking situation, assistance from any agency would be more than welcomed. It is ironic too that the Californian, Captain Lord's ship, warned the Titanic of dangerous conditions on no less than two occasions. Nevertheless, the messages were largely ignored or treated as less than urgent. It was to be just another quirk of fate that was destined to have such serious repercussions for the victims of the Titanic and for Captain Lord.

The following pages show the Titanic's ice messages and also contain extracts from the message book of the Olympic.

The awful truth reaches the public.

Booth — Titanic Signals Archive

Titanic Ice Messages — 12-14 April

Signal No.	Sender	Receiving Vessel	Date	Time
1	La Touraine	Titanic	12 April	7. 10 p.m. GMT
2	Titanic	La Touraine	12 April	7. 45 p.m. GMT
3	Caronia	Captain Titanic	14 April	7. 10 p.m. GMT
4	Smith	Captain Caronia	14 April	1. 26 p.m. GMT
5	Knuth	Hydrographic Office, Washington D.C.	14 April	11.45 a.m. NYT
Via Cape Race				
6	Amerika	Titanic	14 April	7. 30 p.m. NYT
7	Baltic	Captain Smith Titanic	14 April	11. 52 a.m. NYT
8	Smith	Commander Baltic	14 April	12. 55 p.m. NYT
9	Noordam (Krol)	Captain Titanic	14 April	2.30 p.m. GMT
Via Caronia				
10	Noordam	Captain Titanic	14 April	2.45 p.m. GMT
11	Smith	Captain Noordam	14 April	3. 29 p.m. GMT
12	Titanic	Noordam via Caronia	14 April	3. 50 p.m. GMT
13	Mesaba	Titanic	14 April	7. 50 p.m. NYT
14	Mesaba	New York (covering letter contains three ice reports)	23 April	
15/16	Pages blank, marked 'Nothing missing'			
17	Californian	Antillian	14 April	5.35 p.m. NYT
18	Antillian	Californian (heard Titanic)	14 April	6. 00 p.m. NYT

Commanders of Above Vessels

TITANIC	Captain Edward Smith
LA TOURAINE	Captain Coussin
CARONIA	Captain Barr
AMERIKA	Captain Knuth
NOORDAM	Captain Krol
MESABA	Captain Clark
CALIFORNIAN	Captain Lord

ANTILLIAN	Captain Japha
GMT	Greenwich Mean Time
NYT	New York Time

Calls Signs

Titanic	(MGY)
Caronia	(MSG)
Baltic	(MBC)

Booth — Titanic Signals Archive Call Signs

Call letters used by wireless shore stations and vessels involved with the disaster. Taken from signals in the archive. Ice warnings sent to the Titanic are marked with an asterisk (★). See Titanic Ice Message Book 12-14 April 1912.

Wireless shore stations

Cape Race	Newfoundland	MCE
Sable Island	Nova Scotia	MSD
Sea Gate	New York	MSE
Sagaponack	New York	MSK
Siasconset	Massachusetts	MSC
Cape Sable	Nova Scotia	MSB

Vessel Call Letters

Survivor Messages (Carpathia)		via MEA/MSD
Antillian	Capt Japha	MJL
Amerika	Capt Knuth	DDR
Asian	Capt Wood	MKL
Baltic★		MBC
Blucher		DDB
Birma		SBA
Californian (2)★	Capt S. Lord	MWL
Caronia	Capt Barr	MSF
Carpathia	Capt A.H. Rostron	MPA
Celtic		MLC

Cedric		MDC
USS Chester	Capt S.G. Decker	NDG
Franconia	Capt Smith	MEA
Frankfurt		DFT
Empress of Britain		MPB
La Touraine★	Capt Coussin	MLT
Titanic	Capt E.J. Smith	MGY
Mount Temple		MLQ
Mesaba★	Capt Clark	MMU
Minnehaha		MMA
Minnewaska	Capt Gates	MMW
Noordam★	Capt Krol	MRA?
Olympic	Capt Haddock	MKC
Parisian	Capt Hains	MZN
Prinz Friedrich Wilhelm		DFK
Virginian	Capt Gambell	MGN

NB: International distress calls CQD and SOS.

Olympic Message Book

Thirty-seven message-forms, all of the Marconi International Marine Communication Co. Ltd, of London. All typed in purple ink throughout.

1. Titanic to Olympic, 14 April, 11 p.m. New York Time.
   Titanic sending out signals of distress answered his calls. Titanic replies and gives me his position 41°46' N 50° 14'W and says: 'We have struck an iceberg. Our distance from Titanic 505 miles.'
2. Titanic to Olympic, 14 April, 11.20 p.m. NYT.
   Exchanged signals with the Titanic. He says tell Captain get your boats ready and what is your position?
3. Olympic to Titanic, 14 April, sent 11.35 p.m. NYT.
   Commander Titanic.
   4.24 a.m. GMT 40 °32' N 61° 18'W. Are you steering southerly to meet us? Haddock.
4. Titanic to Olympic, 14 April, 11.40 p.m. NYT.
   Titanic says tell Captain we are putting the passengers off in small boats.

11.45 p.m. NYT asked the Titanic what weather he had. He says clear and calm.

5. Olympic to Titanic 14 April, sent 11.50 p.m. NYT.
Commander Titanic.
Am lighting up all possible boilers as fast as can – Haddock. Handwritten note at foot of form: 'This was our last communication with Titanic.'

6. Sable Island to Olympic, forwarded from New York, 15 April. Received Olympic 5 a.m. NYT.
Captain Haddock Olympic.
Endeavour communicate with Titanic and ascertain time and position reply as soon as possible to Ismay New York.
F.W. Redway.

7. Olympic to Sable Island for Cape Race, 15 April, sent 5.20 a.m. EST.
Operator Cape Race.
Have you any particulars of the Titanic?
Commander.

8. Sable Island to Olympic, forwarded from New York, 15 April, received Olympic 7.35 a.m. NYT.
Commander Olympic.
Keep us posted fully regarding Titanic.
Franklin.

9. Olympic to Sable Island, 15 April, sent 7.45 a.m. Eastern Standard.
Ismay New York. Since midnight when her position was 41° 46' N 50°14'W have been unable to communicate we are now 310 miles from her I am under full power will inform you at once if hear anything.
Commander.

10. Olympic to Asian, 15 April, sent 7.50 a.m. EST.
Captain Asian.
Can you give me any information Titanic and if any ships standing by her?
Commander.

11. Asian to Olympic, 15 April, received 8.35 a.m. NYT.
Captain Olympic.
Titanic signalling Cape Race on and off from 8 to 10 p.m. local time Sunday messages too faint to read finished calling SOS midnight position given as lat. 41°46' long. 50°14'. No further information Asian then 300 miles west of Titanic and towing oil tanker to Halifax.
Regards Wood.

12. Asian to Olympic, 15 April, received 8.36 a.m. NYT.
    13th April iceberg reported in lat. 41°50' long. 50° 20'.
    Regards Wood.

13. Parisian to Olympic, 15 April, received 9.30 a.m. EST.
    Parisian sent messages to Titanic at eight thirty last night and heard
    Titanic sending traffic to Cape Race just before Parisian opera-
    tor went to bed at eleven fifteen ship's time Californian was about
    fifty miles astern of Parisian. Heard following this morning at six
    o'clock: According to information picked up Carpathia has picked
    up twenty boats with passengers. Baltic is returning to give assist-
    ance. As regards Titanic I have heard nothing. Don't know if she is
    sunk.

14. Mesaba to Olympic, 15 April, received 10.12 a.m. NYT.
    Captain Olympic: In lat. 42° to lat. 41° 25' N long. 49° W to long. 50°
    35' W. Saw heavy pack ice and a large number icebergs also some field
    ice weather has been very fine and clear.
    Compliments Clark.

15. Sable Island to Olympic, 15 April, received 10.17 a.m. EST.
    Olympic Cape Race says no further news Titanic we have batch traffic
    for you and your signs good readable here.

16. Olympic to Sable Island for New York, 15 April, sent 10.25 a.m.
    EST.
    Ismay New York
    SS Parisian reports Carpathia in attendance and picked up twenty boats
    of passengers and Baltic returning to give assistance position not given.
    Haddock.

17. Parisian to Olympic, 15 April, received 10.35 a.m. NYT.
    Captain Olympic
    Field ice extends to lat. 41° 22' heavy to the NW of that and bergs very
    numerous of all sizes. Had fine clear weather.
    Hains.

18. Olympic to Parisian, 15 April, sent 12.25 p.m. EST.
    Captain Parisian
    Many thanks for message can we steer to 41°22' N 50°14' W from
    Westward and then North to Titanic fairly free from ice we are due
    there at midnight should appreciate Titanic correct position if you can
    give it me.
    Haddock.

19. Parisian to Olympic, 15 April, recd 12.50 p.m. NYT.

Captain Olympic

Safe from field ice to 41° 22' 50° 14' as the ice was yesterday you would need to steer from that position about NE and N to about lat 41° 43' and 50° 00' then approach his position from the Eastward steering about WNW my knowledge of the Titanic's position at midnight was derived from your own message to New York in which you gave it as 41° 47' 50° 20' if such were correct she would be in heavy field ice and numerous bergs. Hope and trust matters are not as bad as they appear.

Regards, Hains.

20. Carpathia to Olympic, 15 April recd 2.10 p.m. NYT.

Olympic

We received distress signal call from the Titanic at eleven twenty and proceeded right to spot mentioned. On arrival at daybreak we saw ice 25 miles long apparently solid, quantity of wreckage and number of boats full of lives. We raised about six hundred and seventy souls. Titanic has sunk she went down in two hours, Captain and all Engineers our Captain sent order that there was no need for Baltic to come any further so with that she returned on her course to Liverpool. We have two or three officers aboard and the second Marconi operator who had been creeping his way through water at 30 degrees for several hours. Mr Ismay is aboard.

21. Olympic to Carpathia, 15 April, sent 2.35 p.m. NYT.

Commander Carpathia 7.12 pm GMT Our position 41° 17' N 53° 53' W. Shall I meet you and where? Steering East true – Haddock.

22. Carpathia to Olympic, 15 April, recd 3.15 p.m. NYT.

Captain Olympic

7.30 GMT Carpathia lat 41° 15' N 51° 45' W. Am steering South 87 West true. Returning to New York with Titanic's passengers.

Rostron.

23. Carpathia to Olympic, 15 April, recd 3.18 p.m. NYT.

Mr Bruce Ismay is under an opiate.

Rostron.

24. Carpathia to Olympic, 15 April, recd 3.20 p.m. NYT.

Commander Olympic

Do you think it is advisable Titanic's passengers see Olympic. Personally I say not.

Rostron.

25. Carpathia to Olympic, 15 April, recd 3.22 p.m. NYT.
    Commander Olympic
    Mr Ismay orders Olympic not to be seen by Carpathia. No transfer to take place.
    Rostron.

26. Olympic to Carpathia, 15 April, sent 3.55 p.m. NYT.
    Captain Carpathia
    Kindly inform me if there is the slightest hope in searching Titanic position at daybreak. Agree with you on not meeting. Will stand on present course until you have passed and will then haul more to Southward. Does Parallel of 41° 17' N lead clear of the ice? Have you communicated disaster to our people at New York or Liverpool or shall I do so and what particulars can you give me to send? Sincere thanks for what you have done.
    Haddock.

27. Carpathia to Olympic, 15 April, recd 4 p.m. NYT.
    Captain Haddock Olympic
    South point pack ice 41° 16' N. Don't attempt to go North until 49° 30' W. Many bergs large and small amongst pack also for many miles to Eastward fear absolutely no hope searching Titanic's position. Left Leyland SS Californian searching round. All boats accounted for. About six hundred and seventy souls saved crew and passengers. Latter nearly all women and children. Titanic foundered about 2.20 a.m. 5.47 GMT in 41° 16' N 50° 14' W. Not certain of having got through please forward to White Star Line. Also to Cunard Liverpool and New York that I am returning to New York. Consider this most advisable for many considerations.
    Rostron.

28. Olympic to Cape Race, 15 April, sent 4.35 p.m. EST.
    Ismay New York and Liverpool.
    Carpathia reached Titanic position at daybreak found boats and wreckage only. Titanic had foundered about 2.20 a.m. in 41° 16' N 50° 14' W. All her boats accounted for about 675 souls saved crew and passengers latter nearly all women and children. Leyland Line SS Californian remaining and searching position of disaster. Carpathia returning to New York with survivors please inform Cunard.
    Haddock.

29. Olympic to Cape Race, 15 April, sent 4.40 p.m. EST.
    Franklin Ismay New York.
    Inexpressible sorrow am proceeding straight on voyage. Carpathia

informs me no hope in searching will send names of survivors as obtainable Yamsi on Carpathia.

Haddock.

30. Olympic to Carpathia, 15 April, sent 4.50 p.m. EST.

Captain Carpathia

Can you give me names survivors to forward?

Haddock.

31. Carpathia to Olympic, 15 April, recd 5.37 p.m. EST.

Captain Haddock Olympic

Captain Chief 1st and sixth Officers and all Engineers gone also doctor all pursers one Marconi operator and Chief Steward. We have Second Third Fourth and Fifth Officers one Marconi operator on board.

Rostron.

32. Carpathia to Olympic, 15 April, recd 5.40 p.m. EST.

Will send names immediately we can. You can understand we are working under considerable difficulty everything possible being done for comfort of survivors. Please maintain stand-by.

33. New York to Olympic, 16 April, recd 2.35 a.m. NYT.

Captain Haddock Olympic

It is vitally important that we have names of every survivor on Carpathia immediately if you can expedite this by standing by Carpathia please do so.

Franklin.

34. New York to Olympic, 16 April, recd 2.55 a.m. NYT.

Captain Olympic

Wire us name of every passenger, officer and crew on Carpathia. This is most important keep in communication with Carpathia until you accomplish this. Instruct Californian stand by scene of wreck until she hears from us or is relieved or her coal supply runs short and ascertain Californian's coal and how long she can stand by. Has life raft been accounted for are you absolutely satisfied that Carpathia has all survivors as we had a rumour that Virginian and Parisian also had survivors. Where is Baltic?

Franklin.

35. New York to Olympic, 16 April, recd 3.05 a.m. NYT.

Captain Olympic

Distressed to learn from your message that Carpathia is only steamer with passengers we understood Virginian and Parisian also had passengers and are you in communication with them and can you get any information?

Franklin.

36 Tunisian to Olympic via (not given), 16 April, recd 4.20 a.m. NYT.
Asks this report to be forwarded to Olympic. Crossed 50° W 43° 25' N
from 48° 44'W 44° N. Passed through heavy field ice numerous bergs.
Last berg seen 43° N 40° W twenty-four hours fog in vicinity of ice.

37. Virginian to Olympic, 16 April, recd 8.45 a.m. NYT.
Captain Olympic.

Hear rumours that we have survivors of Titanic on board this is not
so. I have none. At 10 a.m. yesterday when 30 miles from position of
disaster received Marconi from Carpathia as follows: Turn back now
everything OK. We have 800 aboard. Return to your Northern track
– I consequently proceeded on my course to Liverpool. Similar instructions were sent at same time from Carpathia to Baltic. I passed a large
quantity of heavy field ice and bergs.

Compliments Gambell.

TWO

Aftermath and Accusations

The loss of the Titanic quite naturally caused a worldwide sensation and had literally every newspaper in all corners of the globe vying with each other for exclusive stories. The result of course was that the general public became more than slightly confused, as all sorts of wild and weird reports began to saturate the western world. The imagination of some of the reports knew no bounds, and more than one lucky survivor had the dubious distinction of reading his own obituary in the papers. Even before the rescue ship Carpathia had docked in New York with her complement of survivors, the press was reporting many of those on board as lost or missing, while other papers reported victims as having been saved. The lack of concrete information did not stop with the confusing list of victims and survivors. Some papers even reported the Titanic as being 'in tow' and heading for Halifax in Nova Scotia, with no loss of life. Others printed a completely different account and had the ship lost with all hands. Speculation and wild conjecture were rife, and in many instances the questionable art of sensationalism was practised to its fullest.

As we shall see later, some of these erroneous reports were to have a sinister and damaging effect with regards to what ships were in the immediate vicinity. In the days and weeks following the disaster, the confusion continued. Anyone who had the slightest connection with the ship was immediately pounced on as a source of information. In all too many cases people were only too happy to relate the 'exclusive story' and, in more than several cases, money changed hands for one. There were many cases of reluctant sources who first had their inhibitions lowered by being treated with free drinks. Not surprisingly, the result was that hundreds of grossly inaccurate accounts of the disaster began to circulate in the popular press. In many instances these accounts were obtained at second- or third-hand and, whether intentional or not, contained more than a few embellishments.

It is quite easy to imagine a harassed reporter, anxious to please his editor and stay one step ahead of his competitors, allowing himself to be subjected to a story's fabrication that was sprinkled with just enough truth to make it believable. Yet other reporters, unable or unwilling to track down an account of the tragedy, often lifted previously published material and, by clever re-writing, managed to further embellish the story.

There were also many unscrupulous people who, aware of the financial gain involved, concocted plausible stories and played them out for all they were worth. The end result of course was that the general public very soon did not know what to believe. The surviving crew members, now virtually trapped in America pending investigation, and penniless, found themselves prime targets for both American and foreign reporters. In many cases these men were only too happy to recount their experiences and accept the cash proffered. It is interesting to note that from the precise moment the Titanic slipped beneath the waves, the White Star Line immediately stopped their wages. They were, in effect, no longer employees of the company.

Emotional headlines, such as 'Saw Both Officers Perish', 'Band Played Its Own Dirge', 'Left To Their Fate' and 'Captain Washed Overboard' were commonplace among other more emotive headings. It was to be merely a matter of weeks and months before books on the disaster began to appear. Apart from a few noted exceptions, these were, in the main, based on newspaper reports and as inaccurate as the sources they had been gleaned from. Nevertheless the books sold exceptionally well and went no small way towards causing even further confusion.

By and large, newspaper editors attempted to substantiate and verify reports prior to publication. However, in many instances this proved to be almost an impossible task as many of the reports were cabled to the head-office and were, at the time, considered to be quite factual. Here follows a brief extract of such a report taken from the archives of the Cork Examiner of the morning of 17 April 1912:

> Little actual light has yet been thrown on the circumstances of the Titanic calamity. It has been learned, however, that the Cunarder Carpathia is putting back to New York with 868 survivors. One telegram says that 200 of these are from the crew. This seems sufficiently likely, as each boat would probably have a crew of six, seven oarsmen and a coxswain.
>
> An alarming feature of the Carpathia's message is the statement that she is threading her way through a field of ice.

TITANIC   CATASTROPHE.

SAVED   ROLL   GROWING

CARPATHIA'S PERIL

SAILING THROUGH ICE FIELD

WITH 868 SURVIVORS

LISTS   OF   RESCUED

NAMES OF CREW

VANISHING HOPES

VIRGINIAN'S DISAPPOINTING
MESSAGE.

Lists of survivors of the first and second class passengers are published. They have been sent by wireless, and are not complete. They do not include the names of Mr W.T. Stead or Mr Jacob Astor, the millionaire.

Steamers cruising in the vicinity of the wreck have seen no bodies. In the House of Commons yesterday Mr Asquith made sympathetic references to the disaster. The names of several Cork men are among the passengers and crew. The names of the third-class passengers have not yet been published.

Other newspapers carried more informative articles, yet they too were not often in full possession of all the facts as, by and large, editors were anxious to publish news of the disaster and to a large extent were obliged to rely on information cabled to them by their correspondents:

There is now unfortunately no doubt whatever that the White Star liner, Titanic, the largest ship in the world, sank after collision with an iceberg in Lat. 41° N, Long. 60° W, while on her maiden voyage from Southampton to New York1. She carried 1,455 passengers and 903 crew, a total of 2,358, and there is every reason to fear that the death toll reaches the awful number of 1,490. The terrible calamity has created consternation not only in this country and in the United States, but also on the Continent, and on all hands great sympathy is expressed for the bereaved.

This last photo was taken on Thursday at Queenstown. It shows the entrance to the Titanic where all who joined her at Queenstown passed through, from the tender to the liner. The photo was taken a few seconds before the door was closed forever. The two officers shown at the entrance were bidding farewell to some of the officials they knew on the tender. Courtesy of Cork Examiner Publications.

In view of the first statements, that no lives had been lost and that the passengers had been transferred to other steamers, a feeling of easiness prevailed, but unhappily this was dispelled as the day advanced. In the early morning a message from St John's, Newfoundland, gave rise to the hope that the Allan liner Virginian had some survivors on board. Another straw eagerly clutched at was a statement made by the operator at Sable Island on Monday night, who, when asked about the possibility of delivering messages to Titanic's passengers, replied that it would be difficult to do so as the passengers were believed to be dispersed among several vessels.

Later, however, the sad intelligence arrived from Montreal, through Reuters, that the Allan Line had received communications to the effect that they were in receipt of a Marconigram, via Cape Race, from Captain Campbell of the Virginian, stating that he had arrived on the scene of the disaster too late to be of service and was proceeding to Liverpool. No mention was made of the rescue of Titanic's passengers. Another message also indicated that the same company's liner, Parisian, had no passengers belonging to the Titanic. According to an official statement which arrived from New York early that evening, the White Star Line announced that they had positive news that the number of survivors from the Titanic was 868. The dispatch was transmitted by the Olympic. It appears that the 868 persons who were onboard the Cunard liner Carpathia would have arrived at New York on Thursday afternoon: 'Although she never actually visited the port, Liverpool was the official port of registry for the Titanic and, although she was, strictly speaking, an American ship, she flew the British flag and was entitled to carry the blue ensign of the RNR.'

A press representative who was among several invited reporters on board to inspect the ship prior to her departure communicated the following incident which occurred at the official luncheon on board:

> The tables had been laid in the centre of one of the rooms and, just a few moments before the short speeches were delivered, one of the tables, for no apparent reason, suddenly collapsed. This unusual occurrence was much commented upon and the hope was expressed that no mishap would happen to the ship after she left port. A little later the general body of pressmen decided to send congratulatory messages, including one to Mr Bruce Ismay – who was elsewhere on board the ship – and finding that all the tables were cluttered with the remnants of the lunch, they wrote their messages on the broken table after employing two waiters to hold up the broken portion.

At London's West End branch of the White Star Line, hundreds of callers made frantic enquiries in the days immediately following the disaster. Overwhelmed and anxious for news of their relatives and friends, they were shown the few brief messages that had filtered through. Many of them read with horror and consternation of the supposed loss of a loved one. Their only consolation at that time was the sympathetic manner of the company's manager, Mr Parton, who placated the worried crowd and observed, 'What discipline must have been maintained. The fact that nearly all those saved are women and children is, I think, evidence of that.' His words of comfort did not placate all of the people present. A little later, when the first official list of names was put on the notice board, many anxious eyes scrutinised it. Trembling fingers ran down the list, followed by a gasp of relief or cry of pain at the presence or absence of names. The sea of faces around the ominous board revealed joy, hope, anxiety and despair. One of those anxious people who enquired repeatedly as to the latest information, with regard to safety of the passengers and crew, was Mr Sydney Buxton, the president of the Board of Trade.

In the days following the disaster, the news agency Reuters experienced one of its busiest times in many years. On Tuesday 16 April 1912, Reuters issued the following reports to various newspapers:

HOPE OF MORE SURVIVORS (New York)
A telegram from St John's, Newfoundland, received at 2.15 this morning gives rise to the hope that the Virginian had some survivors of the Titanic on board. It is said that the Virginian would bring to St John's such survivors as she may rescue. This hope arises from the fact that the Virginian is putting back to St John's, which, as she is eastwards bound, she would scarcely do unless she was on a mission of mercy.

In actual fact, the Virginian was much too late to be of assistance to anyone.

OFFICIAL STATEMENT (New York, Tuesday 16 April)
The White Star Company announce officially that they have received positive news that the number of survivors from the Titanic is 868. The dispatch was transmitted by the Olympic.

EIGHT HUNDRED ABOARD CARPATHIA (New York, Tuesday 16 April)
Captain Rostron has sent a wireless message to the Cunard Company stating the Carpathia has eight hundred survivors aboard, and is slowly proceeding to New York through a field of ice.

CHAIRMAN OF WHITE STAR LINE (London, Tuesday 16 April)
A wireless message from the Olympic to the Central News correspondent states that Mr Joseph Bruce Ismay, Chairman of the White Star Line, is safe.

LONDON CORRESPONDENT (London, Tuesday night, 16 April)
The news in London tonight that overshadows all else is that of the confirmation of the appalling catastrophe which has destroyed the Titanic on her maiden voyage. The messages which were received last night that the passengers and crew were saved unhappily proved to be unfounded, and the latest cablegrams leave no doubt that nearly 1,400 souls have perished with the huge ship. When the intelligence of the disaster was confirmed here the feel-

ings of the public were numbed in the attempt to grasp the enormity of what it meant, but this soon gave way to consternation when the full force of the calamity was realised. The short career of the vessel and the enormous death roll furnish undoubtedly the greatest shipping disaster recorded in the history of the world. Those who saw the huge liner sailing out of Southampton less than a week ago, or who had an opportunity of seeing her in Cork Harbour on last Thursday, will fully appreciate the perils of the sea when they now learn that she and the majority of the human freight which she carried are no more.

The full details of the disaster are not yet to hand, but there is ample reason to believe that whatever news is to come will have no mitigating effect upon that which is already available. The offices of the White Star Line in London were today besieged by anxious enquirers who wished to ascertain the fate of relatives or friends, but could not obtain any information that was not to be found in the frequent editions of the evening papers which hourly gave to the public the latest details to hand of the terrible catastrophe.

Apart from the human point of view, the awful calamity is bound to have a world-wide effect, as it is almost certain that amongst the passengers lost are six millionaires whose combined capital exceeds 70 millions, and this, in the world of finance, constitutes a catastrophe which it would be hard to esti-mate. According to the latest advices a notable passenger, who is unaccounted for, and who it is feared is lost, is Mr W. T. Stead, the well-known journalist. America is the greatest sufferer by the disaster from the point of view of the numbers and influence of those who went down with the Titanic, but on an occasion such as this the sympathy of the world will be extended to the relatives of the lost. The proud boast that the vessel was unsinkable has proved to be a vain one, and the disaster supplies another terrible lesson that human science and ingenuity, even at its highest perfection in the twentieth century, avails little against the forces of nature.

There is an interesting little footnote to the report of the tragedy in several editions of the daily papers. In all editions, the report was unobtrusively tucked away in a tiny paragraph under the political section. Concerning yet another ship belonging to the White Star Company, it ran:

FIRE ON ADRIATIC (From our Correspondent, Liverpool, Tuesday 16 April) A fire broke out tonight on the White Star Liner Adriatic, lying in West Canada Dock, Liverpool. Fortunately, it was not serious. The woodwork of three cabins caught fire, but the fire engines promptly attended, and what might have been a serious outbreak was checked. The liner sails for New York on Thursday at 1.00 a.m.

While no reason was given for the fire, it must be considered as more than slightly suspicious that a ship owned by the White Star Company should suddenly and unaccountably burst into flames. It is even more suspicious that the same ship should be berthed in Liverpool, where a vast majority of victims sailed from and where the Titanic was registered and, the fact that the ship was due to sail to New York a few days later. These incidents, coupled with the fact that the fire broke out in three different places, can only lead to the thought that somebody, possibly with a grudge against the company, had deliberately started the fire. For their part – and it can only lead to confirmation of this suspicion – the White Star Line played down the incident and nobody was charged with a crime. Apparently the company did not want any further notoriety and possibly even wanted to forestall any possibility of setting a precedent.

Understandably, varying and sometimes grossly inaccurate reports of the disaster later went the rounds of the general public, and, as a consequence, yet another brave man found himself maligned and castigated; Joseph Bruce Ismay was destined to become as much a victim of the Titanic tragedy as Captain Lord did. Much of the popular press of the time reported a story – later proved to be a fabrication – of a man dressing in women's clothes and attempting to take a place in one of the lifeboats. It was generally intimated that the man in question was Ismay. As ridiculous as it may seem, people actually believed fervently in the story and the unfortunate Ismay found himself branded a coward. Even though, in his defence of the nonsensical charge, Ismay pointed out that he was a man of considerable stature – almost 6ft tall – and that he sported a moustache which would make him an unconvincing-looking woman, he still had the utmost difficulty in disproving the charge. In fact, as Ismay was fortunate enough to be in a position to prove his claims, he was one of the last to reluctantly leave his section of the ship in the last lifeboat. Previous to leaving the ship, he had worked very hard trying to get people off the ship and into lifeboats. Nevertheless, in spite of being able to prove this fact to the satisfaction of the inquiry, Ismay still found himself maligned and labelled for life. It mattered not that the accusations had been refuted and that Ismay had produced several witnesses to testify to his actions. People simply believed what they wanted to believe.

Speculation and rumour continued to follow Bruce Ismay all the days of his life – perhaps it was a case of the distinctive mark of thrown mud. In any event, rumours and innuendoes continued. It was later reported that he resigned his position as chairman of the White Star Line and became a recluse in Ireland after the disaster. In fact, nothing could be further from the truth. Ismay decided to resign from his position as chairman before the loss of the Titanic, but retained most of his numerous directorships. While he did live in Ireland for a period of time, he actually continued to live in London with his American wife, frequently travelling to Liverpool in connection with his work. It was in London that he died in 1937.

It was perhaps unfortunate that the subsequent newspaper reports drew heavily for their 'facts' from both the British and American investigations into the affair. This led, particularly in the case of the American inquiry, to a situation approaching an utter farce and resulted in nothing less than a 'kangaroo court', insofar as Captain Lord was concerned. To appreciate the seriousness of the situation, it is advisable at this stage to delve into the relevant sections of the American inquiry.

The rescue ship Carpathia docked in New York at exactly 9.35 p.m. on 18 April with her decks crowded with survivors from the disaster. Even before the ship had made landfall, a hastily convened inquiry was being organised by the Americans headed by Senator Alden Smith. Smith had been appointed by his fellow senators to chair the subcommittee which was to investigate the loss of the Titanic. The senator had been given this appointment as a result of a resolution which he himself had put to other members of the Senate. An accusation was levelled against the senator that he, in true political tradition, saw the golden opportunity to take advantage of the tremendous amount of publicity that would inevitably attach itself to the inquiry. He was not about to miss out on anything that could help his career. Whether this was a fair comment to make, the fact still remains that Senator Smith had absolutely no knowledge, or scope required, of maritime matters and must have been only too well aware that a considerable amount of technical expertise would have been a prerequisite for such an important undertaking. In this respect, Smith was patently unqualified to handle such an inquiry. Nevertheless he was successful in obtaining a hurried meeting with President Taft and managed to convince the president of the necessity for an investigation. Possibly the most important item that brought the president around to the senator's way of thinking was the fact that, as Smith pointed out forcefully, the Titanic was in effect an American ship, insofar as her owner, the White Star Line, was in turn owned by the parent company of J.P. Morgan's International Mercantile Marine. Wisely, Smith neglected to point out that he had as an ulterior motive behind his obvious enthusiasm to chair the inquiry. Both Smith and Morgan were, apparently, long-time adversaries – some would say outright enemies – and here, clearly, was a golden opportunity for the senator to have a go at Morgan in the public eye.

President Taft duly gave his permission for the inquiry and appointed Attorney General Wickersham to assist Senator Smith by allowing Smith to subpoena the British witnesses while they were on American soil. Aware that he would have to move quickly before the Britons left for home, the senator immediately issued writs to all the officers and crew of the Titanic, and also one to Bruce Ismay whom he saw as an indirect employee of J.P. Morgan. Because of this dubious connection, Ismay was singled out for 'special treatment' and was to be considerably harassed before finally being allowed to sail for home.

Those officers and crewmembers fortunate enough to have survived the disaster now found themselves to be virtual prisoners in that they had been legally summoned and, until such time as the senator permitted, were not to be allowed to leave the United States. Smith now set about picking his subcommittee and, in what appeared a feeble attempt to achieve some semblance of balance, he picked six senators from six different states. The fact that none of the six, like Smith, had any previous experience of such matters and therefore were unqualified as their chairman, apparently raised not one dissenting eyebrow. The six picked by Senator Smith were Senator Duncan U. Fletcher of Florida; Senator Jonathan Bourne of Oregon; Senator George C. Perkins of California; Senator Furnifold M. Simmons of North Carolina; Senator Theodore Burton of Ohio and Senator Francis G. Newlands of Nevada.

Of the seven senators, including Smith, only four could be said to be remotely familiar with the sea, and only because they lived adjacent to it. The idea of appointing the senators from Nevada and Oregon, which is predominantly desert and scrubland, far removed from maritime matters, seemed almost idiotic. Nevertheless, unqualified as these men were, Senator Smith made his choice. These were the men duly appointed to sit in judgement on the officers and crew of the Titanic and Californian, men who, by and large, had literally centuries of seafaring blood running through their veins. It was only a matter of time before it became obvious to even the

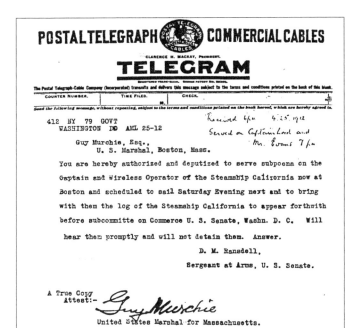

POSTAL TELEGRAPH COMMERCIAL CABLES

TELEGRAM

The Postal Telegraph-Cable Company (Incorporated) transmits and delivers this message subject to the terms and conditions printed on the back of this blank.

COUNTER NUMBER.	TIME FILED.	CHECK.

Send the following message, without repeating, subject to the terms and conditions printed on the back hereof, which are hereby agreed to.

412 NY 79 GOVT
WASHINGTON DC AML 25-12

Received 6pm 4.25.1912
Served on Captain Lord and
Mr. Evans 7pm

Guy Murchie, Esq.,
U. S. Marshal, Boston, Mass.

You are hereby authorized and deputized to serve subpoena on the Captain and Wireless Operator of the Steamship California now at Boston and scheduled to sail Saturday Evening next and to bring with them the log of the Steamship California to appear forthwith before subcommitte on Commerce U. S. Senate, Washn. D. C. Will hear them promptly and will not detain them. Answer.

D. M. Ransdell,

Sergeant at Arms, U. S. Senate.

A True Copy
Attest:- *Guy Murchie*

United States Marshal for Massachusetts.

The subpoena which was served on Captain Lord and wireless operator Evans ordering them to appear before the subcommittee of the U.S. Senate.

most casual onlooker that the entire affair was nothing more than a political football. It was even suggested that Senator Smith used his position as chairman of the investigation to score points over his archenemy, J.P. Morgan. People, particularly some of the British and American reporters, began to write scathing reports of the inquiry. Many emotional articles found their way into print. Without exception, all made a mockery of the rather grandiose term 'investigation'.

Initially, Senator Smith's immediate intention was to get Bruce Ismay to admit negligence by either the Titanic's owners or operators. Smith was so determined to achieve this that he couldn't even wait until the investigation had officially commenced. No sooner had the Carpathia docked than Smith immediately boarded her, surrounded by an entourage of newspaper reporters, and promptly began to question Ismay in the surgeon's cabin, where the chairman of the line was still receiving care for exhaustion and hypothermia. Previous to boarding the rescue ship, Smith had assured reporters that he saw 'no difficulties or obstacles raised by the White Star Line or by British authorities which would impede his investigation.' He was both forcefully and immediately disappointed. Ismay refused to answer any questions or to even discuss the tragedy until the actual inquiry had commenced, and ended by asking the crestfallen senator to leave. Somewhat deflated, and seeing that things were not going to be as smooth as he had at first thought, Smith reluctantly left the ship and had to be content with watching the Titanic's third-class passengers being examined by the port's immigration authorities.

The incident, witnessed by the press, was a devastating blow to the senator's ego. He was obviously disappointed that he had been unable to get Ismay to admit to negligence onboard the ship. Had he been successful in doing this he would then have been in the strong position to have obtained the right to sue J.P. Morgan's IMM company, which, considering the enormity of the tragedy, would have greatly damaged the Morgan empire, if not topple it down altogether. There would have been a further bonus had his ploy worked. He would have been seen to have been working for the financial gain of some of his constituents by bringing about a situation which would have enabled interested parties and individuals the opportunity of suing IMM for substantial damages. This would have been made possible under the Harter Act, which was enacted following the loss of the La Bourgogne in 1898. This law stated that if a company which owned a steamship had knowledge of any negligence aboard the ship, which led to an accident, the individual passengers or surviving next of kin could sue the company for damages. The Titanic, effectively owned by IMM, would have come under this Act, and, whether Ismay was aware of this fact or not, he was saying nothing that might incriminate the company. There is no doubt that Ismay was well aware of the dangerous conditions in the vicinity of the Titanic and that the ship was travelling at a rate which might have been considered to be excessive – knowledge which could be construed as an awareness of negligence.

Perhaps Ismay's stance on the question of negligence can be understood and credited to his benefit when we accept that he was, often in a very brash manner, browbeaten by the senator. Whatever his reasons, Ismay took great exception to his treatment and, quite possibly felt it his duty to remain loyal to the White Star Line in view of the fact that he was still chairman and managing director of the company. Perhaps too he felt some deeper emotion for those who perished in the disaster. However, Ismay was to remain tight-lipped on this one aspect throughout the entire inquiry and retained his stance against frequent and often hostile questioning.

As far as could be ascertained, Ismay never told outright lies during his questioning. Rather, he skilfully managed to evade issues that might have lead to the charge of negligence. There was no doubt that he was only too aware that the ship was travelling at an excessive speed in view of the surrounding conditions and of the several ice warnings which the ship had received. Knowing these facts, Ismay could be said to have been economical with the truth. At times Ismay found the senator's questioning, not only forceful, but downright offensive, and he reacted accordingly. Taking their cue from the chairman, and quite obviously feeling a substantial amount of animosity to some of the more leading questions, the officers and crew, when questioned about negligence, suddenly developed a total loss of memory. Not one person who was questioned admitted that they were aware of any negligence on the ship. The truth of the matter was that most of the crew, and certainly all of the officers, were well aware of the dangerous speed and conditions they were sailing under. In this context they were, strictly speaking, well aware of negligence and, by denying that fact, in effect, all lied.

The entire issue is rather misleading. Of course, Senator Smith knew, with the benefit of hindsight, that Titanic's speed had been excessive under the prevailing conditions, although she had not attempted or even been designed to establish a new record. Her owners had relinquished the quest for the famous Blue Riband as far back as 1890 in favour of other lines. Cunard's Lusitania and Mauretania, both of 1907, were fifty per cent smaller and far more powerful than Olympic and Titanic, but competition between White Star, Cunard, Norddeutscher Lloyd, Hapag and especially Cie Générale Transatlantique was fierce. A huge, fast, luxurious ocean liner that could boast reliability in swift crossings brought enormous prestige, and money, to its owners. Back in 1898-99, the 12,481-ton NDL liner Kaiser Friedrich[2] had been refused by her owners and, ultimately, returned to her builders permanently because she failed to achieve the twenty-two knots required to make her a suitable running mate for the Kaiser Wilhelm der Grosse, Blue Riband holder from 1897 until 1900. Kaiser Friedrich had scarcely managed to achieve twenty knots instead.

By taking this stance, those who were questioned were in fact committing themselves to repeating their 'evidence' at any and all subsequent inquiries. Obviously they could hardly say one thing at one inquiry and then say another thing later. Finding a reason for their attitude is not easy. It could hardly be attributed to their loyalty to the White Star Line, who had stopped their wages the moment the ship sank and was the reason they were stranded in America and penniless. Perhaps it was through some inherent sense of what they saw as their 'patriotic duty' or even loyalty to Ismay, who was a popular figure with them. It is also likely that they resented the manner in which Ismay was being singled out for special attention. They gave him their total support. In any event, not one person ever admitted negligence on anyone's part.

The inquiry dragged on for seventeen days during which eighty-two witnesses were asked various, and sometimes idiotic questions, first in New York, then in Washington and finally back in New York again. At every opportunity Senator Smith repeatedly inundated Ismay with questions relating to negligence to which he invariably received the same weary reply, 'I know of no negligence aboard the ship.'

Early in the proceedings, it became obvious to Senator Smith that Ismay had dug his heels in and that Smith was not about to elicit any incriminating evidence from him. On Saturday 20 April, the second day of the inquiry, desperate to find somebody who would admit knowledge of negligence on the Titanic, the senator issued federal subpoenas to twenty-nine more crew members of the ship just as they were about to sail for Liverpool aboard the Lapland. Obviously disgusted, the men duly presented themselves to Smith and complained bitterly of being virtually held prisoners onboard the Lapland since they had disembarked from the Carpathia two days earlier. Apart from being allowed to attend a service for their dead companions on the previous day, their movements had been severely restricted and they had not been allowed to leave the ship on which they had been placed. Initially, their complaints had been totally ignored as the senator now set about questioning the twenty-nine men. Not surprisingly, he received the usual answer to his questions: 'I know of no negligence aboard the Titanic.' A little later, much to his horror, Smith discovered that yet another five crew members had not been subpoenaed and actually sailed for home aboard the Lapland. On the off-chance that one of these men might give him the break he was seeking so desperately, Smith immediately contacted the Navy Yard at Brooklyn and instructed them to send a radio message to the Lapland to stop and await a boarding party. This was immediately complied with and some time later a federal marshal reached the Liverpool-bound ship by tug boat and the five seamen were officially detained and brought back to New York. It was to prove an exercise in futility. Not only did the five men complain bitterly and forcefully at their treatment, but all gave Smith the now familiar reply to his questions, and disclaimed all knowledge of any negligence on board the Titanic. They further ruffled his feathers by objecting to having been treated like criminals. Contrary to his expectations, the senator now had – including Ismay – thirty-five potentially hostile witnesses.

Although the inquiry was only into its second day, Ismay reminded the court that he had several times given all the evidence he had and now he wished to return to England where another inquiry awaited him. Smith promptly refused the permission and told Ismay that he would require further questioning at a later date. On the following day, Sunday, the sub-committee decided to reconvene the inquiry in the capital city and the entire court took off for Washington in a collection of trains and various vehicles. It was to be here that the ugly spectre of class distinction reared its head and that the great British tradition of 'them and us' came to the fore.

Booked into the reasonably opulent Continental Hotel, the officers immediately began to object to having to double-up in the rooms. They also made it quite clear that they didn't like the idea of crewmembers sharing the same floor. The crew also objected to the close proximity of the officers, and the situation was finally resolved by putting the officers on a different floor. The following morning the crew was moved to another hotel.

The inquiry recommenced on Monday morning and immediately took on the aspect of a farce, as the chief witnesses actually had difficulty in getting into the room due to the huge number of newspaper reporters present. Eventually, and before the inquiry could even begin, the Sergeant-at-Arms was forced to establish order in the noisy throng. When order had finally been established, a hush fell on the room as Fourth Officer Joseph G. Boxhall[3] in describing how the lifeboats were loaded, made the first official mention of a 'mystery ship' in the vicinity (this aspect will be covered in a later chapter). On Wednesday of that week, Titanic's Fifth Officer Harold G. Lowe gave worthy evidence, pointing to a glaring act of blatant negligence which was directly responsible for the loss of several hundred lives.

Asked why some of the lifeboats had left the Titanic only partially full, and in some cases more than half empty, Lowe replied that the officers in charge of loading the boats were afraid that the combined weight of the passengers, sixty to a boat, would, in their opinion, be too heavy. They were convinced that the boats would buckle and break in two before reaching the water, due to the weight. As a result of this belief they did not actually fill the boats to their capacity. Lowe went on to justify this action by saying that the officers were under the impression that other passengers would be put into the boats at a lower level as the boats neared the water. Later, when the Titanic was within minutes of sinking, the remaining boats were crammed with people, in many cases considerably more than sixty, and all made a safe descent to the water. Contrary to what Lowe expected to happen, that the half-filled boats would pick up further survivors at different levels of the ship, no such thing happened. Neither, as Lowe also expected, did any of the lifeboats remain in the vicinity of the ship to pick up passengers who were floundering in the water. It was only later, when the ship had actually gone down, that a few boats reluctantly returned to the scene to pick up more survivors.

As important and vital as this evidence was, the inquiry appeared to set little importance on it and, after accepting the evidence, the matter was allowed to drop. It was to be a major lost opportunity for Senator Smith to prove negligence and, had he pursued the question of the lifeboats, the inquiry might not have turned out to be the bungling farce, as later dubbed in the press. Clearly, the inexperience and lack of maritime knowledge among the subcommittee led to the matter not being considered as overly important, as they obviously saw their first responsibility as being in a position to appropriate blame for the tragedy. It could be said that the senator and his subcommittee couldn't see the wood for the trees.

The question of the lifeboats, however, received a much more thorough examination at the subsequent British inquiry and a devastating fact emerged. It was on 2 May that Naval Architect Mr Edward Wilding, for the ship's builders, Harland & Wolff, testified that Titanic's lifeboats had been test-lowered at the builder's yard, carrying the equivalent weight of a full complement of passengers. This trial was actually carried out during the testing of the newly installed Welin davits. The result was that all boats were successfully lowered to the ship's plimsoll line without mishap, and both the davits and boats were proved to be in excellent working order and quite capable of taking the weight applied to them. It can only be to the eternal disgrace of the White Star Line that the results of these tests were never made known to the Titanic's officers. Had they been made known, clearly the lifeboats would have been filled to their capacity and tremendous loss of life avoided. This omission then, perhaps not considered important at the time, must of necessity be construed as some vestige of culpable negligence by those in authority for the safety of the ship's complement. Yet, once again, amazingly enough, the British inquiry did not see fit to place any undue emphasis on the matter and, like the American inquiry, allowed the matter to drop.

On the day before Fifth Officer Lowe gave his testimony to the American inquiry, Ismay made yet another appeal to Senator Smith to be allowed to return to England, or to New York where 'company business' awaited him. Once again the request was denied.

TITANIC CALAMITY

QUESTIONS IN PARLIAMENT

WOMEN AND CHILDREN VICTIMS.

TRAGIC MISCARRIAGE

BIG LINER CLOSE BY

WIRELESS OUT OF ORDER.

AMERICAN INQUIRY.

FIFTH OFFICER'S EVIDENCE.

QUARTERMASTER ARRESTED

TITANIC SUNK.

EARLY THIS MORNING.

1,683 LOST.

675 SAVED

187 IRISH

MANY FROM CORK

OFFICIAL ADMISSION.

NEARLY 1,700 MSSING.

New York, 9.50 p.m.

The White Star officials now admit that probably only 675 out of the 2,358 passengers an dcrew onboard the Titanic have been saved.

This confirms Reuter's advices from Cape Ace as to the time of sinking.—Reuter.

Persistent, Ismay then arrived at Senator Smith's office the following morning with an attorney and again demanded to be allowed to leave. It was to no avail. Smith still resolutely refused the permission and a very angry and irate Ismay stormed out of the office. Aware that oral pleas were falling on deaf ears, Ismay now adopted a different approach and wrote the senator a letter in which he complained bitterly of the unfairness of being kept in America against his will. He strongly pointed out that he had 'no further contributions or evidence' to offer the inquiry. For his part, Smith replied with a letter of his own in which he stated very forcefully that he 'would tolerate no outside or individual interference with his pursuit of the truth'. He went on to say that, 'I am sure the message will be received in the same spirit in which it is written.'

Senator Smith's seemingly polite reply could be construed as a sarcastic reference to the fact that the British press, both in the States and in England, now began to slate Smith and his subcommittee for their inefficient handling of the inquiry and also that none of the investigators was suitably qualified to conduct such an important hearing. Ismay was convinced that the senator's reply was no more than a thinly disguised tongue-in-cheek remark which actually meant, 'Take this what way you will, I'm not about to become pressurised by you or the British press in this matter.' There is little doubt but that this attitude of the senator's was due to the London Daily Express calling Smith 'asinine', while other British papers had gone even further and made references to legality of the proceedings. Some of the papers questioned the lack of qualification of Smith and his committee members, and some even went out on a libellous limb and questioned Smith's personal integrity. Under one of its many headings, the Daily Express called the inquiry a 'parody of Judicial Inquiry'. Considering the almost casual manner in which the inquiry had been conducted, it was difficult, if not impossible, not to agree with some of the sentiments expressed by the British press.

Nevertheless, in spite of all the opposition by the vast majority of the British media, Senator Smith too had his own fair share of supporters in both Britain and America. As the furore of public opinion grew, most of it fanned into life by the press. Some papers, British and American, rushed to the defence of the senator insisting that he only wanted to get at the 'facts' of the case. Smith dismissed all press criticisms as 'gross inaccuracies and half-truthful information cabled to England by imaginative reporters'. An editorial comment in the New York Herald supported the senator against the British 'attack':

Nothing has been more sympathetic, more gentle in its highest sense than the conduct of the Inquiry by the senate committee, and yet self-complacent moguls in England call this impertinent ... This country intends to find out why so many American lives were wasted by the incompetence of British seamen, and why women and children were sent to their deaths while so many in a British crew have been saved.

There can be absolutely no doubt that if such highly inflammatory reports were to appear in present-day papers in relation to a disaster or inquiry of this nature, then the court would immediately place heavy reporting restrictions on the media. In 1912, however, no such methods were applied and the inquiry was as much conducted in the press as it was in the court room. Because of this, and the public's angry opinions, it soon became evident that there was much more involved here than just the loss of the Titanic. Clearly, personalities and politics were involved. High finance became an important factor, and the future of many a person and company was at stake. There were also remnants of the old rivalry between America and England, and many old wounds were re-opened. Amid all this, the question of the loss of Titanic seemed to take second place.

Amid all the confusion and bickering that went on back and forth in the newspapers, and in the inquiry, nobody thought to ask Ismay why he was so determined to return to England. Indeed, to this day it has never been satisfactorily explained why Ismay consistently insisted in being allowed to leave America and, consequently, leave the inquiry. Could it have been possible that the persistent line of questioning was beginning to wear him down? Was he afraid that sooner or later he would 'slip up' and reveal something that either he or the White Star Line might regret? To speculate on these questions would be unfair, as the simple answer might be that the man was just plain fed up with the idiotic way in which the inquiry was being conducted.

Senator Smith finally came to the inevitable conclusion that he was patently achieving nothing more than the animosity of a lot of people in both England and America by his handling of the inquiry. As a result, he decided to change his tactics. Psychology was called for, and applied with some success. Acknowledging that he would not be able to establish blame under the Harter Act with incriminating statements relating to negligence, Smith now adopted a slightly different approach which, he hoped, might lead to the Morgan empire being held responsible. The senator was obviously obsessed with the possibility of proving negligence aboard the Titanic and seemed reluctant to let the matter drop. His new approach to the problem was also destined to fail miserably and leave the senator somewhat frustrated in his efforts. His argument was based rather loosely on the moral aspect of the case and, although a lot of what he argued made moral sense, it did not impress the defending lawyers, who were quick to point out that they were dealing with matters of legalities, not of morals.

The Californian on the morning of 15 April 1912 after meeting with the Carpathia. The photograph was taken by Mrs James A. Fenwick, a passenger. It was arranged between Lord and Rostron that the Californian continue her search for possible survivors, while Carpathia returned to New York. Courtesy of Titanic Historical Society, Inc.

A politician is nothing if he is not versatile. In this respect Senator Smith was no exception to the rule. Realising that if he were to save anything from this mess, he would have to change his methods. Smith did exactly that. Where he had previously adopted an austere, sometimes loud and brash officious tone with the witnesses, he now tried a much softer approach.

In spite of the fact that the officers of the Titanic were, like Ismay, anxious to leave for home, the crew of the ship was now beginning to enjoy their unexpected stay in Washington. Smith, obviously working on the premise that some members of the crew might prove to be the weak link in the chain, he now began to call each man by his first name and encouraged them to address him as Bill or Al. Having gained what he understood to be the respect and friendship of the men, Smith then arranged for their daily expenses to be raised from $3.00 a day (12s) to the princely sum of $5.00 a day (£1.00). Restrictions on travel were lifted and the crew suddenly found themselves to be the centre of attraction. They became guests of various organisations in Washington and were treated to a special visit to the Washington Lodge of the Benevolent and Protective Order of Elks. From being almost broke, virtual prisoners, they now were given free bus tours of the city and were guests of honour at several different large church denominations.

Senator Smith pulled no punches in his blatant attempts to woo the English seamen. Everywhere they went they were both lauded and applauded. Unfortunately, both for the crew and the senator, their newfound freedom left them with one major problem. In spite of their increased finances, despite more freedom and time on their hands, they couldn't manage to survive on the daily $3 allowance. In spite of the increase that the senator arranged for them, they were still invariably broke and constantly found themselves with less than sufficient cash to enjoy the delights the capital city had to offer. Aware that no additional money would be forthcoming from the American government coffers, they hit on a novel and profitable way of raising more money. The manager of the local Imperial Theatre, a popular music hall of the period, agreed to pay the crew for appearing in a sideshow attraction and allowed them to mix freely with the patrons after their appearance. The arrangement worked out mutually satisfactorily and the grateful audience, upon being told of the sad financial situation of the Titanic's crew, usually took up a collection for them. So popular did the sideshow become that the theatre manager had posters put up around the city which showed some of the crew and added the caption, 'The crew will receive the entire proceeds from the first show.' The audiences in the theatre almost quadrupled as people crowded in to see the crew of the Titanic in the flesh. They would sit, entranced and all agog as the crew recounted some of their experiences and, whether they realised it or not, more than one 'experience' would be recalled with various embellishments and additions. In fact, it was in these circumstances that many a gullible reporter penned a fascinating 'exclusive' of the disaster.

Amid all the debatable distraction, the inquiry continued and now took on, if not a more sinister aspect, then certainly a more suspect one. Senator Smith was now apparently under the impression that he had softened up the crewmembers sufficiently for them to be a little more forthcoming with their information. On Thursday 25 April, they were questioned individually by members of the subcommittee. The day's activities ended at 10.00 p.m. with Senator Smith putting leading questions to Evans, Hemming and Haines, three other members of the crew. Sadly for the senator, his attempts at psychology failed and every crewman resolutely and consistently denied any knowledge of negligence aboard the Titanic.

APPALLING DISASTER

TITANIC LOST

COLLIDES WITH ICEBERG.

2,358 ON BOARD

ONLY 675 SAVED

187 IRISH PASSENGERS

MEAGRE DETAILS

CONFLICTING MESSAGES

News received shortly before going to Press makes it only too probable that one of the most appalling disasters in the history of the sea has to be recorded.

The White Star Liner Titanic, the largest in the world, which left Queenstown on Thursday with 2,358 souls on board, was in collision on Sunday night with an iceberg off Newfoundland.

It was at first reported that the liner had sunk. Later it was declared that her watertight compartments held so well that she was able to make for Halifax, accompanied by several liners, whose aid she had summoned by wireless telegraphy.

All the passengers were believed to be safe.

Mr. and Mrs. Phillips, of Farncombe, Godalming, parents of the wireless telegraphing operator on the Titanic, last night received the following message from their son—"Making slowly for Halifax; practically unsinkable. Don't worry."

Unhappily, in the early hours of this morning cables from Reuter's Agency stated that the liner had sunk, and that only 675 were saved. As she had 2,358 on board at Queenstown, the death-roll must be nearly 1,700, unless by some happy chance some steamer may have picked up more survivors. 187 of the passengers were Irish.

On the following morning, Smith, still no doubt angry that he had not managed to elicit any dawning evidence, now turned his attention to the Leyland ship Californian. Like the Titanic, the Californian also came under the umbrella of the Morgan empire. First to testify was the master, Captain Stanley Lord and two crewmembers, wireless operator Cyril Evans and donkeyman Ernest Gill. The lack of maritime qualifications became immediately obvious on the part of the senator and his committee and led to considerable confusion. This was in connection with the exact status of Ernest Gill. Gill had been variously listed as a 'donkey man', 'deckhand', 'assistant engineer' and 'fireman' on the ship's official papers. With the exception of the title, 'deckhand', all the other terms referred to the same job. Gill actually worked as a stoker and had additional responsibilities in the engine room. At times he doubled as a deckhand and this is undoubtedly the reason for the confusion about his status. When this confusion was sorted out, Gill was put on the stand to give evidence. He swore that an affidavit which he had given in Boston on 24 April was his, and that it was correct and true in every respect. Gill had given sworn testimony that he had seen 'a large ship near the Californian and what appeared to be two rockets fired from a distance of about ten miles away'. Surprisingly, Gill was not asked to elaborate on his statement or to describe this 'large ship' he had seen. Neither was he asked what he meant by 'what appeared to be two rockets' or indeed, how he calculated the distance of 'ten miles'. Captain Lord was next to be questioned. He gave evidence regarding his position on the night/morning of the 14/15 April, telling the court of his repeated attempts to contact a nearby ship by Morse lamp and not receiving a reply. He impressed upon the court that it was highly probable that those onboard the other ship totally ignored the Morse lamp signals (this point will be dealt with in a later chapter).

Finally, Cyril Evans, Californian's wireless operator, gave his testimony and related his account of how, on Captain Lord's orders, he contacted the Titanic and warned of ice in the vicinity. He also confirmed that the Californian's apprentice had informed Lord on three separate occasions about the rockets seen by Gill and other members of the crew. While this in itself was not as damning a statement as first appeared, because Lord had said that he had been aware of the rockets, it nevertheless gave Senator Smith his long-awaited opportunity. He immediately and vigorously pounced on the matter, ending with the remarks which were to prove so decisive to Captain Lord's case and setting the tone for the subsequent British investigation (examined in detail in Chapter 3).

In effect, Senator Smith's words had put the first nail in the coffin of Captain Lord. Many more were destined to follow in quick succession. In spite of the fact that Lord had stated that there had been a third ship between he and the Titanic, which proved to be true, the senator simply brushed aside this statement as being of no importance to the case and concluded that 'Captain Lord has deluded himself about the presence of another ship between himself and the Titanic. There was no such ship. He bore a heavy responsibility'. What the senator was saying, in effect, was that there were only the Titanic and the Californian in close proximity to each other in that busy shipping lane. It was, to say the least, a very irresponsible statement to make and only served to emphasize the senator's obvious lack of qualification to deal with the case. As it happened, there were in excess of twenty ships in the area, seven in the immediate vicinity, and no less than two ships between Titanic and the Californian, one of which was assumed to be the Californian.

In spite of this glaring fact, Smith was reluctant to let go of his one chance to apportion blame. He was not about to allow himself to be side-tracked. Notwithstanding the fact that Lord only appeared before the subcommittee as a witness, as opposed to being on 'trial', the senator, seizing what appeared to him a golden opportunity, went on to systematically condemn Lord for his negligence in failing to respond to what were obviously distress signals from the Titanic. This sweeping and highly inflammatory statement was of course, totally without foundation and mainly consisted of a lot of speculation and a complete disregard for the facts of the case. Apparently it mattered not to Senator Smith that he was firstly, condemning a man without benefit of trial and secondly, that he had no legal right to make sweeping and defamatory statements, completely ignoring the democratic and legal rights of Captain Lord. Smith indulged in a lot of speculation and conjecture in regard to the case.

A few weeks later in the British inquiry, echoing the senator's words and opinion, and impressed or influenced by the sensationalism of the media, Lord Mersey made the following statement:

> There are contradictions and inconsistencies in the story as told by the different witnesses. But the truth of the matter is plain. The Titanic collided with an iceberg at 11.40 p.m. The vessel seen by the Californian stopped at this time. The rockets sent up from the Titanic were distress signals. The Californian saw distress signals. The number sent up by the Titanic was about eight. The Californian saw eight. The time over which the rockets from the Titanic were sent up was from about 12.45 a.m. to 1.45 a.m. It was about this time that the Californian saw the rockets. At 2.40 a.m., Mr Stone (the Californian's second officer) called to the master (Lord) that the ship from which he had seen the rockets had disappeared. At 2.20 a.m., the Titanic had foundered. It was suggested that the rockets seen by the Californian were from some other ship, not the Titanic. But no other ship to fit this theory has ever been heard of.

TITANIC CALAMITY

205 BODIES FOUND

MOUNT ROYAL'S POSITION

CAPTAIN'S DEPOSITION

AMERICAN INQUIRY

MR. MARCONI EXAMINED

THE WIRELESS MESSAGES.

The Senatorial Inquiry into the Titanic disaster was resumed yesterday. Mr. Marconi was the first witness. He said the wireless station at Cape Race had a radius up to a thousand miles. There was no alarm signal on the wireless instruments to attract attention. He did not hear of the sinking of the Titanic until the evening of April 15th, and he did not suppress messages from the Carpathia. He was in favour of regulating the use of wireless telegraphy.

Mr. Cottam, operator on the Carpathia, recalled, repeated the statements made by him in New York regarding signals. He added that he himself got into communication with six or seven ships, but he could not tell how far away some of them were. After the Titanic's survivors were picked up witness was too busy sending messages for passengers to give information to others.

Up to last evening the London Mansion House Titanic Fund amounted to £147,000.

These circumstances convince me that the ship seen by the Californian was the Titanic, and if so, according to Captain Lord, the two vessels were about five miles apart at the time of the disaster. The evidence from the Titanic corroborates this estimate, but I am advised that the distance was probably greater, though not more than eight to ten miles. The ice by which the Californian was surrounded was loose ice extending for a distance of not more than two or three miles in the direction of the Titanic. The night was clear and the sea was smooth. When she first saw the rockets the Californian could have pushed through the ice to open water without serious risk to herself and so have come to the assistance of the Titanic. Had she done so, she might have saved many if not all of the lives that were lost.

On 18 April 1912, the Daily Mirror reported the official statement by the White Star Line that junior operator Harold Bride was among the rescued.

Lord Mersey's statement, clearly blaming Captain Lord for the appalling loss of life, was in itself riddled with inconsistencies, gross inaccuracies and a lot of speculation. Taken at face value it would seem to be a damning indictment against Lord, however, it was far removed from the truth. Once again Lord found himself on trial, despite the fact that he only appeared as a witness in the case. Yet again, he was not given effective legal representation and, to add insult to injury, especially his character, he was not given the basic opportunity to defend himself against Lord Mersey's remarks. As a result, nail number two was firmly driven home.

The American inquiry finally drew to a close and had in effect achieved nothing concrete, apart from castigating Lord for his alleged inaction. Senator Smith had to be content with making several recommendations to the senate, one of which was that a medal be struck and presented to Captain Rostron of the Carpathia for his rescue of the survivors of the tragedy. The recommendation was duly passed and an award was later made to Rostron. In castigating Captain Lord, the inquiry apparently forgot to mention that it was, among others, the Californian which had warned the Titanic of the danger of icebergs in the area. It also conveniently forgot to mention that the Californian also came to the rescue, albeit too late, of the sinking Titanic. Nevertheless, the inquiry chose to ignore the fact that in so doing the Californian endangered herself considerably by ploughing through the huge ice field, not just once, but on two separate occasions, while other ships preferred to sail around the tip of the extended ice in a more cautious manner (see charts on pages 93 and 95).

A few days before the American inquiry ended officially, the officers and crew of the Titanic were finally allowed to return home and, on 30 April, Ismay also finally received the permission he had waited for and joined his countrymen aboard the Baltic. Two days later, a much relieved and slightly apprehensive collection of men sailed for Liverpool to face yet another inquiry.

REFERENCES

1 In actual fact, the position reported and initially given by Titanic was incorrect.

2 Kaiser Friedrich remained laid up at Hamburg from October 1900 until mid-1912. She was bought in May of that year by the Cie. de Navigation Sud Atlantique. Reboilered and renamed Burdigala, she entered the South Atlantic service, but was rejected again in 1913. Requisitioned by the French Navy in 1915, she was converted into a troop transport and later into a merchant cruiser. On 14 November 1916 she struck a mine laid by the German sub U-73 two miles SW of St Nicolo (Kea Channel) and sank. Ironically, exactly one week later, HMHS Britannic, Titanic's second sister, came to rest nearby after hitting a mine laid by the very same U-boat. Burdigala's wreck has not been discovered.

3 Boxhall was the last surviving officer of the Titanic. He died in June 1967 and his ashes, in accordance with his last wish, were scattered over the site of the Titanic wreck. Ironically, the ashes were scattered over the wrong area.

THREE

The British Investigation

It should be noted from the Copy of Proceedings that Mr C. Robertson Dunlop watched the proceedings on behalf of the owners and officers of the SS Californian. The operative word here is 'watched' as opposed to 'defended'. It is advisable to make this distinction because, as we have seen, Lord merely appeared as a witness and was never actually charged with any crime. Likewise, it is also not necessary or indeed possible, to reproduce the entire text of the inquiry. To do so would be impractical as it would run to several hundred pages. In view of this, it is best if we confine ourselves to that section of the inquiry which deals specifically with the Lord aspect and any other incidents directly related to it. Following is that section of the inquiry dealing with the circumstances surrounding the Californian. Officially entitled, 'Lord Mersey's Report', it is reproduced faithfully and verbatim:

(5) The Circumstances In Connection With The SS Californian (Pages 43-46)

On the 14th of April, the SS Californian of the Leyland Line, Mr Stanley Lord, master, was on her passage from London, which port she left on April 5th, to Boston, U.S. where she subsequently arrived on April 19th. She was a vessel of 6,223 tons gross and 4,038 net. Her full speed was 12½ to 13 knots. She had a passenger certificate, but was not carrying any passengers at the time. She belonged to the International Mercantile Marine Company, the owners of the Titanic.

At 7.30 p.m., ship's time, on 14 April, a wireless message was sent from this ship to the Antillian: 'To Captain, Antillian, 6.30 p.m., apparent ship's time, lat. 42° 3' N, Long., 49° 9' W. Three large bergs, 5 miles to southward of us, Regards – Lord.' (Evans, 8941 – 8943) [the numbers and names indicate the person and question number at the inquiry].

> The message was intercepted by the Titanic and when the Marconi operator of the Californian (Evans) offered this ice report to the Marconi operator of the Titanic, shortly after 7.30 p.m., the latter replied, 'It is alright. I heard you sending it to the Antillian, and I have got it.' (Lord, 8972 & 6710)

The Californian proceeded on her course S 89° W. true until 10.20 p.m. ship's time, when she was obliged to stop and reverse engines because she was running into field ice, which stretched as far as could be seen to the northward and southward.

> The master told the court that he had made her position at that time to be 42° 05' N, 50° 07' W. This position is recorded in the logbook, which was written up from the scrap logbook by the chief officer. The scrap log is destroyed. It is a position about 19 miles N. by E. of the position of the Titanic when she foundered, and is said to have been fixed by dead reckoning and verified observations. I am satisfied that this position is not accurate. The master 'twisted her head' to ENE by the compass and she remained stationary until 5.15 a.m. on the following morning. The ship was slowly swinging round to starboard during the night. (Lord 6713, Groves 8249)

> At about 11.00 p.m. a steamer's light was seen approaching from the eastward. The master went to Evans' room and asked, 'What ships he had.' The latter replied, 'I think the Titanic is near us. I have got her'. The master said, 'You had better advise the Titanic we are stopped and surrounded with ice'. This Evans did, calling up the Titanic and sending: 'We are stopped and surrounded by ice'. The Titanic replied: 'Keep out'. The Titanic was in communication with Cape Race, which station was then sending messages to her. The reason why the Titanic answered 'Keep out' was that her Marconi operator could not hear what Cape Race was saying, as from her proximity, the message from the Californian was much stronger than any message being taken in by the Titanic from Cape Race, which was much further off. Evans heard the Titanic continuing to communicate with Cape Race up to the time he turned in at 11.30 pm.
>
> The master of the Californian states that when observing the approaching steamer as she got nearer, he saw more lights, a few deck lights, and also her

LIST OF
WITNESSES IN THE ORDER IN WHICH THEY APPEARED.

Date.	Name of Witness	Description.	Numbers of Questions.	Page.
2nd day (3rd May, 1912).	1. ARCHIE JEWELL	Lookout man	1 to 331	16 to 21
3rd day	2. JOSEPH SCARROTT	Able seaman	332 to 651	22 to 29
3rd day (7th May).	3. GEORGE WILLIAM BEAUCHAMP	Fireman	652 to 892	31 to 36
	4. ROBERT HITCHINS	Quartermaster	893 to 1385	36 to 46
	5. WILLIAM LUCAS	Able seaman	1386 to 1834	46 to 53
	6. FREDERICK BARRETT	Leading stoker	1834 to 2075	53 to 60
4th day (8th May).	FREDERICK BARRETT (continued)		2076 to 2361	61 to 66
	7. REGINALD ROBINSON LEE	Lookout man	2362 to 2761	66 to 74
	8. JOHN POINGDESTRE	Able seaman	2762 to 3339	74 to 83
	9. JAMES JOHNSON	Night watchman in 1st saloon	3340 to 3508	83 to 86
5th day (9th May).	JAMES JOHNSON (continued)		3509 to 3707	87 to 91
	10. THOMAS PATRICK DILLON	Trimmer	3708 to 3980	91 to 95
	11. THOMAS RANGER	Greaser	3981 to 4181	96 to 99
	12. GEORGE CAVELL	Trimmer	4182 to 4501	99 to 104
	13. ALFRED SHIERS	Fireman	4502 to 4830	104 to 109
	14. CHARLES HENDRICKSON	Leading fireman	4831 to 5274	109 to 116
6th day (10th May).	15. FRANK HERBERT MORRIS	Bathroom steward	5275 to 5505	117 to 121
	16. FREDERICK SCOTT	Greaser	5506 to 5906	121 to 130
	17. CHARLES JOUGHIN	Chief baker	5907 to 6366	130 to 139
	18. SAMUEL JAMES RULE	Bathroom steward	6367 to 6669	139 to 144
7th day (14th May).	19. STANLEY LORD	Master of ss. "Californian"	6670 to 7411	145 to 160
	20. JAMES GIBSON	Apprentice of the ss. "Californian."	7412 to 7802	160 to 166
	21. HERBERT STONE	2nd Officer of the ss. "Californian."	7803 to 8110	166 to 172
8th day (15th May).	22. CHARLES VICTOR GROVES	3rd Officer of the ss. "Californian."	8111 to 8564	172 to 181
	23. GEORGE FREDERICK STEWART	Chief Officer of the ss. "Californian."	8565 to 8918	181 to 187
	CHARLES VICTOR GROVES (recalled)		8919 to 8923	188
	24. CYRIL F. EVANS	Marconi operator on the ss. "Californian."	8924 to 9218	188 to 193
	25. JAMES HENRY MOORE	Master of the ss. "Mount Temple."	9219 to 9415	194 to 197
	26. JOHN DURRANT	Marconi operator on the ss. "Mount Temple."	9416 to 9590	198 to 201
9th day (16th May).	JOHN DURRANT (recalled)		9591 to 9596	202
	SAMUEL RULE (recalled)		9597 to 9832	202 to 207
	27. JOHN EDWARD HART	3rd class steward	9833 to 10325	207 to 216
	28. ALBERT VICTOR PEARCEY	3rd class pantryman	10326 to 10497	216 to 219
	29. EDWARD BROWN	1st class steward	10498 to 10672	219 to 222
	30. CHARLES DONALD MACKAY	Bathroom steward	10673 to 10867	222 to 225
	31. JOSEPH THOMAS WHEAT	Assistant 2nd steward	10868 to 11071	226 to 230
10th day (17th May).	CHARLES HENDRICKSON (recalled)		11072 to 11302	232 to 236
	32. GEORGE SYMONS	Able seaman	11303 to 12007	237 to 252
	33. JAMES TAYLOR	Fireman	12008 to 12304	252 to 257
	34. JAMES CLAYTON BARR	Master of the ss. "Caronia"	12305 to 12318	257
	35. ALBERT EDWARD JAMES HORSWILL	Able seaman	12319 to 12447	258 to 260
	36. Sir COSMO DUFF-GORDON	Passenger	12448 to 12591	260 to 268
11th day (20th May).	Sir COSMO DUFF-GORDON (continued).		12592 to 12868	268 to 271
	37. Lady DUFF-GORDON	Passenger	12869 to 12970	271 to 273
	38. SAMUEL COLLINS	Fireman	12971 to 13053	274 to 275
	39. FREDERICK SHEATH	Trimmer	13054 to 13092	276
	40. ROBERT WILLIAM PUSEY	Fireman	13093 to 13155	276 to 277
	41. Mrs. ELIZABETH LEATHER	1st class stewardess	13156 to 13185	278
	JOSEPH JAMES WHEAT (recalled)		13186 to 13271	278 to 280
	42. Mrs. ANNIE ROBINSON	1st class stewardess	13272 to 13314	280 to 281
	43. WALTER WYNN	Quartermaster	13315 to 13407	281 to 283
	44. CHARLES HERBERT LIGHTOLLER	2nd Officer	13408 to 13796	283 to 292
12th day (21st May).	CHARLES HERBERT LIGHTOLLER (continued).		13797 to 14910	293 to 325
13th day (22nd May).	45. HERBERT JOHN PITMAN	3rd Officer	14911 to 15304	325 to 333
	46. JOSEPH GROVE BOXALL	4th Officer	15305 to 15766	334 to 345
	47. HAROLD GODFREY LOWE	5th Officer	15767 to 16019	345 to 350
	48. GEORGE ELLIOTT TURNBULL	Deputy Manager of the Marconi International Marine Communication Company.	16020 to 16087	351 to 352
14th day (23rd May).	GEORGE ELLIOTT TURNBULL (continued)		16088 to 16284	353 to 361
	49. HAROLD BRIDE	Marconi operator	16285 to 16286	361
	GEORGE ELLIOTT TURNBULL (recalled)		16287 to 16322	361 to 362
	HAROLD BRIDE (recalled)		16323 to 16801	362 to 372
	CHARLES HERBERT LIGHTOLLER (recalled)		16802 to 16906	372 to 376
	JOSEPH GROVE BOXALL (recalled)		16907 to 17017	376 to 378
	HERBERT JOHN PITMAN (recalled)		17018 to 17040	379
	HAROLD GODFREY LOWE (recalled)		17041 to 17052	380

LIST OF WITNESSES—continued.

Date.	Name of Witness.	Description.	Numbers of Questions.	Page.
15th day (24th May).	50. HAROLD THOMAS COTTAM	Marconi operator on ss. "Carpathia."	17053 to 17215	380 to 386
	51. FREDERICK FLEET	Lookout man ...	17216 to 17480	386 to 392
	52. GEORGE ALFRED HOGG	Able seaman	17481 to 17572	392 to 394
	53. GEORGE THOMAS ROWE	Quartermaster	17573 to 17701	394 to 398
	54. SAMUEL HEMMING	Lamp trimmer	17702 to 17784	398 to 399
	55. WILFRID SEWARD	2nd class pantry steward ...	17785 to 17828	399 to 400
16th day (4th June).	56. ALFRED CRAWFORD	1st class bedroom steward ...	17829 to 18092	400 to 406
	57. EDWARD JOHN BULEY	Able seaman	18093 to 18111	406 to 407
	58. ERNEST ARCHER	Able seaman	18112 to 18128	407
	59. ERNEST GILL	Donkeyman on ss. "California."	18129 to 18223	407 to 409
17th day (5th June).	60. JOSEPH BRUCE ISMAY	Passenger ...	18224 to 18896	410 to 429
	JOSEPH BRUCE ISMAY (continued)		18897 to 19073	429 to 438
	61. HAROLD ARTHUR SANDERSON ...	Director of Messrs. Ismay, Imrie & Co.	19074 to 19365	440 to 453
18th day (6th June).	HAROLD ARTHUR SANDERSON (continued)		19366 to 19788	454 to 470
	62. EDWARD WILDING	Architect to Messrs. Harland & Wolff.	19789 to 20073	471 to 478
	63. PAUL MAUGÉ	Secretary to the chef of the Restaurant à la carte.	20074 to 20187	479 to 481
	EDWARD WILDING (recalled)		20188 to 20748	481 to 502
20th day (10th June).	EDWARD WILDING (continued)		20749 to 21038	503 to 513
	64. LEONARD PESKETT	Naval Architect to Cunard Company.	21039 to 21254	513 to 519
	65. The Right Hon. A. M. CARLISLE	Member of the Merchant Shipping Advisory Committee, 1911.	21255 to 21529	519 to 527
	LEONARD PESKETT (recalled)		21530	527
21st day (11th June).	66. CHARLES ALFRED BARTLETT	Marine Superintendent, White Star Line, Liverpool.	21531 to 21792	529 to 536
	67. BERTRAM FOX HAYES	Master Mariner, White Star Line.	21793 to 21851	537 to 539
	68. FREDERICK PASSOW	Master of the ss. "St. Paul," American-Inman Line.	21852 to 21905	539 to 540
	69. FRANCIS SPURSTOW MILLER	Assistant Hydrographer at the Admiralty.	21906 to 21942	540 to 542
	70. BENJAMIN STEEL	Master Mariner, Marine Superintendent, White Star Line, Southampton.	21943 to 22021	542 to 544
	71. STANLEY HOWARD ADAMS	Marconi operator on ss. "Mesaba."	22022 to 22088	544 to 546
	72. Sir WALTER J. HOWELL	Assistant Secretary to the Board of Trade and Chief of the Marine Department.	22089 to 22267	547 to 557
22nd day (12th June).	Sir WALTER J. HOWELL (continued).		22268 to 22719	557 to 583
23rd day (13th June).	Sir WALTER J. HOWELL (continued).		22720 to 22842	583 to 590
	73. Sir ALFRED CHALMERS	Late Professional Member of the Marine Department of the Board of Trade.	22843 to 23138	592 to 601
	74. ALFRED YOUNG	Professional Member of the Board of Trade.	23139 to 23343	602 to 609
24th day (14th June).	ALFRED YOUNG (continued)		23344 to 23587	612 to 624
	75. RICHARD OWEN JONES	Master of the ss. "Canada."	23590 to 23713	625 to 627
	76. EDWIN GALTON CANNONS	Master Mariner, Atlantic Transport Company.	23714 to 23850	628 to 631
	77. FRANCIS CARRUTHERS	Engineer and Ship Surveyor to the Board of Trade at Belfast.	23851 to 24020	631 to 636
25th day (17th June).	FRANCIS CARRUTHERS (continued)		24021 to 24030	637
	78. WILLIAM HENRY CHANTLER ...	Ship Surveyor to the Board of Trade at Belfast.	24031 to 24070	637 to 638
	79. ALFRED PEACOCK	Engineer and Ship Surveyor to the Board of Trade at Glasgow.	24071 to 24083	638
	80. MAURICE HARVEY CLARKE	Assistant Emigration Officer to the Board of Trade at Southampton.	24084 to 24225	639 to 642
	81. WILLIAM DAVID ARCHER	Principal Ship Surveyor to the Board of Trade.	24226 to 24515	642 to 656
26th day (18th June).	82. ALEXANDER BOYLE	Engineer Surveyor in Chief to the Board of Trade.	24516 to 24532	656
	83. EBER SHARPE	Surveyor to the Board of Trade at Queenstown and Emigration Officer.	24533 to 24543	657
	84. JOSEPH MASSEY HARVEY	Principal Examiner of Masters and Mates to the Board of Trade.	24544 to 24563	657 to 659

Date.	Name of Witness.	Description.	Numbers of Questions.	Page.
26th day (18th June)— continued.	85. SIR NORMAN HILL	Chairman of the Merchant Shipping Advisory Committee.	24564 to 24849	659 to 671
	86. GUGLIELMO MARCONI	Inventor of Wireless Telegraphy.	24850 to 24956	671 to 675
	87. JOSEPH BARLOW RANSON	Master of the ss "Baltic"	24957 to 25013	675 to 677
	88. SIR ERNEST SHACKLETON, C.V.O.	... ...	25014 to 25151	677 to 682
	89. RIVERSDALE SAMPSON FRENCH	Surgeon on the ss. "Oceanic"	25152 to 25167	682
27th day (19th June).	90. JOHN PRITCHARD	Master Mariner, Cunard Line.	25168 to 25219	689
	91. HUGH YOUNG	Retired Master Mariner. Anchor Line.	25220 to 25241	690
	92. WILLIAM STEWART	Retired Master Mariner, Beaver Line.	25242 to 25268	691
	93. JOHN ALEXANDER FAIRFULL	Retired Master Mariner. Allan Line.	25269 to 25282	691
	94. ANDREW BRAES ...	Retired Master Mariner, Allan Line	25283 to 25290	692
	EDWARD WILDING (recalled)	... ...	25291 to 25352	692
28th day (21st June).	95. ARTHUR HENRY ROSTRON	Master of the ss "Carpathia"	25353 to 25574	696 to 702
	96. GERHARD CHRISTOFER AFFELD	Marine Superintendent of the Red Star Line.	25575 to 25617	703 to 704
	97. ARTHUR ERNEST TRIDE	Master of the ss "Manitou"	25618 to 25622	704

LIST OF WITNESSES—continued.

The list of witnesses in the order which they appeared.

green side light. He considered that at 11.00 p.m. she was approximately six or seven miles away, and at some time between 11.00 and 11.30 p.m., he first saw her green light, and she was then about 5 miles off. He noticed that about 11.30 p.m. she stopped. In his opinion this steamer was of about the same size as the Californian; a medium steamer, 'Something like ourselves' (Lord, 6761 & 6752).

From the evidence of Mr Groves, third officer of the Californian, who was the officer of the first watch, it would appear that the master was not actually on the bridge when the steamer was sighted.

Mr Groves made out two masthead lights: the steamer was changing her bearing slowly as she got closer, and as she approached he went to the chart room and reported this to the master; he added, 'She is evidently a passenger steamer.' In fact, Mr Groves never appears to have had any doubt on this subject; in answer to a question during his examination, 'Had she much light?,' he said, 'Yes, a lot of light. There was no doubt of her being a passenger steamer, at least in my mind' (8147, 8174, 8178).

Gill, the assistant donkeyman of the Californian, who was on deck at midnight said, referring to this steamer: 'It could not have been anything but a passenger boat, she was too large' (Gill, 18136).

By the evidence of Mr Groves, the master, in his reply to the report, said: 'Call her up on the Morse lamp, and see if you can get any answer.' This he proceeded to do. The master came up and joined him on the bridge and remarked: 'That does not look like a passenger steamer.' Mr Groves replied: 'It is, Sir. When she stopped her lights seemed to go out, and I supposed they had been put out for the night.' Mr Groves states that these lights went out at 11.40 p.m. and remembers the time because one bell was struck to call the middle watch. The master did not join him on the bridge until shortly afterwards, and consequently after the steamer had stopped (Groves, 8182, 8197, 8203, 8217).

In his examination Mr Groves admitted that if this steamer's head was turning to port after she stopped, it might account for the diminution of lights, by many of them being shut out. Her steaming lights were still visible and also her port light (8228).

The captain only remained upon the bridge for a few minutes. In his evidence he stated that Mr Groves had made no observations to him about the steamer's deck lights going out. Mr Groves' Morse signalling appears to have been ineffectual (although at one moment he thought he was being answered) and he gave up. He remained on the bridge until relieved by Mr Stone, the second officer, just after midnight. In turning the Californian over to him, he pointed out the steamer and said: 'She has been stopped since 11.40; she is a passenger steamer' (8241, 6866, 8244 - 51. Lord & Groves).

(Stone 7810, Groves 8441) At about the moment she stopped she put her lights out. When Mr Groves was in the witness-box the following questions were put to him by me, (Mersey): 'Speaking as an experienced seaman and knowing what you do know now, do you think that steamer that you know was throwing up rockets, and that you say was a passenger steamer, was the Titanic?'

'Do I think it?'

'Yes?'

'From what I have heard consequently?'

'Yes?'

'Most decidedly I do, but I do not put myself as being an experienced man.'

'But that is your opinion as far as your experience goes?'

'Yes, it is, my Lord.'

Mr Stone states (the report continued) that the master, who was also up (but apparently not on the bridge) pointed out the steamer to him with instructions to tell him if her bearings altered or if she got any closer; he also stated that Mr Groves had called her up on the Morse lamp and had received no reply (Stone, 7815).

'Mr Stone had with him during the middle watch an apprentice named Gibson, whose attention was first drawn to the steamer's lights at about 12.20 a.m. He could see a masthead light, her red light (with glasses) and a 'glare of white lights on her after deck'. He first thought her masthead light was flickering and next thought it was a Morse light, 'calling us up'. He replied, but could not get into communication, and finally came to the conclusion that it was, as he had first supposed, the masthead light flickering. Sometime after 12.30 a.m. Gill, the donkeyman, states that he saw two rockets fired from the ship which he had been observing, and about 1.10 a.m. Mr Stone reported to the captain by voice pipe, that he had seen five white rockets from the direction of the steamer. He states that the master answered: 'Are they company's signals?' and that he replied: 'I do not know, but they appear to me to be white rockets'. The master told him to 'go on morsing', and, when he received any information, to send the apprentice down to him with it. Gibson states that Mr Stone informed him that he had reported to the master, and that the master had said the steamer was to be called up by Morse light. This witness thinks the time was 12.55 a.m. He at once proceeded again to call the vessel up by Morse. He got no reply, but the vessel fired three more white rockets: These rockets were also seen by Mr Stone. Both Mr Stone and the apprentice kept the steamer under observation, looking at her from time to time with their glasses. Between 1.00 a.m. and 1.40 a.m., some conversation passed between them. Mr Stone remarked to Gibson: 'Look at her now, she looks very queer out of the water, her lights look queer'. He also is said by Gibson to have remarked, 'a ship is not going to fire rockets at sea for nothing' and admits himself that he may possibly have used that expression (Gibson, 7424, 7443, Gill, 18156 – 61. Stone, 7870, 7879, Gibson, 7479, 7515, 7529, Stone, 7894)'.

Mr Stone states that he saw the last of the rockets fired at about 1.40 a.m. and after watching the steamer for some twenty minutes more he sent Gibson down to the master. 'I told Gibson to go down to the master, and be sure to wake him, and tell him that altogether we had seen eight of these white lights like white rockets in the direction of this other steamer; that this steamer was disappearing in the south-west, that we had called her up repeatedly on the Morse lamp and received no information whatsoever (Stone, 7949)'.

Gibson states that he went down to the chart room and told the master; that the master asked him if all the rockets were white, and also asked him the time. Gibson stated that at this time the master was awake. It was five minutes past two, and Gibson returned to the bridge to Mr Stone and reported. They both continued to keep the ship under observation until she disappeared. Mr Stone describes this as 'a gradual disappearing of all her lights, which would be perfectly natural with a ship steaming away from us' (Gibson, 7553. Stone, 7957).

At about 2.40 a.m. Mr Stone again called up the master by voice pipe and told him that the ship from which he had seen the rockets come had disappeared bearing SW ½ W., the last he had seen of the light; and the master again asked him if he was certain there was no colour in the lights. 'I again assured him they were all white, just white rockets'. There is considerable discrepancy between the evidence of Mr Stone and that of the master. The latter states that he went to the voice pipe at about 1.15 a.m., but was told then of a white rocket (not five white rockets). Moreover, between 1.30 a.m. and 4.30 a.m., when he was called by the Chief Officer (Mr Stewart) he had no recollection of anything being reported to him at all, although he remembered Gibson opening and closing the chart room door (7976, 7999, Lord, 6790, 6859).

Mr Stewart relieved Mr Stone at 4.00 a.m. The latter told him he had seen a ship four or five miles off when he was on deck at 12.00 midnight, and at 1.00 a.m. he had seen some white rockets, and that the moment she started firing them she started to steam away. Just at this time (4.00 am) a steamer came in sight with two masthead lights and a few lights amidships. He asked Mr Stone whether he thought this was the steamer which had fired rockets, and Mr Stone said he did not think it was. At 4.30 a.m. he called the master and informed him that Mr Stone had told him he had seen rockets in the middle watch. The master said: 'Yes, I know, he has been telling me.' The master came at once on to the bridge, and apparently took the fresh steamer for the one which had fired rockets and said: 'She looks alright, she is not making any signals now.' This mistake was not corrected. He, however, had the wireless operator called (Stewart, 8577, 8582, 8598, 8615, 8619, 8632).

At about 6.00 a.m. Captain Lord heard from the Virginian that the Titanic had struck a berg, passengers, passengers in boats, ship sinking and he at once started through the field ice at full speed for the position given (Lord, 7002).

Captain Lord stated that about 7.30 a.m. he passed the Mount Temple stopped, and that she was in the vicinity of the position given him as where the Titanic had collided (Lat. 41° 46' N, Long. 50° 14' W). He saw no wreckage there but did later on near the Carpathia which ship he closed soon afterwards, and he stated that the position where he subsequently left this wreckage was 41° 33' N, 50° 1' W. It is said in the evidence of Mr Stewart that the position of the Californian was verified by stellar observations at 7.30 p.m. on the Sunday evening, and that he verified the captain's position given when the ship stopped (42° 5' N, 50° 7' W) as accurate on the next day. The

position in which the wreckage was said to have been seen on the Monday
morning was verified by sights taken on that morning (7011, 7026, 7030).

All the officers are stated to have taken sights, and Mr Stewart in his evidence remarks that they all agreed. If it is admitted that these positions were
correct, then it follows that the Titanic's position as given by that ship when
making the CQD signal was approximately S 16 W. (true), 19 miles from
the Californian and further that the position in which the Californian was
stopped during the night, was thirty miles away from where the wreckage
was seen by her in the morning, or that the wreckage had drifted eleven miles
in a little more than five hours (Stewart, 8820).

Drawing from the rather flimsy evidence – and quite obviously ignoring or
not recognising several pertinent points, Lord Mersey, in his summary, made
it quite clear that he personally held Captain Lord absolutely responsible for
not coming to the aid of the Titanic (see summary on pages 78-79).

Lord Mersey stated – as we have seen – that there were many 'contradictions and inconsistencies' in the story. While this was obviously quite true,
he failed to see the contradictions and inconsistencies in his own appraisal
of the case. It is therefore essential that Lord Mersey's summation, on the
face of it a damning indictment against Lord, be closely examined and analysed, bearing in mind that this is precisely what Lord would have done had
he been given the opportunity of defending himself.

Unfortunately, unlike Lord Mersey, we do not have the privilege of being
in a position to question the witnesses and so must rely on the written transcripts of the inquiry. It is also well to bear in mind that many and varied
connotations can, and may have been, put on individual words and progressions of words which could quite possibly have led to a totally different
meaning than that which was intended. We must therefore be quite clear
as to the precise meaning of each statement and refrain from putting inferences on them which may not apply. We must also bear in mind that the
inquiry was only watched by a legal adviser on behalf of Captain Lord and
the Leyland Line, as distinct from being defended. We already know that
Lord was denied effective legal representation in the case and refused the
right to appeal the findings on grounds that he only appeared as a witness
and was not himself on trial. This is obviously a point which was evidently
overlooked by Lord Mersey in his summation.

The most obvious contradiction in his report is in section 6710 where
Mersey apparently accepts that the Californian was obliged to stop because

she was running into field ice 'which stretched as far as could then be seen'. Yet, during his summation (in section 7020) he quite clearly stated that the ice by which Californian was surrounded was 'loose ice, extending for a distance of not more than two or three miles'. In reply to question 6704, Lord told the court that he made the Californian's position at that time (10.20 p.m.) to be 42° 5' N, 57° 7' W to which Lord Mersey replied, 'I am satisfied that this position is not accurate'. Once again the apparent lack of nautical matters became glaringly obvious. If we take into account the latitude by pole star (taken at 7.30 p.m. on Sunday evening) and recall that Captain Lord estimated the Californian's position as being 42° 5' N, 50° 07' W, and allow for a current estimation set to the WNW at slightly under one knot, we can then calculate that the distance between the Titanic's official position (41° 46' N, 50° 14' W) and the Californian's estimated position (as above) is of the order of twenty or twenty-one and a half miles (see chart on page 93).

We know that having reached the Titanic's official position, Lord found absolutely no sign of the ship or anything to indicate she had been in the area. The reason for this, of course, was that the Californian had been given the incorrect position of the disaster. The question may well be asked: 'How then did the rescue ship, Carpathia, which had been given the same position, manage to arrive at the correct spot? The answer to this is both simple and obvious. The Carpathia (as we can see from the chart) was steaming N 52° W (true) on the eastern side of the ice field and was in fact heading for the same position as the Californian when she came across the site of the tragedy. Had the Carpathia been on the western side of the ice field, like the Californian, then she too would have found herself in the wrong position.

The fact that Lord Mersey would not accept the position of the Californian as being correct is absurd and falls down to two points. Firstly, when Captain Lord logged his position, both at 7.30 p.m. (by Pole Star) and again when he was obliged to stop his ship at 10.20 p.m. due to the ice, he had no reason to fabricate his position when we bear in mind that at both these times the Titanic was still steaming along and had not yet struck the iceberg. Not being clairvoyant, Lord had no idea of the drama which was about to unfold in a few hours' time. Mersey also chose to totally ignore the corroborative evidence of Captain Lord's officers who had all individually taken independent sightings at the same time as the master, and all of their accounts tallied exactly alike. Secondly, the Californian was not the only ship to arrive at the wrong position. Acting on the information and position given, two other ships, the Mount Temple and Birma, also arrived at the wrong side of the ice field. The obvious question must therefore be asked: Is it possible, or even remotely feasible, that three different ships could all make the same exact mistake in their navigation and still all arrive at the same spot? Not likely. The case for Lord's truthfulness was later reinforced when several other ships also arrived at the same spot. Nevertheless, Lord Mersey chose to ignore these facts.

On page 95 a chart is shown in which we see that allowing for the estimated position of the Californian at 10.20 p.m. With the probable site of the actual tragedy, the distance is further increased to 26 miles. As this is a much too important item to skip over, we shall return to it in more detail in a later chapter. Meanwhile, we shall once again take a further look at some of the contradictions and inconsistencies contained in Lord Mersey's report.

In this area of questioning (Evans, 8982, Lord, 8988), what appears to be a classic case of 'suggestion' occurs to the extent that the impression is given that the Titanic had actually and positively been identified as being in very close proximity to the Californian. Lord Mersey stated that the two ships were no more than five miles apart and then, changing his mind, said that the distance was certainly no more then eight to ten miles. Once again, he gave no reference to the action of Captain Lord in warning the Titanic of the danger nor remarked on the fact that the master of the Californian acted as any reputable captain would have in the same circumstances. He failed to realise that the reason the Titanic's wireless operator could hear the Californian's operator so clear, and told him to 'keep out', was merely because the Californian was much closer than Cape Race, which was a considerable distance away and on dry land.

In question number 6761 Lord stated, in connection with the steamer which approached the Californian: 'She was a medium steamer, something like ourselves.' The idea that Lord, a highly qualified mariner, could mistake a medium-sized steamer for the largest ship in the world is nothing short of ludicrous. Once again, we see that Captain Lord displayed his professionalism by promptly instructing Groves to call the ship up on the Morse lamp (Groves, 8182). As we have seen, he was to do this on several occasions despite being totally ignored by the other ship. Groves stated (8207) that when she stopped, 'her lights seemed to go out' and he supposed that she had put her lights out 'for the night'. This fact alone proves that the ship he was observing could not have been the Titanic, as it is well documented that the Titanic's lights remained on until moments before she sank at 2.20

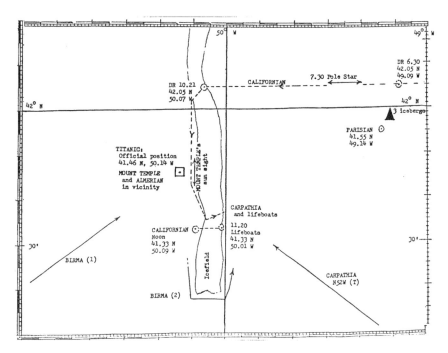

Chart prepared by the captain of the Birma from actual sightings of the ice field and published in the London Daily Telegraph on 25 April 1912. It clearly confirmed the existence and massive scope of the ice. (See also References, page 120.)

a.m. Indeed, the engineers of the Titanic have long been praised for their unselfish act in working so hard in order to keep the lights burning on the doomed ship. Neither, incidentally, did any lights fail on the Titanic after the collision. Much more to the point (as stated by Groves, 8228), the reason the lights appeared to 'go out' was because the ship was turning to port. Again, the whole question of the lights of this 'mystery ship' is somewhat a moot point when we stop and consider the tremendous blaze of lights which must have been aboard the Titanic. Mr Senan Molony, author of that marvellous book *Titanic and the Mystery Ship* (Tempus, 2006) states that she had 10,000 electric lights which were 'not put out in her public rooms before midnight'. Although fitted with considerably fewer electric lights, a mere 260, the Californian also was well lit. It must therefore follow that if the ships were in close proximity to each other, as Lord Mersey insisted, then they could not have failed to see each other. In this respect, the obvious question must be asked: why then did they not contact and respond to each other's signals?

Groves too (7810), became a victim of the same belief and stated that, 'At about the time she stopped, she put her lights out'. Again, this proves he was not observing the White Star liner but some other ship. Yet again, when we consider the blaze of lights that must have emanated from the Titanic, and to a lesser extent the Californian, it is nothing short of unbelievable that the Titanic's perched lookouts, 120ft above the water, could not see the lights of the Californian on such a perfectly clear night with excellent visibility. The reason of course they did not see the Californian's lights was simply because the Californian was not in the immediate vicinity. There is yet another aspect not taken into consideration by the court and it would appear to contradict Groves' statement. Groves stated that he 'saw a ship approaching' from roughly the south and 'I could see her port side and upon stopping, she put out her deck and cabin lights'. Groves, however, when pressed on the matter admitted that the lights might appear to have gone out, due to the ship turning two points to port. If we accept this logi-cal point, it then follows that this 'mystery ship' must have been steering NNW (true) if her bearing was south, and, if her bearing was SE (true), where Stone observed her at 12.15 a.m., then she must have been steering NNE (true) previous to this. If this be the case, then this ship could not have been the Titanic, as that ship was steering S 86° 15'W (true). Groves clearly contradicted himself.

The following chart shows the course of the Californian on 15 April, on her way to the 'reported' position of the Titanic, which, as we have known since October 1987, turned out to be incorrect. We also see that the Almerian and the Mount Temple arrived in the vicinity at approximately the same time. X and Z indicate the positions of the two previously unidentified vessels. The range of port and starboard lights is indicated in the case of the Californian and ship X. A simple calculation will show that the Californian was in loose ice to the north, while the Titanic was among icebergs approx-imately twenty-six miles to the south (as indicated by arrow on right of chart). In hindsight, it is still hard to understand Lord Mersey's stance that no other ships but the Californian was in the immediate vicinity and capable of rendering assistance to the Titanic. The fact that he consistently refused to budge from this view is nothing short of the 'head-in-the-sand' syndrome. If we are to accept the fact that Captain Lord, being the much experi-enced mariner, felt obliged to stop his ship until daylight, due to dangerous conditions, then we can reasonably assume that other responsible ship mas-ters, finding themselves in the same situation, did likewise.

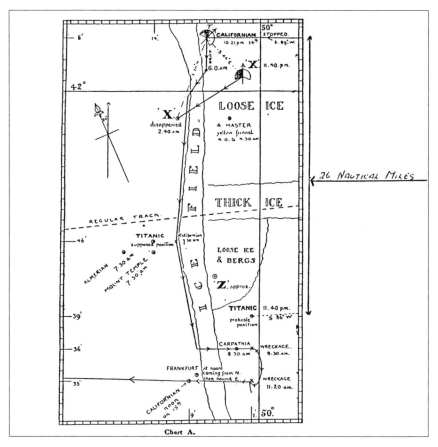

Chart showing the course of the Californian on 15 April on her way to the 'reported' position of the Titanic, which turned out to be incorrect. Note that the Almerian and the Mount Temple arrived in the vicinity at approximately the same time. X and Z indicate the positions of the two previously unidentified vessels. Courtesy of Trinity College Library, Dublin. Foweraker Articles, 1913

Indeed, it may be observed that Captain Smith of the Titanic should have done the same, or at least have reduced his speed, and, had he done so, there is every reason to believe that the tragedy could have been avoided. Sadly, he did neither.

Popular opinion now has it that it has only been since the discovery of the wreck of the Titanic that it can accurately be established that her given position was incorrect and that Lord was telling the truth when he stated that his ship was further away from the site of the tragedy than previously

thought. While the discovery of the wreck has indeed been a very pertinent point in favour of Lord's statement, and instrumental in having the
case reappraised, the fact remains that Lord's name and character should
never have been taken the way it was, and tragically, the evidence which
would have exonerated him from any blame was in place and readily
available after the disaster. It was, sadly, totally ignored by the Board of
Trade and the Court of Inquiry. Following is a short extract from the 1913
Nautical Magazine, entitled 'A Miscarriage of Justice', which points out
the intriguing possibility that the Titanic and the Californian were not
the only ships involved in the disaster and its repercussions, but that two
other ships were directly involved – the ship seen from the Titanic, ship
Z, and the ship seen from the Californian, ship X. If we place both of
these ships between the Titanic and the Californian, it puts a completely
different slant on the entire affair and brings the tragedy down to a more
probable likelihood. Again, this irrefutable evidence was available some
months after Lord was castigated and should have been reason enough
for re-opening the case. Once again it was rejected out of hand by the
authorities.

From the Foweraker Articles, Nautical Magazine, Vol. LXXXLX 1913 (1),
p. 368:

The Differences

The following differences prove that X was not the Titanic:

X was first sighted at 10.55 p.m. (confirmed by Marconi message) and
stopped 5 miles off, bearing SE true at 11.40 p.m. ('One bell to call the middle watch' – Groves). Titanic, going S 86° W at 22 knots, would in this case
have been sighted at a distance of 20 miles, which is impossible.

X on stopping, appeared to put her lights out, but showed her red port
light and masthead light or lights (Groves).

Titanic, on stopping, had all lights burning, and on turning two points to
port would have showed her full starboard broadside to the Californian, the
same relevant positions assumed.

X started firing signals at 12.45 a.m.

Titanic started rockets before this time, probably 12.15 a.m.

X appeared to fire eight signals.

Titanic an indefinite number, 'from half a dozen to a dozen' (Boxhall). (It is submitted that a comparison of the numbers is not conclusive in proving either a resemblance or a difference).

X fired low-lying signals, throwing white stars, which did not explode and did not go as high as her masthead light.

Titanic fired 'socket distress signals' rising many hundreds of feet in the air and exploding (one Titanic witness said they were blue, red and white colours).

X moved from bearing SSE (compass) at 12.45 a.m. to disappear bearing SW ½ S (compass) at 2.40 a.m. She started to move after the first rocket.

Titanic was stationary.

X made no reply to Morse signals made by the Californian.

Titanic was continually morsing the steamer she saw, which we call 'Z'.

The following differences prove that Z was not the Californian:

Z was not in sight when the Titanic struck. One lookout-man said no steamer at all was in sight. The other corroborated, saying that he did not notice the light on the port bow until after he had left the crow's nest.

Californian would have been visible to X.

Z first seen with glasses, two masthead lights in a position to show the red.

Californian showed GREEN to X first. From heading ENE (compass) at 10.30 p.m., she swung through south to WSW at about 2.40 a.m.

Z made no reply to Titanic's Morse signals.

Californian was repeatedly calling up X by Morse light.

Z approached to within about 5 miles and then turned round very slowly and retired, followed by several of Titanic boats as ordered.

Californian was stationary.

The above is ample evidence that X and Z were two unidentified steamers.

The foregoing facts speak for themselves and show that the ship seen from the Titanic could not have been the Californian, and vice versa. In fact, not only are we dealing with just the two central players in the drama. Titanic and Californian, apart from the 'mystery ships', X and Z, we are also dealing with several other unidentified ships in the immediate area of the Titanic and Californian. These other ships number five and, unless two of them were actually X and Z, then there is a possibility of no less than seven ships being in the immediate vicinity of the tragedy. The presence of all these ships was carefully and faithfully recorded by various Masters. Their descriptions are as follows:

1   A four-master steamer with one funnel seen to the northward about 5.00 a.m. by the Carpathia.

2   A four-master steamer with a yellow funnel seen to the southward about 4.30 a.m. by the Californian.

3   A two-master steamer with one funnel also seen by the Carpathia at 5.00 a.m.

4   Two masthead lights bearing N 30° W (true) from the Carpathia at about 3.15 a.m. seen by Captain Rostron. One of the officers also saw her red light.

5   A steamer of about 5,000 tons, black funnel. White band, with some device on it, under observation from about 1.00 to 1.30 a.m. until 9.00 a.m., reported by Captain Moore of the Mount Temple.

We see from the varying descriptions that we are dealing with at least five different ships and, if we include ships X and Z, then the total rises to seven. In spite of this important point, the question of other ships in the area was not entertained at all by Lord Mersey.

Before moving on, let us refer to that part of Lord Mersey's summation in which he concludes: 'When she first saw the rockets the Californian could have pushed through the ice to open water without serious risk and so have come to the assistance of the Titanic.' This was a highly inflammatory and damaging statement based on mere circumstantial evidence, especially in view of all opposing evidence which the court either chose to ignore or declare as inadmissible.

Lord Mersey also clung to his ludicrous insistence that the Titanic and Californian were no more than five miles apart. As we have seen, it was only later that he reluctantly agreed to amend the distance to 'eight or ten miles apart'. It has of course now been conclusively proved, beyond all reasonable doubt, that both ships were about twenty miles apart. Bearing this distance in mind, and recalling that a mere fifty-five minutes had elapsed from the time Captain Lord was first informed of rockets to the moment the Titanic slipped beneath the waves, it would have been nothing short of a miracle for Lord to bring his ship to the Titanic and effect a rescue in such a short space of time. Even if the time difference resulted in sixty-five or seventy minutes, the essential point is still strong. The Californian could never have made it there in time. Realistically, he would have had to get up steam, bring his ship through more than twenty miles of highly dangerous ice in total darkness, and then transfer more than 2,000 people on to his ship. Clearly, even if the distance had been the eight or ten miles suggested by Lord Mersey, for Lord, or any master, to have carried out such a feat in fifty-five minutes would have been impossible. Even if we stretch imagination to its furthest and allow that Lord had been able to reach the tragedy position given, he would still not have been in a position to save anyone because he would have arrived at the wrong position. In fact, the true position of the foundering Titanic was over twelve miles further away on the opposite side of the ice field. It would therefore have been an impossible task on both counts. This point is further strengthened when we realise that upon hearing the news of the disaster the following morning, Captain Lord proceeded to the area at full speed. Nevertheless, it still took the Californian over two and a half hours, in broad daylight, to reach the position given, proving of course that there was no way he could have made the same trip, in darkness, in under one hour. Once again, this blatant and irrefutable fact was totally ignored by the court.

Yet another inconsistency is shown in question twenty-four – 'What vessels had the opportunity of rendering assistance to the Titanic, and, if any, how was it that assistance did not reach the Titanic before the SS Carpathia arrived?' Answer: 'The Californian. She could have reached the Titanic if she had made the attempt when she first saw the rocket. She made no attempt.'

Here again, Lord Mersey chose to ignore the statement that the Californian 'made no attempt'. Obviously, this suggests that the Californian remained stationary, which she did during the night. Yet, Mr Boxhall's evidence clearly states that the ship he observed (Z) approached and retired. We are obviously then speaking of two different ships.

FOUR

Ships that Pass in the Night

The entire case of the Californian, and its subsequent indictment, was based on the false assumption held by Lord Mersey that the Californian must have been close to, and seen the Titanic and vice-versa. Upon this flimsy 'evidence', and apparently ignoring other more conclusive and opposing evidence, he proceeded to discredit Captain Lord's position as inaccurate.

Had Captain Lord been given the opportunity to defend himself, as he undoubtedly would have done had he been charged with any crime, he would have been able to exonerate himself by calling the captains of five other ships as witnesses in his favour. These captains of the Mount Temple, Almerian, Birma, Parisian and Carpathia ships would have been able to verify Lord's statement regarding the position of his ship. We have already seen that Lord logged his position before the Titanic struck the iceberg and that these positions were verified by his officers who had each taken independent sightings. We have also seen that since the publication of the position of the Titanic wreck in October 1987, it has been proved that the position given by the Titanic's wireless operator was incorrect and that the true position was some twelve miles further. This in itself is an indisputable and irrefutable fact and immediately dispels Mersey's assertions that the ships were close to each other. Let us now examine, without speculation, the evidence which the five captains would have given to the inquiry in Lord's defence, had the opportunity been given.

On the afternoon of 14 April 1912, the Allan liner Parisian was some forty miles to the west of the Californian when she sent the following message to the Leyland ship: '41° 55' N, 49° 14' W. Passed three large icebergs'. This signal was acknowledged by the Titanic. Later that night/morning, the Titanic sent the dramatic signal: 'SOS. Come at once. We have struck a berg. Position 41° 46' N, 50° 14' W'. This of course was the incorrect position. The actual position was subsequently located at 41° 44' N, 49° 57' W. If we allow for surface current, which was present on the night of the disaster, set to the south at a rate of slightly under one knot, and the fact that the Titanic hit the iceberg at 11.40 p.m. and sank at 2.20 a.m., the position of the actual impact or collision would be approximately 41° 46' N, 49° 57' W. In other words, if the Californian was, as had been stated, eight to ten miles to the north of that position from 6.30 p.m. until 10.20 p.m. (when stopped for the night), then she would have to have deviated almost fourteen degrees to port out of her course and average a speed of only eight knots. Obviously, such an unlikely scenario is hardly deserving of mention, as it supposes that the Californian's watch keepers would not notice such an unusual occurrence.

We know that Captain Smith of the Titanic instructed his wireless operator to send out distress signals at exactly 11.55 p.m., a fact borne out by the Mount Temple who picked up the message, together with the incorrect position, shortly after midnight. Captain Moore, of Mount Temple, immediately set about turning his ship around and set her course N 65° E (true) for the position given. He estimated the stricken liner to be some fifty miles distant (she was actually more than sixty miles away) and headed in the direction given. Shortly before Mount Temple reached the given position, she encountered a huge field of ice across and, despite cruising around the general area and keeping a sharp lookout, no sign of the Titanic could be seen, and the captain reported that he had not come across any wreckage or lifeboats in the area either. The only other ships Mount Temple saw was the Almerian, which she could not contact because that ship did not carry wireless equipment, and the Carpathia, which she observed at daylight some eight miles away to the east on the opposite side of the ice field which extended, 'as far as the eye could see'. It soon became obvious that Mount Temple had arrived at the incorrect position, yet it was the position given by Titanic's wireless operator. It was several hours later that morning, close to 8.00 a.m., when the Californian was sighted steaming down from the north on the west side of the ice field. She too had arrived at the wrong position (see charts on pp. 93 and 95). Passing within one mile of Mount Temple and observing the Carpathia on the other side of the ice field, and realising her mistake, the Californian immediately changed course, and rather than lose valuable time by sailing around the tip of the ice, steamed straight through it to join the Carpathia. Under normal circumstances this would have been a very foolhardy thing to do but, considering the circumstances, Lord being of the opinion there were still survivors in the water, it must be recognised as a singularly brave action.

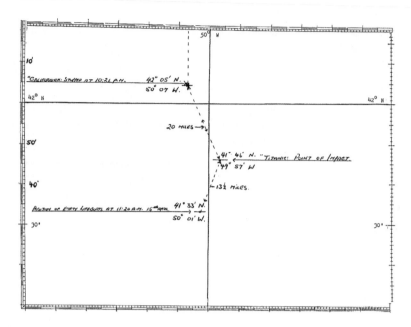

This rough sketch demonstrates that Titanic's estimated point of impact, 41° 46' N 49° 57' W, is over 20 miles distant from Californian's overnight position 42° 05' N 50° 07' W and 13½ miles from 41° 33' N 50° 01' W, the position of the empty lifeboats encountered by the Californian at 11.20 a.m. before she resumed her course towards Boston on 15 April.

The subsequent inquiries, however, did not see fit to even mention this fact. At about this time, a little after 8.00 a.m., longitudes taken by sun sights (one being on the prime vertical) placed the Mount Temple four miles to the east of the Titanic's official position, the incorrect position. Captain Moore later declared himself satisfied with these sights, which were taken by his fourth officer. The sightings put the Mount Temple in longitude 50° 09½' or 50° 09¾' W. Another important witness who could have had much to say was the captain of the Almerian. He was eastbound when, like the Californian, he too encountered the vast ice field and was obliged to stop his ship. Not being equipped with any wireless, the Almerian was obviously unaware of the tragedy and remained hove-to. Nevertheless, she did confirm sighting the Mount Temple cruising on the edge of the ice field and, later, her captain reported:

We saw, apparently at the eastern extremity of the ice field, about 6 or 6½ miles off, a large four-master steamer. With the aid of the telescope we saw she had derricks up at No.1 hatch. We could not distinguish her funnel.

Shortly afterwards we sighted smoke (to the northward) which, on nearer approach, turned out to be a Leyland liner (the Californian). As we got closer and approached her she commenced to steam through the ice field in the direction of the other four-master steamer (Carpathia) which we could see east of the ice field.

The foregoing is clearly a reference to the Californian having been observed steaming through the ice field to reach the Carpathia which was visible from the west side of the ice barrier, and which was also the side of the ice the Titanic had earlier given as her position. Ascertaining that she could not be of any use, the Almerian eventually made her way to clear water in the east and resumed her voyage.

Yet another glaring inconsistency arises when we examine the claims of Captain Rostron of the Carpathia. The Carpathia had been bound for Genoa, out of New York, when she too picked up the Titanic's distress signals. It was a little after midnight and Captain Rostron immediately ordered that the ship be turned and headed for the distress area. Setting a course of N 52° W (true) for the area, Rostron estimated that he had some fifty-eight miles to cover before he would reach the stricken ship. It was a little over three and a half hours later that he encountered the first of the lifeboats. The fact that he was, apparently, able to cover the estimated distance of fifty-eight miles in so short a time has long given rise to the outrageous suggestion that the Carpathia travelled at a speed of seventeen and a half knots. On the face of it, this may seem a perfectly reasonable claim. Seventeen and a half knots was not an exceptionally fast rate of speed for some ships but, for the Carpathia, it was impossible to achieve this speed. This ship was a coal-fired steamer propelled by two quadruple expansion engines of an ostensible 10,000 horsepower, which would in fact only render the ship capable of travelling at a top speed of fourteen knots. In order for the ship to reach a speed of seventeen and a half knots, the engines would have to have been capable of producing no less than 16,000 horsepower, which of course was impossible and must therefore lead us to the obvious deduction that some discrepancy exists in the claim. Indeed, if we accept the Mount Temple's estimate of the position of the lifeboats (41° 46' N, 50° 14'W) then the Carpathia's estimate of fifty-eight miles is considerably reduced to a much more realistic distance and this in turn would bring her speed, and the distance she actually covered, within an acceptable figure and be more in keeping with the output of her engines.

Captain Rostron, in a sworn affidavit on 4 June 1912, stated:

I approached the position of the Titanic, 41° 46' N, 50° 14'W on a course substantially N 52°W (true), reaching the first boat shortly after 4.00 a.m. It was
daylight at about 4.20 a.m. At 5.00 a.m. it was light enough to see all around
the horizon. We then saw two steamships to the northwards, perhaps seven or
eight miles distant. Neither of them was the Californian. One of them was
a four-master steamer with one funnel, and the other a two-master steamer
with one funnel. I never saw the Mount Temple to identify her. The first time
I saw the Californian was at about eight o'clock on the morning of 15 April.
She was then about five to six miles distant, bearing WSW (true) and steaming
towards the Carpathia. The Carpathia was then in substantially the position of
the Titanic at the time of the disaster as given to us by wireless. I consider the
position of the Titanic, as given to us by her officers, to be correct.

Although Rostron stated that he did not see the Mount Temple 'to identify
her', it is probable that the two steamers to which he referred were in fact the
Mount Temple and the Almerian. Regarding his apparently utter conviction
as to the veracity of the position of the Titanic, given by Titanic's officers,
we now know beyond all reasonable doubt that he too was given the incorrect position when we consider the actual location of the wreck and her
estimated point of impact (41° 46' N, 49° 57'W). He was correct about the
time that the Californian arrived on the scene, 'about eight o'clock'. This
statement was corroborated by the captains of both the Mount Temple and
the Almerian. As we have seen in an earlier chapter, yet another vessel, the
Russian East Asiatic Company's passenger ship, Birma, which was bound
for New York from Rotterdam, also picked up the distress signal and arrived
at the scene shortly after daybreak. Like the Mount Temple and Californian,
she too arrived on the wrong side of the ice field. Again, this can only give
credence to the fact that the initial position given by Titanic was wrong.
Anxious to be of assistance to any possible survivors, and realising that she
was on the wrong side of the ice field, the Birma immediately set off to the
south and steamed along and around the lower edge of the ice and joined
the Carpathia. Clearly, the captain of the Birma was not about to take the
risk the Californian did in ploughing directly through the ice field.[1]

It may be a good idea at this stage to deal exclusively with the Californian
and examine her positions in detail, both leading up to the disaster and the
subsequent attempts by her to make all possible haste to the scene.

The Birma (formerly Arundel Castle built in 1894) of the Russian East Asiatic
Co., bound for Rotterdam and Libau, deviated from her course upon receiving
Titanic's distress call and sailed for the SOS position given. Finding the rescue effort
completed, she sailed south along the western edge of the huge ice field, rounded
its tip and resumed her course to the east where she was spotted and photographed
by Mrs James A. Fenwick on board the Carpathia, which had just started her voyage
back to New York. Courtesy of Titanic Historical Society, Inc.

On Sunday 14 April, the Californian was en route from London to Boston,
Massachusetts, making for 42° N, 51° W, in order to avoid the ice which had
been reported by several ships to the west. At 12.00 noon her position, based
on sun sights, was 42° 05' N, 47° 25' W, and her course was altered to S 89°
W (true) to allow for an anticipated set to the WNW of about one knot.
At 5.00 p.m. two sun sights were taken by the second officer and reported
to Captain Lord as these gave a speed of twelve knots since noon, which
was more than expected. At 5.30 p.m. check sights were taken which gave
a much more acceptable average speed of eleven and a half knots since
midday. At 6.30 p.m. in DR (dead reckoning) position 42° 05' N, 49° 09'
W, a distinctive group of three icebergs was sighted five miles to the south.
This fact was conveyed by wireless to the Antillian and the message was also
intercepted and acknowledged by the Titanic. It was apparent to Captain
Lord that these icebergs were probably the same three bergs sighted earlier
that day by the Parisian from 41° 55' N, 49° 14' W. At 7.30 p.m. that same
evening, even though it was a perfectly clear night with a calm sea, the chief

officer of the Californian took a latitude by the Pole Star of 42° 05½' N. Thirty minutes later, anticipating the ice reported by other ships, Lord doubled the lookout, posting a man in the crow's nest, as well as a man on the fo'c's'le head, and then joined the third officer on the bridge.

Cautious to a fault, we now know that Lord's seemingly excessive caution paid off when, at 10.15 p.m., the Californian encountered loose ice on the edge of what was obviously an extensive ice field lying north and south across her track. Unwilling to risk his ship in the dark and dangerous waters, Lord did what any responsible ship's master would do – he stopped his ship to await daylight. The time was exactly 10.21 p.m.

Shortly after midnight, Captain Lord went to the chart room and, fully clothed, lay down on the settee to snatch a rest. It was destined to be brief. During the 12-4 watch, rocket signals were seen which, apparently, came from a ship which had stopped some five or six miles away, shortly before midnight, with this ship being on a south easterly bearing, having arrived from the south and west. The rockets were duly reported to Lord by the second officer but, as the ship then appeared to be steaming away, altering her bearing from SSE to SW½W by standard compass, no action was taken, other than to renew previously unsuccessful attempts to contact the ship and establish her identity by Morse lamp. Yet again the signals were ignored.

At 4.30 a.m. the chief officer called Captain Lord, as per instructions, and the captain went to the bridge. Some time later, dawn began to break and the situation was assessed, with the result that the Californian began to make preparations to proceed westward through the ice field. These preparations however, were put on a more urgent footing when the wireless operator, while attempting to make contact with a four-master steamer in the southwest, learned that the Titanic had struck an iceberg during the night and was in need of urgent assistance. By this time, the Carpathia had already arrived at the scene and was loading survivors from the lifeboats, though Captain Lord was unaware of this. A short time later, another message was received which gave the position of the disaster as being at 41° 46' N, 50° 14' W and, after making some vital calculations of his own, Lord estimated that this position lay about S 16° W (true), a distance of some nineteen and a half miles. The time was approximately 6.00 a.m. and Lord immediately gave orders for the Californian to be put under way. Carefully negotiating through the ice field, she eventually found herself in clearer water at 6.30 a.m. when the captain was able to bring the ship up to her full rate of seventy revolutions, which gave her a top speed of thirteen and a half knots. As we have seen, even at this rate, it still took the Californian one and a half hours to reach the position given, proving to be an incorrect one.

It should also be pointed out that the Californian was anything but a fast ship and, with a top speed of thirteen and a half knots, could even be considered slow. It is also well to take into consideration that when she stopped for the night, at 10.20 p.m., it is likely that the fires were banked in her boilers and steam would therefore have been at a minimum, for lights and heating and any small manoeuvring which might be required to maintain her position during the night. Obviously then, even when she picked up the message about the Titanic being in distress, the Californian would not have been prepared to get under way immediately. Indeed the evidence shows that she had to get up steam first and only then, a little after 4.30 a.m., did she start her engines and begin to move from her position. The fact that the Californian stopped at 10.20 p.m. and remained absolutely stationary until after 4.30 a.m. proves, yet again, that she could not have been the ship which the lookouts on the Titanic state they saw 'approach, stop for while, and then sail away again'. Clearly, they were looking at some other ship. Once again, this vital fact was overlooked by Lord Mersey.

The Californian proceeded to the south along the western edge of the ice field and, as we have seen, eventually passed both the Almerian and the Mount Temple in the official position of the disaster. She then identified and signalled the Carpathia by wireless bearing SSE and was informed that the Carpathia was engaged in picking up survivors from the lifeboats. The Californian then made a frantic and highly dangerous dash right through the ice field in her rush to be of assistance. This, incidentally, was her second time taking such a risk. When she did finally manage to reach the Carpathia on the eastern side of the ice field, it was to be told that all the survivors had been picked up. Nevertheless, Lord kept this ship in the area and began to make what proved a fruitless search for other possible survivors. After about three hours of this fruitless searching, Lord finally decided that there was no point in continuing the quest – all he encountered were some empty lifeboats. He resumed his course for Boston, heading due west through the ice field. Lord took note of the time and position in which he had come across the empty lifeboats and recorded these facts in his log. The time was 11.30 a.m., 15 April, and the position, 41° 33' N, 50° 01' W (see chart on page 102). The fact that the Californian encountered these lifeboats some thirteen and a half miles from the actual site of the disaster does not mean that the boats drifted this distance in the hours since the disaster, some nine hours previous. It is well to appreciate that the survivors from the Titanic pulled away from the ship some considerable distance. Most of them headed after what they took to be a steamer's lights. In many cases lifeboats mistook stars on the horizon for the lights of approaching ships. Also, the Carpathia came across the lifeboats quite some time before actually reaching the site of the disaster. Indeed, were it not for discovering the survivors, there is no doubt but that the Carpathia too would have arrived at the wrong location.

Noon sights taken on board the Californian on 15 April were described by the three navigating officers as 'very good' and placed the Californian in position 41° 33' N, 50° 01' W. From this position, which was later re-checked and verified by the three officers, Captain Lord estimated that he had left the empty lifeboats in position 41° 33' N, 50° 01' W. Again this evidence was ignored by the inquiry.

Still more irrefutable facts emerge as we take a closer look at one of the 'mystery ships'. We see that she did exist, belying both the American and British inquiry assertions, and that she was in fact mistaken for the Californian by the Titanic's officers. Likewise, we have seen how yet another ship had stopped some five or six miles from the Californian, giving rise to the speculation that she was the Titanic, as stated by Groves and Gill. As we have seen, it is now apparent that the Titanic and the Californian were each looking at two different ships and, when we note that both of these ships were of approximately the same size as the Californian, we can begin to see how easy it would have been to have made such a mistake. Even so, the question must be asked: How was it possible that both Groves and Gill assumed that the ship they were looking at was the Titanic? Obviously, the Titanic, being the largest ship in the world and ablaze with lights, could hardly have been mistaken for a smaller steamer with little or no lights. Yet, both men were utterly convinced that the ship they were observing was the Titanic. There is no logical answer to this question, and the only thing we do know for certain is that both men were incorrect in their assumption.

Following is a brief extract from an account written by Mr Lawrence Beesley, a survivor of the tragedy. In connection with other ships in the area, he wrote:

But to return for a time to the means taken to attract the notice of other ships. The wireless operators were now in touch with several ships, and calling to them to come quickly for the water was pouring in and the Titanic was beginning to go down by the head. Bride (one of the wireless operators) testified that the first reply received was from a German boat, the Frankfurt, which was 'All right: stand by' but not giving her position. From comparison of the strength of the signals received from the Frankfurt and from other boats, the operators estimated the Frankfurt was the nearest, but subsequent events proved that this was not so. She was in fact, one hundred and forty miles away and arrived at 10.50 a.m. next morning. The next reply was from the Carpathia, fifty eight miles away [sic] on the outbound route to the Mediterranean, and it was a prompt and welcome one – 'Coming hard', followed by the position (unfortunately, Mr Beesley did not include the position – Author). Then followed the Olympic, and with her they talked for some time, but she was five hundred and sixty miles away on the southeast route, too far to be of any immediate help. At the speed of 23 knots she would expect to be up about 1.00 p.m. next day, and this was about the time that those in boat 13 had calculated. We had always assumed in the boat that the stokers who gave this information had it from one of the officers before they left; but in the absence of any knowledge of the much nearer ship, the Carpathia, it is probable that they knew in a general way where the sister ship, the Olympic, should be, and had made a rough calculation.

Other ships in touch by wireless were the Mount Temple, fifty miles; the Birma, one hundred miles; the Parisian, one hundred and fifty miles, and the Baltic, three hundred miles. But closer than any of these – closer even than the Carpathia – were two ships (a reference to X and Z – Author), the Californian, less than 20 miles away, with the wireless operator off duty and unable to catch the CQD signal which was now making the air for many miles around quiver in its appeal for help, immediate, urgent help, for the hundreds of people who stood on Titanic's deck.

The second vessel was a small steamer some few miles ahead on the port side, without any wireless apparatus, her name and destination still unknown; and yet the evidence for her presence that night seems too strong to be disregarded. Mr Boxhall (fourth officer of the Titanic) states that he and Captain Smith saw her quite plainly some five miles away, and could distinguish the masthead lights and a red port light. They at once hailed her with rockets and Morse electric signals, to which Boxhall saw no reply, but Captain Smith and stewards affirmed they did. The second and third officers saw the signals sent and her lights, the latter from the lifeboat of which he was in charge. Seaman Hopkins testified that he was told by the captain to row for the light; and we in boat 13 certainly saw it in the same position and rowed towards it for some time.

But notwithstanding all the efforts made to attract its attention, it drew slowly away and the lights sank below the horizon.

The pity of it! So near, and so many people waiting for the shelter its decks could have given so easily. It seems impossible to think that this ship ever replied to the signals: those who said so must have been mistaken. The United States Senate Committee in its report does not hesitate to say that this unknown steamer and the Californian are identical, and that the failure on the part of the latter to come to the help of the Titanic is culpable negligence. There is undoubted evidence that some of the crew on the Californian saw our rockets; but it seems impossible to believe that the captain and officers knew of our distress and deliberately ignored it. Judgement on the matter had better be suspended until further information is forthcoming.

Mount Temple was the only one near enough from the point of distance to have arrived in time to be of help, but between her and Titanic lay the enormous ice-floe, and icebergs were near her in addition.

The seven ships which caught the message started at once to help but were all stopped on the way – except the Birma – by the Carpathia's wireless message announcing the fate of the Titanic and the people aboard her.

What a magnificent witness Mr Beesley would have made in favour of Captain Lord's insistence that a third ship, as far as Lord was concerned, was between the Californian and the Titanic on that fateful morning! At this stage it might be time to take a closer look at at least one of those 'mystery ships' which, apparently, acted so furtively before, during, and after the disaster. Of the many and often vital documents concerning the Titanic and its subsequent loss, the following example is just one to have somehow surfaced after years of obscurity. There is the definite possibility that this document, with many others, was, for reasons best known to the people involved, deliberately suppressed for many years. The reason for this will become quite obvious as will the serious implications involved. There is little doubt but that at least one of the mystery ships was the sealing ship Samson, and the following letter and statement is reproduced verbatim from the original document written by Henrik B. Naess, first officer of the Samson. In it, we shall see that his ship was in the general area of the Titanic on the night/morning in question, and the similarities and comparisons made are much too close and accurate to be someone's vivid imagination. It should also be borne in mind that this statement is a sworn affidavit from an honourable man who was decorated on several occasions and whose conscience would not allow him to remain silent on the issue. In reading the following statement we must also realise that Naess had absolutely nothing to gain by his admission, in fact, he probably had more to lose. Yet, right up to his death he always insisted that his statement was true. Indeed, so strong is the evidence in Naess's statement that none but a blind fool would doubt its veracity for one moment.

The Samson

Copy of a letter dated 18 November 1939 from Captain Hendrik B. Naess to professor Adolf Hoel, translated from the Norwegian. This letter is a true translation certified by William D. Shepherd, lawyer & authorised translator:

Trondhjem, 18th November 1939
Mr Adolf Hoel, Oslo

Dear Sir,
    In answer to your letter of the 17th inst. I may inform you as follows. My father, Hans Henrik Naess, was born in Trondhjem (dates to be forwarded later). He was a seaman and a sail maker. My mother, Birgitthe Torbersen, was born in Tromsø (dates to be forwarded later). They are both dead. My wife's maiden name: Birgitthe Amanda Waeraas. She was born in Tromsø 22nd December 1867. We were married 3rd March 1893. My wife's father, Gunerius Waeraas was born in Indherrad, Trondhjem, date unknown. He was a seaman. In the autumn of 1868 he went to sea as Bosun, with the Tromsø ship Statsraad Hegermand and vanished without trace. A seaman's chest which proved to belong to my wife's father, was later found to have drifted ashore. My wife's mother, Hanna Helmine Fredrikke Kjeldsen, a sister of the well-known Arctic navigator, Johan Kjeldsen, was born in Tromsø 5th July 1845 and died in 1926 in Trondhjem.
    It is incorrect that I sailed the Arctic Ocean when I was eight years old, but in 1881 when I was 13½ years old I accompanied my foster-father, Captain Nils Johnsen, who owned the sloop Grøne Haabet and the schooner Søstrene. One year I skippered the sloop Moderen and in 1897 I skippered SS Laura which had been hired from the Englishman Barclay Walker for a hunting trip in the Arctic Ocean. In 1894 I acted as pilot and guide on board the German

passenger ship Stettin of Danzig, in 1897 as pilot and guide on board the English tourist steamer Garonne, in 1896 as pilot and guide on board the sloop Otoria. In June 1898 I moved to Trondhjem and in 1900 I made the first expedition to Svalbard. In 1901 I bought the cutter Alaska with which I continued the coal expeditions, until the Americans took over the fields, and you are acquainted with my activities during the period I worked there.

In 1912 I signed on with the sealing vessel Samson for a sailing expedition to Labrador, as mate and harpoon gunner. The Samson and her sister ship Njørd had been bought by Trondhjem owners. In 1918 I was engaged as a lighthouse keeper at Støtt Lighthouse.

I have been awarded the King's Medal of Merit in gold for pioneering work on the coals in Svalbard, the French Rescue Medal (Bronze) for searching for Roald Amundsen, and the Trondelag Exhibition Silver Medal for designing and constructing a pilot control clock which has been patented.

In 1928 I sailed as Arctic pilot and guide on board the Swedish Mobile Expedition ship Tania of Gothenburg. In 1930 I sailed as Arctic pilot and guide on board Nordenfjeldske's Prins Olav.

In 1935 as Arctic pilot and guide for the Belgian Baron Jean Empaise on his private yacht Heliopolis.

In case it might be of interest, I might inform you that when we were on board the sealing vessel Samson at the south end of the ice south of Cape Hatteras [this has probably become confused in the translation and should read Cape Race – Author] we saw the Titanic at the very moment she fired her rockets just before sinking. But we didn't know that at the time. Had we any idea that it was the Titanic and that there was something wrong, we would have been able to save a lot of lives with our eight big sealing boats, in the fair weather, calm with quite clear air and a very slight swell. We were lying in slack ice with shaded lights during the darkest part of the night, and we were near enough to be able to see the masthead lights from our deck. In fact, we did not dare let ourselves be seen, as we had gone out to catch young seal in Labrador without a licence, and all hands on board, totalling 45, had been hired on their own responsibility in the event that we were caught by the American sealers.

When we arrived at Isafjord in Iceland, the consul there told us the unhappy news, and the local newspaper confirmed the news and gave the position. As I had kept the log, I took it out and compared our position with that of the Titanic, and they corresponded exactly. I admit that both the captain and I felt a bit queer after seeing this, as, had we understood that anything like that was happening before our eyes, we would have been able to perform a won-derful feat. Instead, the whole voyage was a failure.

When I get the dates from my son, I shall promptly forward them to you. It will be interesting to see the outcome of this, when you have put it together the way you want it.

Yours sincerely,
Signed: Henrik B. Naess

Naess obviously felt a great deal of concern, knowing what he knew, and had even gone to the newspapers with his story some eleven years before. We see that in the intervening years, the story only differed slightly in that Naess, in his 1939 account, referred to 'eight big sealing boats', and in his earlier newspaper account he makes reference to 'twelve dories'. There is of course the distinct possibility that this could have been either a newspaper error, a mistake in translation or even a genuine slip on the part of Naess himself. Nevertheless, it is not an important issue and does not detract from the fact that the Samson sealing ship was, apparently, in the area of the dis-aster and was probably mistaken for the Californian. As Naess's newspaper statement is somewhat more detailed than his later affidavit, it is included hereunder from the Arbeideravisa, Trondhjem, 9th June 1928:

… Captain Naess comes from the town of Tromsø and started his Arctic career in 1877 under his foster-father, Captain Nils Johansen, Tromsø. Later, ever since 1913, he has for many years ploughed the Arctic Sea both as whaler and pilot. His name is known from a number of famous expeditions to the Arctic regions. In 1896 he acted as pilot and interpreter with Sir Baden Powell's expedition on the yacht Otoria for studies of the total solar eclipse in the Arctic. It was on the return trip from this expedition that Otoria in August of the same year took on board Fridtjof Nansen in Vardø after Nansen's and Hjalmar Johansen's famous voyage to Frans Josef Land. In 1912, Naess was engaged as harpoon gunner and mate on the well-known Arctic vessel Samson. It was during this expedition that he experienced an event which was far more eerie than the many days and nights in the Arctic.

'We were engaged in sealing operations on prohibited territory', Naess explains. 'One night while the skipper and I were sitting in his cabin, the helmsman reported lights ahead. This was about half an hour before midnight and the weather was clear. I ran up on deck. In fact, we did not feel quite

safe from the Americans. On the horizon, a few miles to the west, we saw a
faint light. "Use your telescope," I said to the helmsman. "I see lots of lights,"
answered the helmsman. We finally became aware that rockets were being
fired and this continued until half an hour after midnight. Then the lights disappeared. About a month later our ship arrived at Iceland. There we were told
that the great steamer Titanic had been lost after colliding with an iceberg
about a month ago, which was exactly the night when we saw the lights out
at sea. The hour and place corresponded precisely to our observations.'

Visibly moved, Captain Naess explains how the report affected him and
others: 'Had we the slightest idea of what was happening out there or had
our vessel been equipped with radio, we would probably have been able,
with our twelve dories to save most of the lives.'

Naess actually submitted a written report to the Norwegian Consul in
the subsequent weeks declaring that he had seen 'two big stars', which he
later identified as 'lanterns and lots of lights'. He went on to state that a few
moments later he noticed several rockets and then all the lights seemed to
disappear. His written report to the Consul went on:

> The Samson's position was such that it feared we might be taken for violat-
> ing territorial waters as there were Americans in the neighbourhood. When
> the lights went out this probably meant we were being observed, the rockets
> being, maybe, signals to other ships. We therefore changed course and hurried
> northwards.

When we superimpose the statement that Naess made and compare it with
the evidence from those aboard the Titanic, we can immediately see the
similarities and must concede that these, taken along with all the other
details, are simply far too close to allow for any coincidence. Considering
this, the Samson may very well have been one of the 'mystery ships' between
the Titanic and the Californian and was, obviously mistaken for Lord's ship.

Naess, in his statements also suggests that there might have been another
'mystery ship' in the area when he says, 'There were Americans in the
neighbourhood.' This of course implies that some form of fishery-protec-
tion vessel or vessels might also have been in the locality.

Obviously not wishing to become involved in what was rapidly becoming an event of major controversy, the Norwegian government conveniently
'lost' Naess's report and for the next fifty years disavowed any knowledge of

The sealing vessel Samson. Courtesy of Claes-Göran Wetterholm Collection, Sweden

it. It was only in 1962, the year Captain Lord and Henrik Naess died, that the information finally became public. The report had managed to surface a few times in the intervening years, in 1928 and 1939, but still the Norwegians consistently denied that they knew anything about the incident. In fact, an approach to the Norwegian embassy in connection with the report (for inclusion in this book) was met with the polite but firm reply, 'The office of this Ministry has no information concerning the sealing ship Samson'. Clearly, even though by then almost eighty years had passed since the tragedy, the Norwegian government still declined to become involved, publicly at least, in the affair. Much more suspicious and thought-provoking is the fact that the official log of the Samson, and the original affidavit made by Naess, mysteriously and suddenly disappeared.

The sad possibility remains that if the British and American inquiries had had access to the Naess Report, and the log of the Samson, during the formal investigation in 1912, then there is the distinct likelihood that a totally different result would have been arrived at and, in all probability, Captain Lord would have been exonerated of the false and damaging accusations. In this respect, yet another government must hang its head in shame for the subsequent events which led to the ruination of Captain Stanley Lord in the eyes of the world.

Editor's note: This was not to be the end of the Samson story. During the process of writing his book, Tom Williams was evidently completely unaware of the fact that in the United States Mr David L. Eno, an investigator with the Federal Credit Union Administration in Washington, specialising in high-dollar embezzlement cases, had already been tracking down Samson's whereabouts that eventful night since 1978. A report on part of the results of his research was published in the Washington Post of Sunday 30 June 1991. Quotes of the relevant sections are reprinted below with permission:

THE SHIP THAT PASSED IN THE NIGHT
by Ken Ringle, Washington Post staff writer

At some point – [Eno] can't remember precisely when – he began thinking of the Titanic less as history than as another police case he wanted to solve. In 1962 he heard of a recurring suspect for the 'mystery ship' – a steam-powered Norwegian schooner called the Samson, reported by one of its officers to have been near the Titanic when the huge liner sank. Citing a tangle of circumstantial evidence, most scholars concluded it couldn't have been there. Eno wasn't so sure.

He set out upon a curiously single-minded quest. During his off-duty hours over the past 13 years, he says, he has assembled a 170-member network of volunteer investigators that researched the Newfoundland fishing and sealing fleets of 1912. He peppered Scandinavian police stations with letters, appealing for investigative help.

[In 1990] Eno flew to Iceland, and there in a nursing home near the Arctic Circle, he says, found two elderly men who remember the Samson and at least part of her voyage.

Eno and his collaborator Lieutenant Commander Craig McLean of the National Oceanic and Atmospheric Administration, believe they have finally dismantled the arguments of those who contend the Samson couldn't have been within visible range of the Titanic on the night it went down, April 14, 1912.

What Eno and Mclean offer is a modest but intriguing addition to the controversy that still engulfs the Titanic. Their evidence is likely to satisfy few Titanic buffs, most of whom have long since positioned themselves immovably in one camp or another. But it will help keep alive and rolling one of the most enduring seafaring mysteries of all time.

The Samson, a Norwegian sealing ship, has long been part of the Titanic lore. After the disaster, its former first officer, one Henrik Naess, told a newspaper in Norway that the Samson had been within sight of the Titanic the night the great ship went down.

According to Naess's story, the 147ft steam-powered schooner with eight [sic] seal-hunting boats and a crew of forty-five onboard, had been cruising in an ice field north of the Titanic's position the night of 14 April, when the crew spotted two masthead lights and rockets on the horizon. Naess sent a man into the crow's nest with binoculars for a better view, and he returned with a report of 'many lights' on the sea where rockets were being fired.

'The Samson had been sealing illegally off the coast of Labrador and Newfoundland, and Captain Carl Johann Ring was wary of being discovered with his cargo, even in international waters,' Naess said.

Having no radio, they had no way of knowing the scope of the disaster unfolding and thought the most discreet move was to leave the scene. Only the following month, when the ship put into Isafjordur, Iceland, for repairs did the ship learn of the Titanic's sinking, Naess said.

Scholars of the Titanic found Neass's story intriguing in some places and simply baffling in others. For example, Naess stated that his ship had been south of Cape Hatteras, which was not only physically impossible but logically confounding. Why would a Norwegian sealer even think of being near Cape Hatteras? It's a thousand miles from his Arctic hunting ground and nowhere near any seals.

Neither Captain Ring, nor other Samson crewmen, apparently ever made any public statement about the Titanic.

Two men in Iceland, older than the Titanic, confirmed that the Samson had been in Isafjordhur in May 1912, and not before, he said.

Eno said, 'the reason they remembered is that the crew of the ship had gone on a spree and almost wrecked the town.' They had accosted women on the street and even gone into people's homes, and in the end a citizens protection league had been formed to round up the sailors, get them back on the ship and force the ship out to sea. It was a highly memorable event in the town's history.

The disputed dates in April, Eno says, displaying affidavits from port authorities, were actually the recorded dates when the ship had been expected to arrive, and when the Norwegian consul had made an advance payment of half the Samson's harbor fees. The 1912 shipping lists from Lloyds of London place the Samson in Isafjordur on May 14.

Eno got further help from Irene Erickson of Leesburg, a Norwegian woman he met in church in Purcellville [Eno's home town; editor] who happened to be from the town of Arendal, Norway, where the Samson was built, and who volunteered further research on the vessel while home on a visit.

She discovered that in Norway, First Officer Naess is still looked on, long after his death, as a man of substance and credibility. He had been a highly skilled seaman and explorer and the most accomplished ice pilot of his day, and had been decorated by both Norway and Sweden for his role in various Arctic rescues. He does not sound like the sort to elaborate stories, Eno says. He had referred to the Titanic incident in his unpublished memoirs and had told his children and grandchildren that he regretted not having had a radio so the Samson might have saved some of the 1,500 Titanic passengers and crew who died that night. He realized, however, that he couldn't have saved them all.

Erickson, Eno said, even learned one of the reasons why no Titanic researcher in the past 70 years had heard from the Samson's captain: Carl Johann Ring died June 22, 1918, after his ship, the Eglantine, was torpedoed by a German U-boat in the North Sea.

As for the Samson itself, the ship went on to fame from its days as a renegade sealer. Uniquely equipped as an ice vessel, with a steel-reinforced bow and a hull as much as 5ft thick in places, it was sought out by Admiral Richard Byrd, the explorer, renamed the City of New York, and shown off in New York and Chicago after service in the Antarctic.

She burned in a fire off Yarmouth, Nova Scotia, in 1952.

'The bow wound up on the beach, and we learned some kid had taken pictures of it the next day', Eno says with a satisfied grin. 'Through a cop in Yarmouth we found the name of the kid. He still lives there. He had the pictures in his attic.'

Just how much all this really means to the story of the Titanic, of course, is problematic. There is, for example, the matter of the Cape Hatteras reference, which Eno and McLean admit they can't explain, and shrug off as an obvious mistaken reference to Cape Race, Newfoundland. And though the Samson could have matched the description of a vessel seen by some of the Titanic's survivors, showing a single white light and appearing to be moving slowly away, it leaves unexplained the vessel seen from the Californian, which was clearly a steamer of some kind.

Eno and Mclean say they're working on that. There are many candidates, they say: the area was a major Atlantic shipping route at the time.

McLean and Eno have come to subscribe to the basic theory of the Lordites – that the rockets seen from the Californian were, in fact, fired from

Captain Lord in retirement in 1930 together with his wife in their beloved North Wales. Photo courtesy of Mrs Muriel Fairweather.

the Titanic, but appeared to be from a separate still unknown vessel, far closer than the sinking ship. In all, says Eno, he's been working for 13 years on 74 'corridors of inquiry' into the unanswered questions of the Titanic. So far, he says, he's found 29 'points of corroboration' tending to substantiate Lord's claim of innocence.

'You read through the record of these inquiries,' McLean says, 'and there are so many contradictions and unanswered questions you just can't believe nobody followed them up. Which is all we're doing. It's like the Kennedy assassination investigation. There was a rush to judgement after the Titanic went down. As a nation we get on these things like we take an escalator. And we always get off at the first floor.'

The editor of this book was part of David Eno's 170-member network. He finally met him and (then) Lieutenant Commander Craig McLean personally before and after their successive speeches about the Samson during the Titanic Historical Society Convention at the Copley Plaza Hotel in Boston on 11 April 1992. The day after this event, a small group of people, including Mr Eno and the editor, even managed to pinpoint the site of the former saloon in Boston Harbor where donkeyman Ernest Gill had spilled his tale about Californian's alleged involvement in the Titanic disaster to a reporter of the Boston American in exchange of $500.00 around 24 April 1912.

The Californian had been docked nearby eighty years before and we were able to retrace Gill's exact steps. Mr Eno and I corresponded for several years more. We exchanged views after Stanley T. Lord's death in December 1994, but, sadly, a detailed work on the issue will not be forthcoming as a result of a fire in Mr Eno's home during which all his documents were destroyed. There is no doubt in this editor's mind that the Samson was operating in the general area of the Titanic's sinking that night for about an hour after the latter's demise, the Mount Temple came across a schooner on a bearing in line with the Titanic's position. At that time, Captain Moore of the Mount Temple estimated that the schooner would have been thirteen miles from Titanic's SOS position. Since this vessel, like Samson, was steaming under auxiliary power, it could have been in the Titanic's vicinity at about the time of the sightings of the unidentified ship. However, Samson did not fit the description of the vessel seen to approach by Fourth Officer Boxhall. It had lit portholes and range lights, which implied electricity. Samson had no portholes to speak of and had doused her lights as she tried to make off like a thief in the night after having carried out illegal operations. This ship could never have given shelter to those 1,500 people still on board the Titanic anyhow. Nine decades have passed and numerous candidates that fitted this role have since emerged and been dismissed. It is likely that we will never know what ship left the Titanic to die. Mr Senan Molony nominates a dozen likely vessels in the third appendix of his book *Titanic and the Mystery Ship* (2006).

REFERENCES

1   The chart previously referred on page 93, though somewhat rough, was prepared by the captain of the Birma from actual sighting of the ice field and was published in the London Daily Telegraph on 25 April 1912. It clearly confirmed the existence and massive scope of the ice. The independent, yet interrelated information provided by the five ships mentioned, is plotted in bold outline, and the navigational evidence of the Californian is superimposed in broken outline. Amazingly, at the British inquiry into the disaster, this chart was submitted to and rejected by Lord Mersey.

**THE DEPARTMENT
OF TRANSPORT**

14 May 1990

Mr T B Williams
1 Quain Tce
Cork Hill
Youghal
Co Cork
Ireland

Dear Mr Williams

TITANIC AND CALIFORNIAN

Your letter of 5 April has been passed to this Branch for reply.

There have been a number of representations made on behalf of Captain Lord, and it is right to tell you that, following a close examination of the evidence now available, it is accepted that CALIFORNIAN was substantially further from TITANIC than Lord Mersey found. The distance was, as you suggest, probably of the order of 20 miles.

At the same time, it is considered inescapable that Capt Lord did merit a degree of censure. When all possible allowances are made, both for the different circumstances of 78 years ago – including the common use of company identification signals – and for the presence of the SAMSON in the vicinity, the fact remains that signals which <u>could</u> have been signals of distress were seen in an area which Capt Lord himself thought hazardous enough to require him to stop his ship until daylight.

The Department does not consider that the Formal Investigation should be re-opened: the investigation was into the loss of the TITANIC, and Capt Lord was not a party. No charge was made against him in any court; as to why this was so, I am afraid that at this distance of time I can offer no answer.

Yours sincerely

J de Coverly

Captain J de Coverly
Deputy Chief Inspector of Marine Accidents

**THE DEPARTMENT
OF TRANSPORT**

20 June 1990

Mr T B Williams
1 Quain Terrace
Cork Hill
Youghal
Co Cork
Ireland

Dear Mr Williams

RMS TITANIC AND SS CALIFORNIAN

You will, I am sure, be glad to know that the Secretary of State has decided that this Branch should commission a re-appraisal of the evidence concerning Captain Lord. The re-appraisal will be conducted by Captain T W Barnett, a recently retired officer with wide experience, and it is intended that a Report will be published when he has completed the task.

Captain Barnett may wish to get in touch with you in the course of his inquiries, and if he does so I am sure you will give him any assistance in your power.

Yours sincerely

Captain J de Coverly
Deputy Chief Inspector of Marine Accidents

**THE DEPARTMENT
OF TRANSPORT**

26 June 1990

Mr.T.B.Williams
1 Quain Terrace
Cork Hill
Youghal
Co Cork
Ireland

Dear Mr.Williams

RMS "TITANIC" AND SS "CALIFORNIAN"

Captain J.de Coverley has written to you to advise that I have been commissioned to re-appraise evidence concerning Captain Lord.

Attached to this letter are my terms of reference.

Although I have had recent experience in marine casualty inquiries, I know very little about the "Titanic" tragedy; however, this may help me to approach the matter with an open mind.

In order for my re-appraisal to bear any weight it will have to refer to source material. I have already been provided with copies of the Wreck Commissioner's Court Minutes of Evidence, and the Report of the Formal Investigation.

I am writing similar letters to this, to those gentlemen whose letters on file show them to be interested in a re-appraisal, and are in a position to assist me in gathering the necessary source material.

I note from your letters on file that you have been conducting intensive research into this casualty for some time, and I would be grateful for any help you can offer. Initially I would be grateful for a copy of the Henrick B Naess statement concerning "Samson" which you kindly offered in your letter of 5 April 1990.

Yours sincerely

Tom Barnett

RMS "TITANIC" AND SS "CALIFORNIAN"
RE-APPRAISAL OF EVIDENCE CONCERNING CAPTAIN LORD

TERMS OF REFERENCE

1   Taking into account the discovery of the wreckage of the "Titanic" and other evidence which has become available since the Formal Investigation into her loss was held, together with recorded evidence given at the Investigation:

    a)   To establish so far as is now possible the positions of the "Titanic" when she struck an iceberg on 14 April 1912 and when she subsequently foundered; to estimate the positions of "Californian" at the same times; and to deduce the distance apart of the two vessels during the period between those times.

    b)   To consider whether "Titanic" was seen by "Californian" during that period, and if so when and by whom.

    c)   To consider whether distress signals from "Titanic" were seen by "Californian" and, if so, whether proper action was taken.

    d)   To assess the action taken by Captain Stanley Lord, Master of "Californian", between about 10pm ship's time on 14 April and the time on 15 April when passage was resumed.

2   To present my findings to the Chief Inspector of Marine Accidents.

3   To prepare a Report.

T.W.Barnett

MARINE ACCIDENT INVESTIGATION BRANCH

5/7 Brunswick Place Southampton Hants SO1 2AN

Switchboard 0703 232424

Direct Line 0703

Telex 477917 MAIB SOG   Fax 0703 232459

THE DEPARTMENT
OF TRANSPORT

23 July 1990

Mr.Thomas B.Williams,
1 Quain Terrace
Cork Hill
Youghal
Co.Cork
Ireland

Dear Mr.Williams,

RMS "TITANIC" AND SS "CALIFORNIAN"

Thank you for your letter of 5 July, together with the documents concerning Captain Naess and the vessel "Samson", which are most useful.

I have taken note of the various points put forward in your letter, and look forward to reading the document you have in preparation.

I shall make sure that you receive a copy of the Report in due course.

Yours sincerely,

T.W.Barnett

MARINE ACCIDENT INVESTIGATION BRANCH

5/7 Brunswick Place Southampton Hants SO1 2AN

Telephone 0703 232424

Telex 477917 MA1B SOG   Fax 0703 232459

THE DEPARTMENT
OF TRANSPORT

15 January 1991

Mr T B Williams
Shipping Researcher & Consultant
1 Quain Tce
Cork Hill
Youghal
Co Cork
Ireland

Dear Mr Williams

CALIFORNIAN

Your letter to Mr Rifkind has been passed to me for reply. It would not be right for Mr Rifkind to discuss the subject and give his personal remarks, as you request, with Captain Barnett's re-appraisal still in progress.

I can advise you that his enquiries are at an advanced stage, and I understand that he hopes to submit his Report to the Chief Inspector within the next few weeks.

Yours sincerely

Captain J de Coverly
Deputy Chief Inspector of Marine Accidents

MARINE ACCIDENT INVESTIGATION BRANCH

21 March 1991

Mr T B Williams
Shipping Researcher & consultant
Cork Hill
Youghal
Co Cork
Ireland

Dear Mr Williams

CALIFORNIAN

Thank you for your letter of 14 March.

Because of pressure of other work, it will be a little time yet before the Report on the CALIFORNIAN is finalised. Your interest has been noted; I am sure the findings will be well publicised when they are available.

Yours sincerely

Captain P B Marriott
Chief Inspector of Marine Accidents

THE DEPARTMENT
OF TRANSPORT

Marine Accident Investigation Branch
Department of Transport
517 Brunswick Place
Southampton
Hants S01 2AN

12 March 1992

The Right Honourable Malcolm Rifkind QC MP Secretary of State for Transport

Sir

Your predecessor, The Right Honourable Cecil Parkinson MP, determined that
MAIB should carry out a reappraisal of the role played by SS CALIFORNIAN at
the time RMS TITANIC was lost in 1912.

Clearly, the case was somewhat outside the ordinary run of MAIB investigations
and, in order to avoid its clashing with our main work, an Inspector from outside
the Branch was appointed to study the evidence and advise me of his
conclusions, after which a Report would be prepared. The Officer appointed to
this task had recently retired from a post as Principal Nautical Surveyor in the
Department of Transport Marine Survey Service and is a very experienced
Master Mariner. I do not fully agree with all the Inspector's findings but this does
not mean that I have any doubt at all as to either the thoroughness of his
enquiries or the fair-mindedness of his approach. It rather serves to emphasize
the difficulty of the task he was set and of reaching absolute conclusions.

However, I considered that some further examination was required and I
instructed the Deputy Chief Inspector of Marine Accidents to undertake this and
report to me. His report, which follows, incorporates his conclusions and those of
the appointed Inspector.

I fully endorse the Deputy Chief Inspector's report and conclusions.

I am, Sir,

Your obedient servant

Captain P B Marriott

Chief Inspector of Marine Accidents

MAIB
MARINE ACCIDENT INVESTIGATION BRANCH

85

2 April 1992

PRESS NOTICE NO.

DATE

RMS 'TITANIC' - RE-APPRAISAL OF EVIDENCE RELATING TO SS 'CALIFORNIAN' REPORT PUBLISHED

The report of the re-appraisal of the evidence relating to the role played by SS CALIFORNIAN at the time RMS TITANIC was lost in 1912 is published today.

On 14 April 1912 at about 2340 hours ship's time the White Star liner TITANIC, on her maiden voyage from Southampton towards New York, struck an iceberg and was severely damaged. She foundered less than two and three quarter hours later, with the loss of 1,490 lives. In response to her radio distress signals, various ships attempted to come to her aid but the first to reach the scene, the Cunard liner CARPATHIA, did not arrive until about 0400 hours, well after TITANIC had sunk.

There is no doubt that other vessels were nearer to hand than CARPATHIA, but in 1912 many ships did not have wireless and those that did, did not necessarily keep continuous watch with their apparatus. One such ship was the British cargo/passenger vessel CALIFORNIAN, whose single wireless operator had gone off duty shortly before the first distress call was sent.

At the Formal Investigation held in London between 2 May and 3 July 1912, evidence was heard from CALIFORNIAN's Master and some of her officers and crew. It was put to the Court that although they had not heard TITANIC's wireless messages, they had seen distress signals which she had fired; and that had they responded to those signals, they might have saved many of the lives lost.

The terms of reference of the re-appraisal were as follows:

To establish so far as is now possible the positions of TITANIC when she struck an iceberg on 14 April 1912, and when she subsequently foundered; to estimate the positions of CALIFORNIAN at the same times; and to deduce the distance apart of the two vessels during the period between those times.

To consider whether TITANIC was seen by CALIFORNIAN during that period, and if so, when and by whom.

To consider whether distress signals from TITANIC were seen by CALIFORNIAN and if so, whether proper action was taken.

To assess the action taken by Captain Stanley Lord, Master of CALIFORNIAN, between about 10.00pm ship's time on 14 April and the time on 15 April when passage was resumed.

The main conclusions reached are:

TITANIC was in approximate position 41 47N 49 55W when she struck the iceberg at 2345 hours 14 April, and in position 41 43.8N 49 56.9W when she foundered.

The position of CALIFORNIAN cannot be deduced so accurately and opinions are divided. However, it is concluded that CALIFORNIAN was probably between 17 and 20 miles from TITANIC.

It is possible that TITANIC was seen by CALIFORNIAN due to abnormal refraction permitting sight beyond the ordinary visible horizon; but more likely that she was not seen.

The Court was asked the specific question:

"What vessels had the opportunity of rendering assistance to the TITANIC and, if any, how was it that assistance did not reach the TITANIC before the SS CARPATHIA arrived?"

The Court's answer was:

"The CALIFORNIAN. She could have reached the TITANIC if she had made the attempt when she saw the first rocket. She made no attempt."

CALIFORNIAN's Master was Captain Stanley Lord and it was upon him that the great weight of the extremely grave accusation implied by the Court's finding fell. Captain Lord always disputed the justice of the finding and he requested a re-hearing of that part of the Inquiry which concerned his ship; the request was rejected, and as no formal charge had been laid against him, and no action had been taken against his Certificate, he had no right of appeal.

For many years the matter rested, but in the mid-1950s the book 'A Night to Remember' appeared; it was widely read and a successful film based upon it was made. The allegations against CALIFORNIAN were repeated and this led Captain Lord, by then over 80 years old, to renew his plea for the matter to be re-examined, and his case was taken up by others. In particular, two petitions were made to the Board of Trade, asking for the inquiry to be re-opened; both were rejected.

In 1985 an expedition discovered the wreck of the TITANIC, in a position some 13 miles from that accepted by the 1912 Inquiry as being the position of the casualty. This 'new evidence' led to further pressure for the Inquiry to be re-opened, and although initially the Department of Transport (who by now had taken responsibility for shipping matters) refused, in 1990 the Secretary of State for Transport determined that the Marine Accident Investigation Branch should make a re-appraisal of the relevant evidence.

TITANIC's distress signals were seen, and that proper action was not taken; however, any reasonable action by Captain Lord would not have led to a different outcome to the tragedy, as CALIFORNIAN would have arrived well after TITANIC had sunk.

Because of the complexity of the investigation, the conclusions above can only be regarded as a summary and it is recommended that the report is studied in its entirety to see the conclusions in their proper perspective.

NOTES TO EDITORS

1. 'RMS TITANIC, Re-appraisal of Evidence Relating to SS CALIFORNIAN' (ISBN 0-11-551111-3) is published today by HMSO, price £7.50. Press copies are available from the Press Office, Department of Transport, 2 Marsham Street, London, SW1P 3EB (tel: 071 276 5172).

2. In the United States, copies are available from HMSO's agents, Unipub, 4611 S Assembly Drive, Lanham, MD 20706, USA.

Press Enquiries: 071 276 0888; out of hours: 071 276 5999
Public Enquiries: 071 276 3000; ask for Public Enquiry Unit

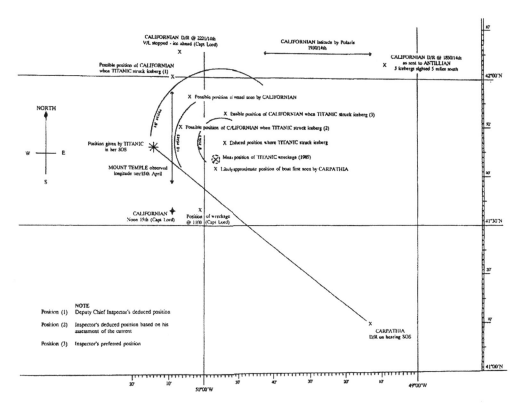

CALIFORNIAN D/R @ 2221/14th
V/L stopped - ice ahead (Capt Lord)
X

CALIFORNIAN latitude by Polaris
1930/14th

CALIFORNIAN D/R @ 1850/14th
as sent to ANTILLIAN
3 icebergs sighted 5 miles south
X

Possible position of CALIFORNIAN
when TITANIC struck iceberg (1)
X

42°00'N

NORTH

X Possible position of vessel seen by CALIFORNIAN

X Possible position of CALIFORNIAN when TITANIC struck iceberg (3)

X Possible position of CALIFORNIAN when TITANIC struck iceberg (2)

10'

W — E

Position given by TITANIC
in her SOS
X

X Deduced position where TITANIC struck iceberg

S

MOUNT TEMPLE observed
longitude am/15th April

Mean position of TITANIC wreckage (1985)

X Likely approximate position of boat first seen by CARPATHIA

40'

CALIFORNIAN
Noon 15th (Capt Lord)

X
Position of wreckage
@ 1100 (Capt Lord)

41°30'N

20'

NOTE
Position (1)   Deputy Chief Inspector's deduced position

Position (2)   Inspector's deduced position based on his
               assessment of the current

10'

X
CARPATHIA
D/R on hearing SOS

Position (3)   Inspector's preferred position

41°00'N

20'   10'   50'   40'   30'   20'   10'
50°00'W   49°00'W

Captain Barnett stated that the formal investigation report of 1912 was correct in deducing that the Californian and the Titanic were no more than between five and seven miles apart. However, Captain Marriott, chief inspector of the Marine Accident Investigation Branch, and Captain de Coverly, the deputy chief inspector, stated more correctly that the Californian was about seventeen to twenty miles away from Titanic during her sinking.

Numbers saved.

The following were the numbers saved :—

1st class.

Adult males	...	...	57	out of 175 or 32.57 per cent.
Adult females	...	...	140	out of 144 or 97.22 ,,
Male children	...	...	5	All saved.
Female children	...	...	1	All saved.

203 out of 325 or 62.46 ,,

2nd class.

Adult males	...	...	14	out of 168 or 8.33 per cent.
Adult females	...	...	80	out of 93 or 86.02 ,,
Male children	...	...	11	All saved.
Female children	...	...	13	All saved.

118 out of 285 or 41.40 ,,

3rd class.

Adult males	...	...	75	out of 462 or 16.23 per cent.
Adult females	...	...	76	out of 165 or 46.06 ,,
Male children	...	...	13	out of 48 or 27.08 ,,
Female children	...	...	14	out of 31 or 45.16 ,,

178 out of 706 or 25.21 ,,

Total ... ... 499 out of 1,316 or 37.94 ,,

Crew saved.

Deck Department ... 43 out of 66 or 65.15 per cent.
Engine Room Department 72 out of 325 or 22.15 ,,
Victualling Department, (including 20 women out of 23) ... ... 97 out of 494 or 19.63 ,,

Total... ... ... 212 out of 885 or 23.95 ,,

Total on board saved. 711 out of 2,201 or 32.30 ,,

Passengers and Crew.

Adult males	...	...	338 out of 1,667 or 20·27 per cent.
Adult females	...	...	316 out of 425 or 74·35 ,,
Children	...	...	57 out of 109 or 52·29 ,,

Total ... ... 711 out of 2,201 or 32·30 ,,

Source: From the Formal Investigation Report. (1912)

RMS TITANIC & OLYMPIC.   TECHNICAL DATA.

ENGINES

No.	H.P.	Consn. Coal d	Speed Coal d	No. of Screws	Description of Engines	If F.D. or N.B.	Wt. of Machy. Tons	Diameter of Cylinders	Stroke	Revs.
400	51,000	825	21 mean	3	Twin 4 cyl. Triple Exp. Rec. + L.P. Turbine	N.B.		54·84·97·97	75	77 R 165 J
401	51,000	825	"	3	"	N.B.		54·84·97·97	75	77 R 163 J

	D.E. BOILERS		S.E. BOILERS							PROPELLERS		
No.	Dia.	Len.	No.	Dia.	Len.	No. of Furnaces	Heating Surf.	Grate Surf.	Steam Pressure	Diar.	Pitch	No.
1 23	13'6" 15'9"	20'0" 20'0"	5	15'9"	11'9"	159	142,454	3,430	215	R 22'9" J 17'0"	36'0" 14'0"	400
24	15'9"	20'0"	5	15'9"	11'9"	159	144,142	3,466	215	R 23'6" J 17'0"	33'0" 14'6"	401

	1ST CLASS ACCOMMN.			2ND CLASS ACCOMMN.			3RD CLASS ACCOMMN.			CREW			HEAD OF		
Rooms	Berths	Sofas	Seats in Saloon	Rooms	Berths & Sofas	Seats in Saloon	In Rooms	Open Berths	Seats in Saloon	Deck	Eng. Rm.	Stewds.	Cattle	Horses	No.
381	844	109	540 132 1st 36 3rd	162	510	402	86 1st 776	164	473	75	325	524	–	–	400
416	928	106	554 132 1st 36 3rd	162	510	402	982	40	473	74	326	524	–	–	401

Courtesy: Harland & Wolff. Belfast.

RMS TITANIC & OLYMPIC.   TECHNICAL DATA.

			WHERE BUILT		DATES						DIMENSIONS				
No	Name	Owners	Hull	Engs.	Order to Proceed	Keel Laid	Launch	Comple- tion	* Surveys	Len. B.P.	Len. O.A.	Br. Mld.	Depth K. to B.	Depth Mld.
400	Olympic	White Star	Belfast	Belfast	30.4.07	16.12.08	20.10.10	29.5.11	None B.T./Pass Eng/cont	850'0"	882'8"	92'0"	64'6" &c	64'3"
401	Titanic	"	Belfast	Belfast	30.4.07	31.3.09	31.5.11	2.4.12	None B.T./Pass Eng/in.	850'0"	882'8"	92'0"	64'6" &c	64'3"

	TONNAGE					LOAD CONDITIONS						LIGHT CONDITIONS				
Frame Spacing	U.D.	Gross	Net	Suez Net	No. B.Hds.	Dft.	Disp.	Tons per Inch	D.W.	Block Coef.	Prism. Coef.	Dft.	Tons per Inch	Trim	G.M.	Block Coef.	No.
36"	17,871 35,043	45,324	24,844	24,744	16	34'7"	52,310	143·8	14,030	·684	·705	26'4"	138·3		·87	·660	400
36"	17,871	46,329	21,831	—	15	34'7"	52,310	143·3	13,550	·684	·705	26'2"	135·5	—	—	—	401

	CAPACITIES								DYNAMOS	
No.	Total Cargo	Insulated	Permt. Bunkers	Res. Bunkers	BALLAST TANKS F.W.	S.W.	Deep Tanks	F.W. Outside D.B.	No.	Capacity K.W.
400	lt 7,589 228,880	25,060 lbrs 22,720 Cargo	6,611 &c	1,201 &c	1,002 796	3,932 820	–	962	4 main 2 Emeg.	1,600 60
401	221,760	25,060 22,720	6,611 &c	1,201 &c	1,002 796 or	3,932 820	–	962	"	"

Courtesy: Harland & Wolff. Belfast. (* Showing Board of Trade pass and no surveys)

SCHEDULE OF EVENTS, 14/15 APRIL 1912

NEW YORK TIME	On board the "Californian"	CALIFORNIAN TIME	On board the "Titanic"	TITANIC TIME
9.58am	–	11.48am	Clocks set 2 hrs 2 mins fast on New York Time (for longitude 44½° West).	Noon
10.10	Clocks set 1 hr 50 mins fast on New York Time (for longitude 47½° West).	Noon	–	12.12pm
8.30pm	Stopped in ice.	10.20pm	Course S86W true, speed 22¼ knots.	10.30
9.05	Ship 'X', approaching from the southwest, watched by Captain Lord, the chief engineer, and the radio officer.	10.55	Nothing in sight.	11.05
9.10	Radio message sent to "Titanic", 'Am stopped in ice'.	11.00	From "Titanic" to "Californian", 'Keep out'.	11.10
9.40	Third officer reports 'X' to captain.	11.30	"Titanic" strikes iceberg and stops.	11.40
9.50	'X' stops bearing SE'ly, 4 to 5 miles away. Morse lamp signals flashed but ignored by 'X'.	11.40	Nothing in sight.	11.50
9.55	Captain joins the third officer on the bridge briefly. Morse lamp signals continued.	11.45	Nothing in sight.	11.55
10.20	'X' under observation by the captain, the second officer, and the third officer.	12.10am	Nos. 5 and 7 lifeboats lowered.	12.20am
10.25	'X' under observation by the second officer; Morse lamp signals still ignored.	12.15	First radio distress calls transmitted, giving position 41° 44' N, 40° 24' W.	12.25
10.30?	–	12.20?	Ship 'Z's lights sighted on port bow.	12.30?
10.35	'X' lying quietly, closely observed by second officer.	12.25	Amended position 41° 46' N, 50° 14' N transmitted. First detonator fired.	12.35
10.50	Second officer tells captain that 'X' is still lying quietly, ignoring Morse lamp signals.	12.40	Detonators being fired and Morse lamp signals flashed.	12.50
10.55	Rocket apparently fired from 'X' seen by second officer.	12.45	'Z' turning away, about 4 to 5 miles off.	12.55
11.25	Second officer tells captain that he has seen five rockets from 'X', which is now steaming away.	1.15	'Z' steaming away, showing sternlight.	1.25
12.10am	Apprentice reports to captain in the chartroom.	2.00	Last lifeboats being launched.	2.10
12.20	'X's' sternlight receding.	2.10	"Titanic" sinks.	2.20
12.30	'X's' sternlight disappears.	2.20		
12.50	Second officer reports to captain that 'X' has gone out of sight.	2.40		

A 'Schedule of Events, 14/15 April 1912'. Courtesy: Mr Leslie Harrison

MINUTES OF EVIDENCE.

14 May, 1912.]　　JAMES GIBSON.　　HERBERT STONE.

Examined by MR. LAING.

7757. I should like to ask one question. Did you hear any explosive signal?—No.

7758. Were those rockets which you saw go up explosives? Did you hear any explosion?—I did not hear any report at all.

(*The Commissioner.*)

7921. Tell me what you said to the Chief Officer?—I have remarked at different times that these rockets did not appear to go very high; they were very low lying; they were only about half the height of the steamer's masthead light and I thought rockets would go higher than that.

7922. Well, anything else?—But that I could not understand why, if the rockets came from a steamer beyond this one, when the steamer altered her bearing the rockets should also alter their bearings.

T I M E　I N T E R V A L　between Stone's first report to Captain Lord of rockets seen and the sinking of the Titanic.

NB: The Titanic's clocks were set twelve minutes fast on the Californian's.

182　　COMMISSION ON THE LOSS OF THE S.S. "TITANIC":

14 May, 1912.]　　HERBERT STONE.　　[*Continued.*

(MR. DUNLOP.)

8041. Did not those come in fairly quick succession one after another?—Yes.

8042. What do you mean by saying that you did not see them coming in quick succession one after another?—I said that the ship was altering her bearing from the time she showed her first rocket; she commenced altering her bearing by the compass.

8043. Is not this accurate? When you came on to your watch at twelve o'clock this ship was stationary?—Yes.

8044. And except for a change in her position towards 2.40 she was stationary all the time?—No she was not stationary.

8045. Was she moving?—She started to move as soon as I saw the first rocket. She was stationary up to that time. She was stationary by our compass, at least so far as I could tell.

8046. Do you mean to say she was swinging about?—She was not swinging so far as I could tell; she was steaming away.

8047. But have not you said to Mr. Aspinall that you only noticed her steam away towards four o'clock?—Certainly not; I made no such remark, I think.

8048. When did you send word to the Captain that you noticed her steaming away.

8049. (*The Commissioner.*) It is 2 o'clock?—At 10 minutes past 1. I reported to the Master that she was altering her bearings, which was the same thing.

8050. (*Mr. Butler Aspinall.*) Altering her bearings did not mean steaming away?—I do not see how two ships can alter their bearings when stopped.

The Commissioner: You need not press this any further.

Mr. Scanlan: No, my Lord.

LOSS OF THE STEAMSHIP "TITANIC."

REPORT OF A FORMAL INVESTIGATION INTO THE CIRCUMSTANCES ATTENDING THE FOUNDERING ON APRIL 15, 1912, OF THE BRITISH STEAMSHIP TITANIC, OF LIVERPOOL, AFTER STRIKING ICE IN OR NEAR LATITUDE 41° 46′ N., LONGITUDE 50° 14′ W., NORTH ATLANTIC OCEAN, WHEREBY LOSS OF LIFE ENSUED.

23. Where and at what time did the *Titanic* founder?

Answer. Two twenty a. m. (ship's time) April 15. Latitude 41° 46′ N., longitude 50° 14′ W.

24. (*a*) What was the cause of the loss of the *Titanic* and of the loss of life which thereby ensued or occurred? (*b*) What vessels had the opportunity of rendering assistance to the *Titanic* and, if any, how was it that assistance did not reach the *Titanic* before the steamship *Carpathia* arrived? (*c*) Was the construction of the vessel and its arrangements such as to make it difficult for any class of passenger or any portion of the crew to take full advantage of any of the existing provisions for safety?

Answer. (*a*) Collision with an iceberg and the subsequent foundering of the ship. (*b*) The *Californian*. She could have reached the *Titanic* if she had made the attempt when she saw the first rocket. She made no attempt. (*c*) No.

At about 11.10 Groves noticed the lights of another ship, racing up <u>from the east</u> on the starboard side. As the new-comer rapidly overhauled the motionless *Californian*, a blaze of deck lights showed she was a large passenger liner.

From
A NIGHT TO REMEMBER
(1956)

From
THE NIGHT LIVES ON
(1986)

Around 11:00 Groves noticed the lights of a distant steamer coming up <u>from the southeast.</u> As it drew closer, he decided it was a large passenger ship.

From
THE BRITISH INQUIRY PROCEEDINGS, 1912

Mr. CHARLES VICTOR GROVES sworn.

Examined by Mr. S. A. T. ROWLATT.

8134. Did you see any ships approaching?— Yes.

8135. Now, what did you see, and when?—As I said before, the stars were showing right down to the horizon. It was very difficult at first to distinguish between the stars and a light, they were so low down. About 11.10, ship's time, I made out a steamer coming up a little bit <u>abaft our starboard beam.</u>

8235. (*The Commissioner.*) Did the captain see these lights disappear?—Not to my knowledge, my Lord.

8236. Was he there when you saw them disappear?—Not on the bridge.

8237. Where was he—in the chart-room?—I could not be certain where he was at that particular moment. When I spoke to him about the steamer coming up astern he was in the chart-room.

8151. You say you were heading about N.E.?— <u>We were heading N.E.</u>

8152. Did you notice that at the time?—Yes.

8153. Was that with a view to see in what direction the steamer was bearing?—No, for my own information.

8154. But it was at that time?—At that time, yes.

8155. Now, how did she bear, how many points abaft the beam did she bear?—Do you mean when I first noticed her?

8156. Yes?—I should think about 3½ points, but I took no actual bearing of her.

8157. That would leave her S. by W.?—We were heading N.E. and she was three points abaft the beam.

8158. Your beam would be?—S.E.

8159. That would bring her about S?—S. or S by W.—<u>S. ½ W.</u>

Mr. HERBERT STONE, Sworn.

Examined by Mr. BUTLER ASPINALL.

7810. Was the captain up?—Yes.

7811. Did you speak to him?—Yes.

7812. Did he tell you anything?—Yes.

7813. What did he tell you?—He told me the ship was stopped, surrounded by ice, and he pointed out another steamer.

7814. He pointed out another steamer. What could you see of the other steamer?—One mast-head light and a red side-light and two or three small indistinct lights.

7815. Did he say anything to you when he pointed her out?—He asked me to tell him if the bearing of the steamer altered or if she got any closer to us.

7816. Is that all he said about her?—And that the Third Officer had called her up on the Morse lamp and received no reply.

7817. He told you that?—Yes.

7818. Did you look and see these lights yourself? —Yes.

7819. How far away did you judge they were?— Approximately about five miles.

7820. And how were they bearing from you at this time?—<u>S.S.E. by the standard compass.</u>

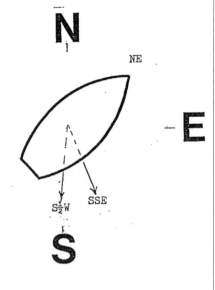

STATEMENT BY MR. BENJAMIN KIRK of Cliff House, Mariners' Park, Wallasey, Cheshire

"I was born in Liverpool on September 30th 1890. I made my first trip to sea as a deck boy in the *Runic*, a White Star boat, in 1905. I did a trip in the *Californian* to New Orleans in March 1912, and came back to London. She was a Leyland liner. I stayed by the ship and went on the next voyage from London to Boston and back to Liverpool. I was on lockout 10 to 12 on the night she stopped, surrounded by field ice. I was on the foc's'l'e head. There was a glare of light from another ship on the starboard beam. I cannot remember when I first saw it but I *did not report it as an approaching ship so think it must have come up from astern*. It was still there when I went off watch at twelve o'clock.

"I came on watch again at four in the morning. There were no icebergs in sight. Later the Chief Officer asked me to go up in a coal basket shackled to a mainmast stay and hoisted by a gantline to look for survivors or wreckage or boats from the *Titanic*. I could see nothing. I remember very plainly first seeing the *Mount Temple* on the port bow and then the *Carpathia*. There were no boats or wreckage in the water, which was calm, but the *Carpathia* had boats on her foredeck. She steamed away and I came down.

"When the *Californian* docked in Liverpool no one questioned me about what had happened. I did not go down to the inquiry.

"This Statement is made of my own free will and to the best of my recollection".

(Signed) Mr. B. Kirk
(Date) 31-1-1969

Signed in the presence of:
(Witness) (Mrs.) Ethel G. Penn
Matron, Mariners' Home, Wallasey

1/ 1913

RETURN OF THE EXPENSES

INCURRED BY

THE BOARD OF TRADE AND OTHER GOVERNMENT DEPARTMENTS

IN CONNECTION WITH

THE INQUIRY INTO THE LOSS OF THE S.S. "TITANIC."

Presented to both Houses of Parliament by Command of His Majesty.

LONDON:
PUBLISHED BY HIS MAJESTY'S STATIONERY OFFICE.
To be purchased, either directly or through any Bookseller, from
WYMAN AND SONS, LIMITED, FETTER LANE, E.C., and 32, ABINGDON STREET, S.W.,
and 54, ST. MARY STREET, CARDIFF; or
H.M. STATIONERY OFFICE (SCOTTISH BRANCH), 23, FORTH STREET, EDINBURGH; or
E. PONSONBY, LIMITED, 116, GRAFTON STREET, DUBLIN;
or from the Agencies in the British Colonies and Dependencies,
the United States of America, the Continent of Europe and Abroad of
T. FISHER UNWIN, LONDON, W.C.

PRINTED BY
DARLING AND SON, LTD., BACON STREET, E.
1913.

"TITANIC" INQUIRY.

(A.) EXPENSES OF INQUIRY PAID BY THE BOARD OF TRADE.

	£	s.	d.
Counsel for the Board of Trade—			
Sir Rufus Isaacs, M.P.	2,458	2	0
Sir J. A Simon, M.P.	2,425	4	0
Mr. Aspinall...	2,345	12	0
Mr. Rowlatt	1,249	3	6
Mr. R. Asquith	864	0	0
Counsel and Solicitors representing other interests—			
Mr. A. Smith	250	0	0
who instructed Mr. Thos. Scanlan, M.P., as Counsel on behalf of the National Sailors' and Firemen's Union	500	0	0
Messrs. Helder, Roberts, & Co. ...	250	0	0
who instructed Mr. A. C. Edwards, M.P., as Counsel on behalf of the Dock, Wharf, Riverside and General Workers' Union	500	0	0
Mr. C. G. P. Farrell	230	0	0
who instructed Mr. H. D. Harbinson as Counsel on behalf of the 3rd Class Passengers ...	400	0	0
Messrs. C. G. Bradshaw and Waterson who instructed Mr. Adair Roche as Counsel on behalf of the Marine Engineers' Association	212	10	7
Messrs. Miller, Taylor and Holmes, Solicitors, who appeared by their Mr. L. S. Holmes on behalf of the Imperial Merchant Service Guild...	250	0	0
Mr. Lewis who appeared on behalf of the British Seafarers' Union	77	0	6
Mr. Cotter who appeared on behalf of the National Union of Stewards	68	2	0
Witnesses (allowances for travelling and subsistence)—			
Sir A. J. G. Chalmers, ex-Professional Officer to the Board of Trade	9	0	0
Officers of the "Titanic"—			
C. H. Lightoller, 2nd Officer	26	2	6
H. J. Pitman, 3rd Officer ...	20	2	6
J. G. Boxhall, 4th Officer ...	20	15	0
H. G. Lowe, 5th Officer ...	20	7	6
Officers of other vessels—			
R. S. Friend, Surgeon, "Oceanic"	3	5	0
C. Evans, 3rd Officer, "Californian"	4	3	0
D. Dow, Master, "Carmania"	0	15	0
C. V. Groves, 2nd Officer, "Californian"	5	8	0
J. B. Ranson, Master, "Baltic"	0	15	0
J. H. Frodsham, 1st Officer, "Tunisian"	0	12	6
J. C. Ban, Master, "Caronia"	5	8	0
R. O. Jones, Master, "Canada"	0	15	0
H. Stone, 1st Officer, "Californian"	4	13	6
G. F. Stewart, 1st Officer, "Californian"	5	3	0
G. T. Gambell, Master, "Virginian"	0	15	0
S. Lord, Master, "Californian"	7	0	6
J. A. Murray, Master, "Empress of Britain"	0	15	0
J. Gibson, Apprentice (acting 4th Officer), "Californian"	4	13	0
J. H. Moore, Master, "Mount Temple"	3	14	9
Carried forward	£12,218	18	4

	£	s.	d.
Brought forward...	12,218	18	4
Witnesses (allowances for travelling and subsistence)—*cont.*			
Crew of "Titanic"—			
S. Humphreys, Quartermaster	9	7	6
W. Wynn, ,,	11	8	0
G. T. Rowe, ,,	6	11	6
A. J. Bright, ,,	6	5	6
R. Hitchens, ,,	3	4	0
A. J. Olliver, ,,	6	5	6
W. J. Perkis, ,,	6	5	6
H. Mailey, Master-at-Arms ...	9	7	6
J. Foley, Storekeeper ...	9	7	6
F. Prentice, ,, ...	11	17	6
A. Harris, Boatswain's Mate	5	9	6
A. E. Jewell, Look-out ...	5	12	6
F. Fleet, ,, ...	8	7	6
G. A. Hogg, ,, ...	5	18	0
R. R. Lee, ,, ...	6	6	6
G. Symons, ,, ...	6	10	10
S. Hemmings, Lamp Trimmer	6	5	6
J. Anderson, A.B. ...	8	12	6
F. Evans, ,, ...	8	12	6
J. Forward, ,, ...	8	12	6
W. Lucas, ,, ...	5	18	0
W. McCarthy, ,, ...	8	12	6
G. McGough, ,, ...	10	6	0
C. H. Pascoe, ,, ...	8	12	6
W. C. Peters, ,, ...	0	15	0
J. Scarrott, ,, ...	5	5	0
W. Weller, ,, ...	8	12	6
A. E. J. Horswell, ,, ...	12	4	0
J. Poingdestre, ,, ...	8	7	6
P. Vigott, ,, ...	8	12	6
E. Archer, ,, ...	7	18	6
E. J. Buley, ,, ...	7	13	0
W. Brice, ,, ...	5	1	0
F. Clinch, ,, ...	5	1	0
F. O. Evans, ,, ...	5	1	0
T. Jones, ,, ...	6	13	0
G. Moore, ,, ...	6	4	6
F. Osman, ,, ...	5	1	0
F. Barrett, Leading Fireman	6	6	0
C. Hendrikson, ,, ,,	13	11	0
T. Threlfall, ,, ,,	11	6	6
G. Beauchamp, Fireman ...	5	4	6
G. Combes, ,, ...	7	16	6
W. Clarke, ,, ...	7	16	6
R. Couper, ,, ...	7	16	6
S. Collins, ,, ...	11	4	0
J. Dilley, ,, ...	7	19	8
F. Doel, ,, ...	7	16	6
F. Dymond, ,, ...	13	16	6
J. Draper, ,, ...	10	3	0
E. Flarty, ,, ...	7	16	6
G. Godley, ,, ...	7	16	6
T. Graham, ,, ...	7	15	0
W. Hurst, ,, ...	9	7	0
J. Haggan, ,, ...	8	1	0
F. Harris, ,, ...	7	18	0
C. Judd, ,, ...	12	13	0
J. Kemish, ,, ...	7	16	6
F. T. Kasper, ,, ...	7	16	6
W. Lindsay, ,, ...	9	0	6
F. Knowles, ,, ...	8	10	0
F. Mason, ,, ...	7	16	6
J. Moore, ,, ...	9	0	6
T. Mayzes, ,, ...	7	16	6
W. Major, ,, ...	9	8	6
W. Murdock, ,, ...	8	1	0
H. Noss, ,, ...	10	4	6
W. Nuttbeam, ,, ...	7	16	6
C. Othen, ,, ...	7	16	6
H. Oliver, ,, ...	7	16	6
F. O'Connor, ,, ...	10	4	6
J. Pearce, ,, ...	7	16	6
J. Priest, ,, ...	7	16	6
J. Podesta ,, ...	7	16	6
Carried forward	£12,808	3	4

	£	s.	d.
Brought forward...	12,808	3	4
Witnesses (allowances for travelling and subsistence)—*cont.*			
Crew of "Titanic"—*cont.*			
R. Pusey, Fireman ...	9	18	6
C. Rice, ,, ...	7	16	6
H. Spackman, ,, ...	11	10	0
A. Spiers, ,, ...	5	6	0
A. Strur, ,, ...	7	16	6
E. Self, ,, ...	7	16	6
H. Senior, ,, ...	7	18	0
G. Thresher, ,, ...	7	16	6
R. Triggs, ,, ...	7	16	6
J. Taylor, ,, ...	10	1	6
W. H. Taylor, ,, ...	4	11	6
J. Thompson, Trimmer ...	3	16	6
J. Avery, ,, ...	7	16	6
E. Allen, ,, ...	7	16	6
W. Binstead, ,, ...	7	16	6
P. Blake, ,, ...	9	7	0
G. Cavell, ,, ...	11	0	6
A. Dore, ,, ...	7	16	6
W. Fredericks, ,, ...	7	16	6
A. Fryer, ,, ...	7	16	6
A. Hunt, ,, ...	7	16	6
A. Hebb, ,, ...	7	16	6
J. McGann, ,, ...	8	17	0
E. Perry, ,, ...	7	16	6
G. Petham, ,, ...	8	19	0
F. Sheath, ,, ...	9	18	6
E. Snow, ,, ...	9	7	0
W. White, ,, ...	9	7	0
T. P. Dillon, ,, ...	5	16	0
W. McIntyre, ,, ...	4	11	6
G. Pregnell, Greaser ...	9	7	6
F. Scott, ,, ...	11	16	6
A. White, ,, ...	9	7	6
T. Ranger, ,, ...	7	0	6
W. S. Halford, Steward ...	0	13	0
E. Brown, ,, ...	15	2	6
A. Baggott, ,, ...	11	17	6
F. Crafter, ,, ...	14	15	6
F. Hartnell, ,, ...	14	15	6
A. Harrison, ,, ...	11	17	6
C. Cullen, ,, ...	11	15	0
R. Pfropper, ,, ...	9	9	0
W. C. Foley, ,, ...	10	4	6
J. W. Gibbons, ,, ...	10	7	0
J. Hart, ,, ...	9	13	0
L. Heyland, ,, ...	7	18	0
J. Johnston, ,, ...	7	10	6
G. Knight, ,, ...	11	17	6
P. Keene, ,, ...	11	17	6
W. Lucas, ,, ...	12	4	0
A. Littlejohn, ,, ...	11	12	6
A. Lewis, ,, ...	7	18	0
W. S. Faulkner, ,, ...	11	15	0
S. Daniels, ,, ...	9	10	6
C. Mackay, ,, ...	15	5	0
A. McMicken, ,, ...	11	17	6
F. Morris, ,, ...	10	11	6
W. H. Nichols, ,, ...	9	9	0
F. Port, ,, ...	7	18	0
W. J. Prior, ,, ...	7	19	8
A. Pugh, ,, ...	10	4	6
S. Rule, ,, ...	12	13	6
W. E. Ryerson, ,, ...	9	10	6
O. Savage, ,, ...	7	18	0
A. Thessinger, ,, ...	9	9	0
F. Terrell, ,, ...	9	9	0
J. Wheat, ,, ...	16	2	6
W. William, ,, ...	9	9	0
J. Witter, ,, ...	9	9	0
W. Wright, ,, ...	7	13	0
H. Yearsley, ,, ...	11	17	6
H. Phillamore, ,, ...	9	9	0
C. W. Fitzpatrick, ,, ...	9	9	0
F. Toms, ,, ...	11	17	6
B. Thomas, ,, ...	11	17	6
A. C. Thomas, ,, ...	11	17	6
A. Burrage, ,, ...	7	18	0
J. Chapman, ,, ...	12	2	6
A. Pearcey, ,, ...	8	12	6
J. Stewart, ,, ...	15	0	6
W. Seward, ,, ...	10	8	0
C. E. Andrews ,, ...	5	14	0
W. Burke, ,, ...	7	2	6
Carried forward	£1,596	8	10

	£	s.	d.
Brought forward...	13,596	8	10
Witnesses (allowances for travelling and subsistence)—*cont.*			
Crew of "Titanic"—*cont.*			
G. F. Crowe, Steward ...	6	17	6
A. Cunningham, ,, ...	6	17	6
A. Crawford, ,, ...	14	2	0
H. Etches, ,, ...	6	17	6
J. Hardy, ,, ...	6	17	6
F. P. Ray, ,, ...	7	2	6
E. Wheelton, ,, ...	6	17	6
W. Ward, ,, ...	6	17	6
J. G. Widgery, Bath Room Steward	5	12	6
V. C. Jessop, Stewardess ...	7	1	0
B. Lavington, ,, ...	0	13	0
Mrs. Bennett, ,, ...	7	7	0
Mrs. Gold, ,, ...	7	7	0
Miss Gregson, ,, ...	7	4	0
Mrs. Leather, ,, ...	12	15	0
Mrs. A. Martin, ,, ...	7	1	0
Miss Marsden, ,, ...	8	12	6
Mrs. McLaun, ,, ...	7	7	0
Mrs. Pritchard, ,, ...	7	6	0
Mrs. Roberts, ,, ...	8	12	6
Mrs. Robinson, ,, ...	11	0	0
Miss Stap, ,, ...	7	2	6
Miss Sloan, ,, ...	8	12	6
Miss Smith, ,, ...	7	7	0
Mrs. Bliss, ,, ...	7	9	6
Miss Caton, Turkish Bath Attendant	6	1	0
Miss Slocombe, Turkish Bath Attendant	6	1	0
Miss R. Bowker, Cashier ...	9	0	0
Miss Martin, Assistant Cashier	7	4	0
J. Ellis, Cook	9	9	0
J. Collins, ,, ...	5	8	0
J. Windebank, Assistant Cook	9	9	0
I. Maynard, Entree Cook ...	9	9	0
C. Joughin, Chief Baker ...	14	19	0
C. Burgess, Baker	9	9	0
C. Mills, Assistant Baker ...	7	18	0
H. Neal, ,, ,, ...	9	9	0
J. Colgan, Scullion	7	18	0
F. Martin, ,, ...	6	8	6
H. Ross, ,, ...	7	18	6
A. Simmons, ,, ...	10	6	0
P. Ball, Plate Washer ...	6	7	0
R. Hardwick, Kitchen Porter	7	18	0
J. Guy, Assistant Boots ...	9	9	0
W. Harder, Window Cleaner	7	16	6
P. Mauge, Secretary to Chef	0	15	0
H. S. Bride, Marconi Wireless Operator	4	5	0
Tram fares of 28 of crew paid by Receiver of Wreck, Southampton	0	4	3
Cab fares of injured members of crew paid by Receiver of Wreck, Southampton ...	0	2	6
Crew of other vessels—			
E. Gill, Donkeyman, "Californian"	9	18	0
W. Ross, A.B., "Californian"	3	2	6
G. Glenn, Fireman, ,,	3	7	6
W. Thomas, Greaser, ,,	6	14	0
Mr. H. Wolferstan, Solicitor's Agent at Plymouth, expenses incurred in taking depositions at Plymouth ...	205	15	10
Marconi Wireless Company for charts, particulars of telegrams, and work of, and attendance at Inquiry of, their Deputy Manager	173	13	9
Messrs. Harland and Wolff for plans, models, and attendance at Inquiry of Mr. Wilding and three others in their service	574	11	0
Messrs. Malby and Sons for enlarging and mounting charts	10	0	0
Messrs. J. D. Potter for charts ...	1	4	0
Service of Summonses—			
Customs Officers at Plymouth ...	0	1	6
,, ,, ,, Southampton	3	4	6
,, ,, ,, Liverpool ...	0	19	6
,, ,, ,, London, Dock Street, E.	0	3	0
Carried forward	£14,953	8	1

	£	s.	d.
Brought forward...	14,953	8	1
Affidavits—			
Various Commissioners at Liverpool	0	13	6
Various Commissioners at Southampton	3	8	6
Consular Expenses—			
H.M. Consul-General at Havre ...	5	13	0
H.M. Consul at Philadelphia ...	5	16	2
H.M. Consul-General at New York—			
Cables	6	15	8
Travelling and expenses of Vice-Consul	29	7	8
Charles Fox, Esq. (legal) ...	154	6	5
Stenographer for notes of evidence of certain witnesses	48	4	4
Shorthand notes of proceedings of United States Committee	308	3	0
Fees for taking depositions...	9	0	0
Carried forward	£15,524	16	4

	£	s.	d.
Brought forward...	15,524	16	4
J. Swan, packing cases for evidence...	7	3	6
Cost of reproduction of evidence taken by United States Senate Committee	201	9	4
Cunard Steamship Company, expenses in securing attendance of Captain Rostron, of S.S. "Carpathia"	77	14	7
Remuneration for the staff of the Board of Trade Solicitor for additional work:—			
Mr. G. C. Vaux	126	0	0
Mr. L. J. Block	63	0	0
Mr. R. A. Macaskill	52	10	0
Mr. F. Studley	42	0	0
Mr. W. H. Biggs	31	10	0
Telegrams and cablegrams	15	12	9
Copying and typing	175	0	0
Incidentals (including cabs, &c.) ...	15	0	0
	£16,331	16	6

(B.) EXPENSES PAID BY THE TREASURY FROM THE VOTE FOR MISCELLANEOUS LEGAL EXPENSES.

	£	s.	d.
Wreck Commissioner (Right Hon. Lord Mersey)	1,050	0	0
Wreck Commissioner's Secretary (The Hon. Clive Bigham)	125	0	0
Wreck Commissioner's Clerk (Mr. A. Dones)	95	0	0
Assessors (remuneration and travelling and subsistence allowances)—			
Professor J. H. Biles, D.Sc., LL.D.	500	0	0
Rear-Admiral Hon. A. Gough-Calthorpe, C.V.O., R.N. ...	139	2	0
Mr. E. C. Chaston, R.N.R. ...	156	17	8
Carried forward			

	£	s.	d.
Brought forward			
Assessors (remuneration and travelling and subsistence allowances)—*cont.*			
Captain A. W. Clarke	80	19	6
Commander F. C. A. Lyon, R.N.R.	73	18	0
Shorthand writing	622	15	6
Clerical assistance, indexing, &c. ...	78	12	11
Travelling and incidental expenses ...	39	3	8
Hire of Hall and Offices (including cost of fitting up Hall as Court)	341	7	1
	£3,282	16	4

(C.) CHARGES FOR STATIONERY AND PRINTING.

	£	s.	d.	£	s.	d.
Cost of printing Report and Evidence	1,147	3	0			
Cost of Miscellaneous Stationery	67	10	0			
	1,214	13	0			
Less proceeds from sale of copies of Report and Evidence (estimate)	280	0	0			
				934	13	0

	£	s.	d.
(A.) Total paid by the Board of Trade	16,331	16	6
(B.) Total paid by the Treasury from the Miscellaneous Legal Expenses Vote ...	3,282	16	4
(C.) Charges for Stationery and Printing	934	13	0
	£20,549	5	10

FIVE

Rockets and Questions

Today, a rocket fired from a ship at sea generally means only one thing – that the ship is in some form of difficulty and requires assistance. However, in examining the question of the rockets fired by the Titanic, it would be totally inaccurate to look at these rockets of 1912 through present-day eyes. At that time, rockets had many different meanings and were of an entire kaleidoscopic host of colours and varieties. At present, radio and sophisticated electronic equipment have all but rendered the use of rockets a rarity. We would, however, do well to remember that in 1912 radio (wireless) was a relatively new form of communication between shipping and not every ship was equipped with the apparatus. In fact, it was only the Californian's second trip with wireless. Consequently, many ships depended on an elaborate system of coloured rockets to identify and communicate with each other. It is quite possible that this practice may have been misinterpreted by the various witnesses on the night/morning of the disaster – remember, Naess and his shipmates thought that the rockets they were observing might have been signals to other ships. To enable the reader to appreciate why Lord continually enquired as to the colour of the rockets, it will be necessary to take a look at the many uses and varieties of rockets in vogue at the time, from *A History of Fireworks* by A.H. Brock, Harrap, 1949:

> Wireless has rendered practically obsolete the elaborate, not to say pictur-
> esque, system of identification formerly used by vessels of all nations to make
> themselves known when passing Lloyd's stations at night and on similar
> occasions. Each line had its characteristic pyrotechnic display, consisting of
> Roman candles, rockets, hand and Costan lights. The last-mentioned are cases
> charged with fire of various colours in layers, so that any required combina-
> tion of colour may be burned in succession from one unit. These are more
> frequently in use by foreign shipping. A glance at the Universal Guide, setting

out the signals employed, makes one realise that their passing has taken something from the colour of nightlife at sea. The following are a few examples taken at random: The Zuid–Amerika Line of Amsterdam employed a white light at stern, green at bridge, and blue at bow; the White Star Line a green light at bow and green at stern; W. Johnson & Co., a green light, followed by a Roman candle throwing three red and three blue stars, followed by a white light; the Aberdeen, a red light, followed by a Roman candle throwing red, white and blue stars three times successively shown from aft; J.L. Burnham and Co., a blue light changing to white, then to red, followed by a red star; a vessel of the Cunard Line when off the coast of Ireland fired a blue light followed by two golden star-rockets; the Ulster Steamship Co. Ltd, three lights, yellow, blue and red above one another, followed by two Roman candles fired together, each throwing two yellow, two blue, and two red stars. As suffixes to the identification signal, a red light indicated 'all's well', a green signified 'Wish to communicate'. Elder's and Fyffe's banana-boats employed a code of their own, designed to advise the quantity and condition of their cargoes; the number of bunches carried, and condition of their cargoes; the number of bunches carried, 'ripe', 'green', or 'ripe and turning'.

We know immediately see of course from the beginning that the sudden appearance of rockets at sea in 1912 did not necessarily mean that a ship was in difficulty. It also brings home to us the obvious problem a captain would have in dealing with spoken reports of such rockets. In many cases, he would be relying totally on what was effectively, second-hand information. In the event that the captain, like the case of Lord, did not, in the first instance observe the rockets, he would then have to take the report at face value and act accordingly. We see that Captain Lord did ask if there were any colour in the lights which were reported to him and if the officer was certain of this.

Before we progress to the actual questions relating to the rockets, it will be of assistance if we set out the internationally agreed distress signals which were used at night in 1912:

- A gun or other explosive signal fired at intervals of approximately one minute.
- Flames on the vessel.
- Rockets or shells, throwing stars of any colour or description, fired one at a time, at short intervals.
- A continuous sounding with any fog-signal apparatus.

In relation to the above signal agreement it is vital to point out the following:

1. No explosive signals were heard by anyone on board the Californian.
2. At no time were any flames seen on the other vessel by the Californian.
3. The rockets seen by the Californian (eight) were not fired 'one at a time at short intervals', but spasmodically, over a lengthy period of time.
4. No sound of any fog signal or siren was heard on the Californian.

In the following pages there will be many references to 'rockets'. Rockets not only send out stars of various colours but also detonate with a resounding explosion! Let us remind ourselves of the weather conditions which prevailed on that night/morning: no wind, a calm sea and clear. Obviously then, these extraordinary conditions would insure that the sound of any detonating 'rocket' would have travelled many miles. Yet, nowhere in their evidence, did any member of the Californian's crew state that they heard any form of explosion. Clearly, if both ships were in a radius of five, eight or ten miles, the crew of the Californian could not help but hear the explosions.

Lawrence Beesley, second class passenger on the Titanic and a science master and trained observer, writes on page 79 of his book *The Loss of the Titanic* (7 C's Press edition, 1973):

> Suddenly a rush of light from the forward deck, a hissing roar that made us all turn from watching the boats, and a rocket leapt upwards to where the stars blinked and twinkled above us. Up it went, higher and higher, with a sea of faces upturned to watch it, and then an explosion that seemed to split the night in two, and a shower of stars sank slowly down and went out one by one. And with a gasping sigh one word escaped the lips of the crowd: 'Rockets!'

Referring for a moment back to the unidentified ships, X and Z, we recall that ship X, seen by the Californian, fired 'low-lying' rockets or Roman candles, and that the Titanic's rockets are quite clearly stated to have gone 'many hundreds of feet into the air'. This leads to only one possible conclusion – the reason the rockets appeared to be 'low-lying' was because the ship from which they had been fired, the Titanic, was many miles away. We must then reach the logical conclusion that Lord was probably correct in not regarding the signals seen from the Californian as being 'signals of distress'. The entire question of the 'rockets' is covered in more thorough detail in an article published by the Mercantile Marine Service Association which was, in effect, Captain Lord's union. It states:

In this article it is claimed that the first of the Titanic's distress rockets was fired at 22.25 New York Time, i.e. at 12.25 a.m. Titanic apparent time or 12.15 a.m. Californian apparent time, and not as held by the 1912 British Court of Inquiry, at 12.45 a.m. Titanic time (chart showing the schedule of events and different times on page 132). Apart from the important question of the timing of the Titanic's first distress rocket, the article also claims that there is confirmatory evidence from the Mount Temple, Birma and Carpathia that the navigational evidence from the Californian was right and accurate and accordingly should not have been rejected by the British and American Inquiries. The following summarises the main evidence upon which these assertions are based:

THE FIRST DISTRESS ROCKET

There appears to be no precise evidence as to the time at which the Titanic's first radio distress messages were sent out. However, it was established that the original position of 41° 46' N, 50° 24' W, given in these messages was subsequently amended to 41° 46' N, 50° 14' W. This amendment followed action taken by Mr Boxhall, the Titanic's fourth officer, which is described in the following passage from the official record of the British Inquiry proceedings, questioned by Mr Raymond Asquith:

Question 15384 'When the order to clear the boats was given what did you do: did you go to any particular boat?'

Boxhall 'No, I went right along the line of boats and I saw the men starting, the watch on deck, our watch.'

15385 'Which side of the ship?'

Boxhall 'The port side, I went along the port side, and afterwards I was down the starboard side as well but for how long I cannot remember. I was unlacing covers on the port side myself and I saw a lot of men come along – the watch I presume. They started to screw some boats out on the after part of the port side; I was just going along there and seeing all the men were well established with their work, well under way with it, and I heard someone report a light, a light ahead, I went on the bridge and had a look to see what the light was.'

15386 'Someone reported a light ahead?'

Boxhall 'Yes; I do not know who reported it. There were quite a lot of men on the bridge at the time.'

15387 'What sort of light was it?'

Boxhall 'It was two masthead lights of a steamer. But before I saw this light I went to the chart-room and worked out the ship's position.'

15389 'Is that the position we have been given already – 41° 46' N, 50° 14' W?'

Boxhall 'That is right, but after seeing the men continuing with their work I saw all the officers were out, and I went into the chart-room to work out its position.'

15390 'Was it after that you saw the light?'

Boxhall 'It was after that, yes, because I must have been to the Marconi office with the position after I saw the light.'

15391 'You took it to the Marconi office in order that it might be sent by the wireless operator?'

Boxhall 'I submitted the position to the captain first, and he told me to take it to the Marconi room.'

15392 'And then you saw this light, which you say looked like a masthead light?'

Boxhall 'Yes, it was two masthead lights of a steamer.'

15393 'Could you see it distinctly with the naked eye?'

Boxhall 'No, I could see the light with the naked eye, but I could not define what it was, but by the aid of a pair of glasses it was the two masthead lights of a vessel probably about half a point on the port bow, and in the position (where) she would be showing her red if it were visible, but she was too far off then.'

15394 'Could you see how far off she was?'

Boxhall 'No, I could not, but I had sent in the meantime for some rockets, and I told the captain I had sent for some rockets, and told him I would send them off, and told him when I had seen this light. He said, "Yes, carry on with it". I was sending the rockets off and watching the steamer. Between the time of sending the rockets off and watching the

	steamer approach us I was making myself generally useful round the port side of the deck.'
15395	'How many rockets did you send up about?'
Boxhall	'I could not say, between half a dozen and a dozen, I should say, as near as I could tell.'

Unknowingly perhaps, Boxhall had made two very important points in favour of Captain Lord yet, because Lord was not allowed to question any witnesses or to pursue any matter, the vital evidence was allowed to slip into obscurity. Obviously, if Boxhall was of the opinion that the steamer in question had actually approached the Titanic, then it will be abundantly clear that this ship could not have been the Californian, as that ship had remained stationary all night and had not moved until several hours after the Titanic foundered. Amazingly, nobody even bothered to place any importance on the fact that Boxhall admitted that initially he gave the wrong position of the Titanic and only later amended the position. The line of questioning was, at best, somewhat haphazard. Eventually it was concluded, with Boxhall candidly admitting, that he couldn't say exactly how many rockets had been fired from the sinking ship. Yet, Lord Mersey, in his summation, clearly and categorically stated that the number was 'about eight'. Was this then a dangerous and foolhardy assumption based on the knowledge that the Californian crew had reported seeing eight rockets? When one considers that Lord Mersey had previously changed his mind concerning the distance that the Californian was alleged to have been from the Titanic, from five, to eight or ten miles, the impression is given that he was, at best, unsure of his facts and, at worst, most anxious to see that the evidence at hand fitted his impressions of the disaster.

In relation to the amended position spoken of by Boxhall, a specific time for the transmission of this position (the amended position) was given in evidence at the British inquiry by Mr J. Durrant, radio officer with the Mount Temple, examined by the solicitor general:

Question 9450	'Now let us take the story in order of time, as you recorded it with the help of your Marconi apparatus. I am going to add one hour and forty-six minutes to your time, so as to keep your ship's time all the way through.'
Durrant	'In this copy I have New York time and ship's time both together.'

9451	'That is very convenient. Now tell us the ship's time when you first got a message as to the Titanic being in distress?'
Durrant	'12.11 a.m. (or 22.25 New York time).'
9452	'Just read your account, as you have it there, of that message.'
Durrant (reading)	'Titanic sending CQD answer him, but he says, "Cannot read you, old man. Here is my position, 41° 46' N 50° 14' W. Come at once, have struck berg". I advised my captain.'

It is advisable to point out that at the time the position was given to the Mount Temple (12.11 a.m.) the Californian's only wireless operator had shut down his radio for the night and therefore had no way of knowing that the air was later to vibrate with distress calls. The Californian's operator had no reason to remain at his post as the ship had already stopped for the night and his services would therefore not be needed. Likewise, as he was the only wireless operator on the ship, he had, naturally, to get some respite from his work and sleep was as important to him as to anybody else.

There is supporting evidence that the first lifeboat had been lowered and the first rocket fired by 22.25 New York time, as officially recorded from Mr G. T. Rowe, Titanic quartermaster at the United States Congressional Inquiry, page 519:

It was then twenty minutes to twelve (when the collision occurred). I then remained on the after-bridge to await orders through the telephone. No orders came down, and I remained until twenty-five minutes past twelve, when I saw a boat (lifeboat) on the starboard beam. I telephoned to the forebridge to know if they knew there was a boat lowered. They replied asking me if I was the third officer. I replied, 'No, I am the quartermaster'. They told me to bring over detonators, which are used in firing distress signals. I took them to the fore-bridge and turned them over to the fourth officer (Mr Boxhall).

This statement is in fact corroborated by Boxhall at the later British inquiry into the disaster. In his testimony, Boxhall states:

I knew one of the boats had gone away, because I happened to be putting the firing lanyard inside the wheelhouse after sending off a rocket, and the telephone bell rang. Somebody telephoned to say that one of the starboard boats had left and I was surprised".

There would appear to be a slight contradiction of the timing of the first rocket here when we recall that Gill, of the Californian, in his sworn affidavit, states that he had first seen two rockets 'sometime after 12.30 a.m.'. Stone, for his part, states that he had reported to Captain Lord the fact that he had seen rockets, numbering five, fired from the ship at 'about 1.10 a.m.'! This would obviously make a total of seven rockets. Yet, Stone was later to recall and report seeing three more rockets, making a total of ten rockets altogether. While the actual number of rockets is something of a moot point, there is considerable discrepancy concerning the timing of the sightings which can only suggest that the men clearly had no idea of the precise time of the rockets.

Mr H.J. Pitman, third officer of the Titanic, testified at the U.S. inquiry that No.7 boat was the first to leave the ship (p.304) two or three minutes previous to No.5 boat, with No.3 boat next. He stated that he saw the first rocket fired 'shortly after' No.5 boat had left the Titanic and, at the British inquiry, said that the time 'would be about 12.30 a.m. when No.5 boat reached the water' several minutes after No.7 boat. This of course suggests that the first rocket must have been fired on or before 12.30 a.m. In contrast to this testimony, apart from the fact that Gill also stated that the two white rockets he said he saw 'might have been just white flashes in the sky', yet another contradiction comes to light in the evidence of Mr H.G. Lowe, Titanic's fifth officer, in the U.S. inquiry, p. 401:

Lowe	'I pursued the same course in filling No.3 boat as in No.5.'
Senator Smith	'Did Mr Ismay assist in loading the boat?'
Lowe	'Yes, he assisted there too.'
Senator Smith	'You found him there when you turned from No.5 to No.3?'
Lowe	'He was there, and I distinctly remember seeing him alongside me – that is, by my side – when the first detonator went off. I will tell you how I happen to remember it so distinctly. It was because the flash of the detonator lit up the whole deck. I did not know who Mr Ismay was then, but I learned afterwards who he was, and he was standing alongside me.'

The contradiction is quite obvious. We have seen that the third officer of the Titanic, Mr Pitman, stated that he saw the first rocket 'shortly after No. 5 boat had left the Titanic'. Yet, in his testimony, Mr Lowe expressly states that he remembered seeing Mr Ismay when he turned from No. 5 boat to No. 3, and he is quite adamant that the reason he remembered it was when he turned 'the first detonator went off'. This then clearly means that the first rocket was fired while boat No. 5 was still aboard the ship and not, as Mr Pitman stated, 'shortly after No. 5 boat had left'. If we accept this statement then it follows that the first rocket was fired at almost exactly 12.30 a.m.

We see that yet another inconsistency arises in the evidence of Mr G. Symons, one of the Titanic's lookouts, during question 11721 of the British inquiry, read by the attorney general from a deposition dated 2 may 1912:

> Shortly after I had got on the boat deck I noticed rockets being fired at very frequent intervals from the bridge, Morse signals being used; and at about 12.30 a.m. I saw about one point on the port bow distant some five or six miles a light which I took to be the stern light of a Cod Bank fisherman.

In this statement, Mr Symons clearly states that he observed rockets being fired 'at frequent intervals'. Yet, the rockets observed from the Californian were erratic and not at all frequent.

Sir Cosmo Duff Gordon, a passenger on the ship, also made a statement to the British inquiry regarding the rockets, answering the attorney general's question 12496, 'Were they firing rocket at the time?' by saying 'Yes, they had just begun while they were lowing No. 3 lifeboat.' His statement also conflicts with previous statements given at the hearing.

Obviously, what we are dealing with here is an absolute confusion of times. We see that in his testimony, Mr Pitman said that boat No. 7 was the first to leave the ship, 'two or three minutes previous to No. 5 boat, with No. 3 boat next'. He went on to say that he saw the first rocket 'shortly after' No. 5 boat left the ship. Yet, we know that No. 5 boat left before No. 3 and that Mr Lowe states that the first rocket went off while boats No. 5 and 3 were still on the deck. Obviously somebody was mistaken, but who?

In an extract from his book *The Truth about the Titanic*, Colonel Archibald Gracie states: 'From my own conclusions, and those of others, it appears that about forty-five minutes had now elapsed since the collision when Captain Smith's orders were transmitted to the crew to lower the lifeboats, loaded with women and children first.'

If we add these forty-five minutes to the time of impact with the iceberg, we get a time of 12.25 a.m. for the order to lower the lifeboats given by Smith. Yet, in his testimony, the quartermaster, Mr Rowe, clearly states that he 'remained until twenty-five minutes past twelve when I saw a boat (lifeboat) on the starboard beam'. This of course suggests that at least one lifeboat had been lowered before 12.25 a.m., which is evidently contradictory. Likewise, yet another conflicting account is contained in Mr Lawrence Beesley's authoritative account of the disaster in his book *The Loss of the Titanic* (Star Books, 1912). Mr Beesley states that lifeboats nine, eleven, thirteen and fifteen were being 'cleared and swung out at 12.20 a.m.' and that the first rocket was seen shortly before they began to lower them, and, that by 12.40 a.m. and 12.45 a.m., when Mr Beesley was called into boat No.13 as it was being lowered, 'several' of Titanic's lifeboats could be seen in the water.

If we are to accept Mr Beesley's account, then we must naturally arrive at the implication that the first rocket was fired before or close to 12.15 a.m. If we were to likewise accept that at the time the wireless officer on board the Mount Temple received the CQD (exactly 12.11 a.m.), the lifeboats were simultaneously being lowered from the Titanic, which is a reasonable assumption, considering the ship was sinking and assistance sought, then the first rocket must have been fired between 12.11 a.m. and 12.20 a.m.

Timing

The attention paid by both the American and British inquiries to the differing apparent times being kept by the various ships involved was casual in the extreme. And perhaps this only served to highlight their respective lack of understanding of maritime matters. The British inquiry report accepts a time difference of only one hour and fifty minutes between New York time and the apparent time being kept by the Titanic. To be valid this would have meant that on Sunday 14 April, the Titanic's noon longitude would have been 47½° W. In fact, this was almost the exact noon longitude of the Californian which was also westward bound, but only with the approximated half speed of the Titanic.

Even more inexplicable, and in stark contrast to this, the American inquiry accepted a time difference of one hour and thirty-three minutes between New York time and the Titanic's apparent time! In this case, such a difference would only have been possible if the Titanic's noon position on 14 April had been in longitude 51¾° W, a position thirty-three miles further to the west than the erroneous position in which she was thought to have sunk.

Finally, regarding the vital need to establish the correct relationship between the differing times, which, evidently, helped to incriminate the Californian, it is necessary to examine the full text of the exchange which took place on the last day of the British inquiry between Lord Mersey, the president of the court, and Attorney General Rufus Isaacs. We take up the discussion as the latter was concluding his submission to the court that the Californian could have rescued 'many, if not all of the lives which were lost'. Although in this passage, he obviously misinterprets the evidence from the Californian:

Attorney general	'It is said, for example, in this case that this white rocket, the first distress signal, was not seen till a quarter past one. It is very difficult to explain that, in view of the evidence from the Titanic, which is that they were sending up these rockets from about 12.45 a.m. I should have thought upon this evidence and upon the evidence which follows it, that the estimate of time must be quite wrong.'
Lord Mersey	'There might be some difference in the clocks of the two vessels.'
Attorney General	'Yes. Certainly there might be.'
Lord Mersey	'That might partly account for it.'
Attorney General	'Yes, it might.'

The Titanic's Heading

On the Titanic's heading when she sank, Lawrence Beesley writes in *The Loss of the Titanic* (7 C's Press edition, 1973, pp. 124-25):

So in the absence of any plan of action, we rowed slowly forward – or what we thought was forward, for it was the direction the Titanic's bows were pointing before she sank. I see now that we must have been pointing northwest, for we presently saw the Northern Lights on the starboard, and again, when the Carpathia came from the south, we saw her behind us on the southeast, and turned our boat around to get to her.

This means that Titanic's 'mystery ship' was at a compass bearing of 303¼ to 291½ degrees by compass, or one to two points off the port bow as stated by the witnesses. The Californian was NNW on a bearing reciprocal to the ship she saw, which was SSE of her. This bearing would be 157½ degrees, or over 2 points to starboard of the Titanic.

The Californian's Navigation

Both the British and United States inquiries rejected the Californian's navigational evidence showing that she was nineteen and a half miles from the reported position of the Titanic and approximately thirty-three miles from the actual position in which the lifeboats were found. Yet the inaccuracy of the reported position and probability that the actual position was given by the Californian in evidence is supported by testimony from the Mount Temple and Birma and, likewise, by inference from the time taken by the Carpathia to reach the Titanic's lifeboats, as follows:

The Mount Temple

The United States Inquiry, pp. 777/8

Captain H. Moore	'I think, after all, the Titanic was further east than she gave her position, sir. In fact, I am certain she was.'
Senator Smith	'East or South?'
Capt. Moore	'East, sir.'
Senator Smith	'How much further away?'
Capt. Moore	'I should think at least eight miles sir, of longitude.'
Senator Smith	'What makes you think so?'
Capt. Moore	'Because when I got the position in the morning I got a prime vertical sight; that is a sight taken when the sun is bearing due east. That position gave me 50° 9½' West. I got two observations. I took one before the prime vertical and also on the prime vertical. We were steering north at the time, steering north to go round this pack (ice) again, to look out to see if we could find a hole through the ice, and we took these two positions, and they both came to within a quarter of a mile of each other; so that the Titanic

must have been on the other side of that field of ice, and then her position was not right which she gave.'

Senator Smith	'Does the fact that you found no evidence of the wreck when you got to the Titanic's reported position tend to confirm you in the idea that her position was 8 miles further to the southward?'
Capt. Moore	'No; to the eastward.'
Senator Smith	'To the eastward?'
Capt. Moore	'Yes.'
Senator Smith	'That tends to confirm you in that belief?'
Capt. Moore	'Yes, sir. My observation was this; my fourth officer took two observations, and of course he is a navigator, and also an Extra Master's certificate is held by him, which is a better certificate than mine, and he took the observations both times, and both of them tallied. One came 50° 9½'West, and the other came 50° 9¾'West. Of course, it proved afterwards when, after coming southward and trying to find some place I could get through, on the way back again – I suppose about 6 o' clock in the morning – that I sighted the Carpathia on the other side of this great ice pack, and there is where I understand he picked up the boats. So this great pack of ice was between us and the Titanic's position.'
Senator Smith	'As given by her?'
Capt. Moore	'No, sir. I was in that position. I was to the eastward of the position the Titanic gave me, but she must have been to the eastward still, because she could not have been through this pack of ice.'
Senator Smith	'As I recollect, the captain of the Californian, who was sworn yesterday, and who went to the position given by the Titanic in the CQD also said that he found nothing there, but cruised around this position.'
Capt. Moore	'I saw the Californian myself cruising around there, sir.'

The British Inquiry

Mr Butler Aspinall, Question 9240	'And at about daylight did you come up to the position? (i.e. 41° 46' N, 50° 14'W).'

Capt. Moore	'In the vicinity of that position.'
9241	'In the vicinity of the position you had been given?'
Capt. Moore	'Yes.'
9242	'Did you see any signs of wreckage?'
Capt. Moore	'None whatever.'

The Birma

Almost the entire page sixteen of the London Daily Telegraph for Thursday 25 April 1912 is given to an account by Mr Charles E. Walters of the movements of the Russian East Asiatic Company's liner Birma, which attempted to join in rescue operations after learning by radio of the Titanic tragedy. She went initially to the reported position but, like the Mount Temple and Californian, found nothing. She then steamed southward, rounded the tip of the ice field and continued up the eastern edge until she eventually came to the Carpathia (see chart on page 93 which shows the Birma's movements and position of the lifeboats as estimated by the Californian and the Mount Temple). The chart, incidentally, was authenticated by a certificate signed by the Birma's captain, first officer, purser and two British radio officers.

The Carpathia

Captain Rostron of the Carpathia originally estimated that he had fifty-eight miles to run before he reached the position broadcast by the sinking Titanic. The journey took Rostron some three hours and twenty-five minutes to complete and, as we have seen, it was claimed that he did this at an average speed of seventeen knots, a profoundly impossible feat for his engines. Apart from the fact that the Carpathia's normal maximum speed was just fourteen knots, an additional 8 minutes of the time he took was taken at half speed and 25 minutes, the last stages of the final approach to the lifeboats, was taken at slow speed, navigating 'cautiously' to avoid the icebergs (see *Tramps and Ladies* by Sir James Bisset, pp. 282/4). Flares from the lifeboats were seen on board the Carpathia as long as one and a half hours before the first boat was reached. The inescapable conclusion is that the distance covered by the Carpathia was not, as originally claimed, fifty-eight miles, but much more likely to have been between forty and forty-eight miles. Based on this calculation, and the fact that the Carpathia could not have achieved a speed of seventeen knots, it is much more likely that the true position of the lifeboats, and of the disaster, was to the south-east of the broadcast position, as confirmed by the Mount Temple and the Birma, and as claimed by Captain Lord. In these circumstances, the action of both the British and American inquiries, in utterly rejecting the navigational evidence of the Californian, was quite unwarranted and without foundation.

We clearly gather from the foregoing that there was simply no way in which Lord could have got his timing, his position and his navigation wrong. If the court said that he did, which they did by rejecting his evidence, then it follows that they should also have rejected the navigational evidence of the other ships involved.

At this stage of the British inquiry yet another ugly nail was firmly hammered home in Lord's coffin by Attorney General Rufus Isaacs. Isaacs, when told of how Captain Lord went to the chartroom for a rest, made the remark that it 'would not do to enquire too closely into what was going on in the chartroom and captain's cabin that night'. Implications that Lord had been drinking were quite clear and were not lost on the members of the press who were present. The fact that Lord was actually a teetotaller made the thoughtless statement all the more upsetting. Obviously hurt by the remark, Lord took it upon himself to write the attorney general and voice his objections to the unfounded remark. Instead of the abject apology which was his due, he received a curt reply from the attorney general's office that Rufus Isaacs was 'out of the country' and that 'no correspondence was being forwarded'. The damage had been done. No sooner did the press get wind of the implied allegation than, almost within hours, Lord found himself branded an uncouth and uncaring drunkard. Although there was not one iota of truth in the remark, it was blown out of proportion and became a major drama in the headlines of the world. The old adage still applied, 'Mud, when it's thrown, leaves a distinct mark'.

Returning to the important question of 'lights' having been seen at varying times, by many people, it is vital that we examine all the possibilities. A brief extract from Mr Beesley's book *The Loss of The Titanic* deals with lights, alleged and otherwise, seen from the lifeboats:

> That night the stars seemed really to be alive and to talk. The complete absence of haze produced a phenomenon I had never seen before; where the sky met the sea the line was as clear and defined as the edge of a knife, so that the water and the air merged gradually into each other and blended to a softened rounded horizon, but each element was so exclusively separate that where a star came low down in the sky near the clear-cut edge of the water-

line, it still lost none of its brilliance. As the earth revolved and the water edge came up and partially covered the star, as it were, it simply cut the star in two, the upper half continuing to sparkle as long as it was not entirely hidden, and throwing a long beam of light along the sea to us.

In the evidence before the United States Senate Committee the captain of one of the ships near us that night said the stars were so extraordinarily bright near the horizon that he was deceived into thinking that they were ship's lights; he did not remember seeing such a night before. Those who were afloat will all agree with that statement: we were often deceived into thinking they were lights of a ship.

All night long we had watched the horizon with eager eyes for signs of a steamer's lights; we heard from a stoker that the first appearance would be a single light on the horizon, the masthead-light, followed shortly by a second one, lower down, on the deck; if these two remained in vertical alignment and the distance between them increased as the lights drew nearer, we might be certain it was a steamer. But what a night to see that first light on the horizon! We saw it many times as the earth revolved, and some stars rose on the clear horizon and others sank down to it; there were 'lights' on every quarter. Some we watched and followed until we saw the deception and grew wiser; some were lights from those of our boats that were fortunate enough to have lanterns, but these were generally easily detected, as they rose and fell in the near distance. Once they raised our hopes, only to sink them again to zero. Near what seemed to be the horizon on the port quarter we saw two lights close together, and thought this must be our double light; but as we gazed across the miles that separated us, the lights slowly drew apart and we realised that they were two boat's lanterns at different distances from us, in line, one behind the other. They were probably the forward port boats that had to return so many miles next morning across the Titanic's graveyard.

Here again is yet more conclusive proof that the lifeboats were several miles from the actual site of the disaster, 'the forward port boats had to return so many miles next morning', and were in fact, so far down on the horizon that other lifeboats mistook them, because of their lanterns, to be approaching ships. This would of course account for the fact that many of the witnesses were so emphatic that they observed the lights of a nearby ship or ships.

The question of timing remains of vital interest and the fact that so little attention was paid to it at the investigations is something which can only be deplored. In fact, if we examine the question of whether or not any rocket

signals or flares seen by the second officer of the Californian could have origi-
nated from the Titanic, we must once again revert to timing. We have already
seen the almost casual and off-hand manner in which Lord Mersey and Rufus
Isaacs referred to the timing when they agreed that there might have been
some difference in the clocks of the two vessels. Had this entire question of
timing been given the scrutiny and attention it deserved, it would have shown
beyond all doubt that whatever ship those on board the Californian were
observing that night/morning, it could not have been the Titanic. It is true
to say that if the ship's apparent times only are taken into consideration, there
would then be some evident coincidences. However, it must be remembered
that the time on both ships differed by some twelve minutes and, while this
might seem to be of little or no importance, it completely rules out any possibility of coincidence. To put this twelve minute factor into context, let us refer
to Gill's testimony when he stated: 'I saw a large steamer going at full speed
after 11.56 p.m.' In making this statement, Gill was obviously going by the time
on the Californian's clocks, which were a full twelve minutes behind those of
the Titanic. This of course would make the time, on the Titanic, exactly 12.08
a.m. and, as we know, the Titanic, by that ship's timing, struck the iceberg at
precisely 11.40 p.m. and did not move again. If therefore, Gill, or anyone else
on board the Californian, said that they saw a steamer moving after this time,
then clearly it could not have been the Titanic (to appreciate the entire question of the differing timing, refer to the Schedule of Events on page 132).

During the initial investigations in both America and England, both
courts refused to accept the possibility of any other ships being in the
immediate area of the tragedy. Yet, in his sworn statement, signed in New
York on 4 June 1912, which was subsequently read at the British inquiry,
Captain Rostron clearly stated: 'Neither of the steamers seen at 5.00 a.m.
(on the morning of the 15th) was the Californian'. Clearly this is a reference
to the fact that other steamers had been observed by the Carpathia and
this indeed, has been proved to have been the case. We have also seen how
Lord Mersey utterly rejected the Californian's position. It is perhaps just as
well that Mersey did not attempt to give a reason or explanation for this
decision. Had he done so, he would undoubtedly have realised that he was
at the same time rejecting the navigational evidence available to him from
three independent and honourable witnesses, namely, the captains of the
Mount Temple, Birma and Carpathia, each of whose testimony confirms
that Lord's navigation was correct and which also shows that the Titanic's
reported position was incorrect.

Returning to the question of rockets for a moment, let us now look at the sworn evidence of two of the Californian's watch keepers, James Gibson and Herbert Stone from the minutes of evidence, British inquiry, 14 May 1912:

Gibson examined by Mr Laing:

Question 7757	'I should like to ask one question. Did you hear any explosive signal?'
Gibson	'No.'
7758	'Were those rockets which you saw go up explosives? Did you hear any explosion?'
Gibson	'I did not hear any report at all.'

Stone examined by the commissioner:

7921	'Tell me what you said to the chief officer?'
Stone	'I have remarked at different times that these rockets did not appear to go very high; they were low-lying; they were only about half the height of the steamer's masthead light and I thought rockets would go higher than that.'
7922	'Well, anything else?'
Stone	'But that I could not understand why, if the rockets came from a steamer beyond this one, when the steamer altered her bearings the rockets should also alter their bearings.'

Perhaps unknown to himself, what Stone was suggesting was that the rockets seen from the Californian, and thought to have been coming from the ship they had been observing, were in fact coming from the Titanic many miles away. His reference to the fact that the rockets only seemed to go half as high 'as the masthead light' confirms this possibility and also highlights the fact that nobody at the inquiry saw fit to allow for the natural curvature of the earth and its effect on visibility at any great distance. Apparently, they also put no great emphasis on Stone's reference to the fact that when the ship altered her bearings, the rockets should also alter with her. The questioning continued with Mr Scanlan addressing Stone:

Question 8041	'Did not these rockets come in fairly quick succession one after another?'
Stone	'Yes.'
8042	'What do you mean by saying that you did not see

	them coming in quick succession one after another?'
Stone	'I said that the ship was altering her bearings from the time she showed her first rocket; she commenced altering her bearings by the compass.'
8043	'Is not this accurate: When you came on to your watch at 12.00 p.m. this ship was stationary?'
Stone	'Yes.'
8044	'And except for a change in her position towards 2.40 a.m. she was stationary all the time?'
Stone	'No, she was not stationary.'
8045	'Was she moving?'
Stone	'She started to move as soon as I saw the first rocket. She was stationary up to that time. She was stationary by our compass, at least so far as I could tell.'
8046	'Do you mean to say she was swinging about?'
Stone	'She was not swinging so far as I could tell; she was steaming away.'
8047	'But have you not said to Mr Aspinall that you only noticed her steam away towards four o'clock?'
Stone	'Certainly not; I made no such remark, I think.'
3048 (the commissioner)	'Was it two o'clock?'
Stone	'At ten minutes past one. I reported to the Master that she was altering her bearings, which was the same thing.'
8050 (Mr Butler Aspinall)	'Altering her bearings did not mean steaming away.'
Stone	'I do not see how two ships can alter their bearings when stopped.'
The commissioner	'You need not press this any further.'
Mr Scanlan	'No, my Lord.'

Once again the members of the inquiry only served to display their lack of qualifications in dealing with nautical matters. Obviously finding themselves in something of a quandary, the line of questioning was abruptly discontinued.

Further conclusive evidence came to light with the discovery of the wreck of the Titanic. An extract from Dr Robert Ballard's book *The Discovery of the*

Chart showing the range of visibility from the vantage points of the
"Titanic" and the "Californian"

Explanatory note;

" Longitude " = distance from East or West from standard Meridan.

" Latitude " = distance on Meridan reckoned North or South from Equater.

" Meridan " = relating to Noon, or Sun's position at noon.

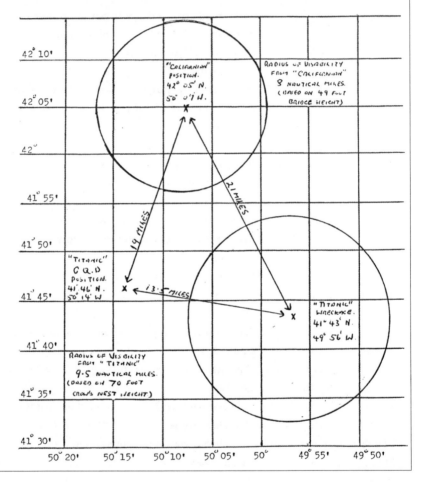

Chart showing the range of visibility from the vantage points of the Titanic and the Californian.

Explanatory note:
Longitude = distance from east or west from standard Meridian.
Latitude = distance on Meridan reckoned north or south from equator.
Meridan = relating to noon, or the sun's position at noon.

Titanic should silence forever those who still believe that the two ships were within sight of each other:

> Until now (the discovery of the wreck) the two great unknowns in the tale were the actual position of the Titanic and the actual position of the Californian. At least now the Titanic's final position can be stated with reasonable certainty – assuming the wreck lies pretty well directly below it. Since the stern and boilers likely fell almost straight down, these probably are closest to the ship's surface position at the time of the sinking. The stern section sits on the ocean bottom at 49° 56' 54' W, 41° 43' 35' N, and the centre of the boiler field is at 49° 56' 49' W, 41° 43' 32' N (the centre of the bow section is at 49° 56' 49' W, 41° 53' 57' N). This means the Titanic sank roughly 13.5 miles east-southeast of her CQD position. She is just south of her calculated course, but well to the east. So the navigators on board overestimated the Titanic's speed by roughly 2 knots: instead of travelling at about 22.5 knots as fourth officer Boxhall had supposed, she was travelling at about 20.5 knots. This position therefore puts the Californian's logged position 21 miles to the north-north-west. An interesting sidelight here – and part of the reason Jack Grimm didn't find the wreck – is that the actual position of the ship is five and a half miles northeast of where the first lifeboat was picked up by the Carpathia …

It was destined to be still several years before the Department of Transport finally agreed to reappraise the evidence surrounding Captain Lord and the Californian.

The accompanying chart shows the radius of visibility of both ships and serves to emphasise that it would have been impossible to see the other in view of the distance apart. This fact holds true even if the Titanic had been at her CQD position. Also, contrary to what the two inquiries would have us believe, there were considerably more ships in this area than just the two central characters in the drama. It should be borne in mind that, as well as being a regular sea lane, the Grand Banks of Newfoundland were also a huge fishing and sealing area. At any given time, this area of the North Atlantic would have substantial shipping engaged in various activities. It is well to recall that in 1912 only more modern ships would have been equipped with electricity and radio apparatus. Apart from these few ships so equipped, there would have also been a whole host of sailing vessels, tramp steamers, poachers and various fishing vessels in the area. The idea then that only two ships were in this area is simply bordering on the absurd.

SIX

Gibson, Gill and Groves

There are many contradictions in the evidence given by Gill, the donkeyman, and while we delve into this evidence in some detail, we must bear in mind that it was publicly stated at the United States Congressional Investigation that Gill sold his account of the tragedy to a Boston newspaper. The Californian's wireless operator, Cyril Evans, stated that Gill said to him 'I think I'll make about $500.00 on this.' Whether he actually made $500.00 is not known. However, it is known that he did manage to sell his account of the tragedy and later deserted his ship. It is obvious that a sum as substantial as $500.00, equal to a year's pay, would have been a tremendous incentive to Gill, whose wages on the Californian amounted to just £5 10s per month.

Gill, upon having his sworn affidavit read back to him at the U.S. inquiry, agreed that was his evidence. He stated that he had been working in the engine room of the Californian when he checked the clock and saw it was 11.56 p.m. He 'immediately left the engine room' to call the man who was to relieve him at midnight. The Californian, he said, had stopped for 'about an hour and a half'. This would in fact be in keeping with Captain Lord's statement that he stopped his ship at 10.21 p.m. Gill went on to say that during the brief moment he was on the open deck en route to the quarters, he looked over the ship's side and saw 'the lights of a very large steamer at a distance of about ten miles'. Later, at the British inquiry, Gill was to improve on this statement and said that he could see 'two rows of lights and several groups of lights which I took to be saloon or deck lights'. He went on to say that the steamer he observed was travelling 'at full speed'. Amazingly, nobody bothered to ask how a twenty-nine-year-old donkeyman could, with just a brief glance over the ship's rail, determine that the ship he was looking at was a large passenger steamer, taking particular note of her lighting, estimate that she was ten miles distant, and even arrive at the conclusion that the ship was travelling at full speed. Suffice it to say that this feat would have been impossible. Although he was certain that he was looking at the Titanic, it never apparently occurred to Gill that had he in fact really been observing the White Star liner, then he would have been looking at a ship showing about ten thousand lights and that these lights would, of necessity, have cast a massive glare on the surrounding water.

After handing over the watch to his relief, Gill stated that he went to bed but could not sleep. At 'about 12.30 a.m.' (he never appeared to be specific with times) he decided to go on deck to smoke a cigarette. While he was so engaged 'for about ten minutes' he said he saw a white rocket 'at a considerable distance, away on the starboard side'. Curiously enough, he didn't commit himself to any given distance for this sighting and went on to add that the steamer which he had seen a little over a half-hour before, was no longer in sight. The rocket, he said, 'did come from the general direction' relative to the Californian's heading in which he had seen the ship he took to be the Titanic. No more than 'seven or eight minutes later' and prior to disposing of his cigarette, he observed a second white rocket, which, apparently, made no great impression on him. Evidently it did not occur to him to report this matter to his superiors, as one would expect a responsible crewmember to do. Instead, Gill simply went off to bed. Strange behaviour, when one considers that his own ship had stopped because of the dangerous conditions prevailing.

There is also some discrepancy in Gill's statement concerning his smoking habit. He said that he had been smoking 'for about ten minutes' when he saw the first rocket and that, 'seven or eight minutes later', after he had seen the second rocket, he disposed of his cigarette and went to bed. This, obviously, and as any smoker will attest, is completely untrue. Gill would have us believe that he spent up to eighteen minutes smoking a cigarette, while allegedly wearing only pyjamas in the freezing cold, yet, experiments show that it takes exactly seven minutes to smoke a cigarette indoors. Outside, the time is drastically reduced by wind to less than six minutes. We can only conclude that Gill's cigarette must have been at least eight inches long!

For some reason best known to himself, $500.00 perhaps, Gill was extremely critical of his captain and made a point of concluding his testimony with the remark, 'I am quite sure that the Californian was less than twenty miles from the Titanic which the officers report to have been our position. I could not have seen her if she had been more than ten miles distant, and I saw her very plainly'. There is little doubt that Gill did in fact see a ship, but, for reasons explained above, and in other areas, that ship could not have been the Titanic. Nevertheless, from this contentious piece of supposition, Gill gave the court the distinct impression that he could almost read the nameplate on the ship's side.

When we compare the irrefutable facts of the case against Gill's evidence, we see that his assertions simply fall apart and cannot have any substance. We have already seen, and is necessary to repeat, that the Titanic's clocks were operating a full twelve minutes ahead of the clocks of the Californian. So, when Gill said that he saw a very large steamer going at full speed after 11.56 p.m., the actual time on the Titanic would have been 12.08 a.m. and, as we know, the Titanic struck the iceberg well before midnight and remained stationary until she sank.

Gill also passed the boundaries of belief when he claimed that with just a cursory glance over the ship's rail, he was able to determine that the ship he was looking at, was firstly, moving at top speed; secondly, was ten miles distant and thirdly, this ship was the Titanic. This feat, as any mariner worth his salt will tell, is patently impossible. As we have ascertained, the lights on the Titanic did not go out at any stage prior to her foundering and, consequently, would have literally been lit up like a small town. Nevertheless, Gill, either unaware or uncaring of the idiocy of his statement went on to describe individual cabin and deck lights on the ship and seemed oblivious of the fact that lights on any ship at this distance would not be discernible but would fuse into one large glare.

Even more extraordinary is the fact that the evidence of Groves, the Californian's third officer, greatly differed from that of Gill. Yet both men were observing the same ship! Clearly, if the laws of average applied, as they should have done, and we accept that both Gill and Groves were looking at the same horizon, they should have witnessed the same incidents. However, such, apparently, was not the case. Groves stated that he saw a 'passenger steamer' and that she was stopped and had put out all her lights at 11.40 p.m. This of course, was exactly sixteen minutes before Gill had even left the engine room. This situation prompts the obvious question – was one, or both, of the men badly mistaken? In any event, the court seemed impressed with the evidence of Gill, and basing its decision on his statement, found Lord responsible for the loss of more than fifteen hundred lives.

There is, however, ample evidence to contradict Gill's story which was provided by other crew members of the ship. In 'Man of Californian – "I Saw

Titanic's Signals" by Eugene Seder (*Titanic Commutator*, Spring 1985), the following information was revealed:

The members of the crew, several of whom were interviewed by [a] (Boston) Herald reporter, declared they had heard nothing of any ship in distress and that they considered it remarkably queer that Gill had said nothing about it to them and that he had not reported it to the watch on duty. It was said by several members of the crew that forecastle talk was to the effect that Gill received a good round sum for his affidavit. William Thomas, a donkeyman, was Gill's 'bunkie' and was highly indignant yesterday that his name had been brought into the affidavit. 'I knew nothing about this affidavit,' he said, 'and I am positive that Gill said nothing to me about the steamer in distress, if he saw such a thing. I believe he would have told the watch, for I can't see an Englishman letting others drown without making some move to help them.'

'Gill woke me up soon after 12 o'clock that night, and I asked him why he was so late. "It's all right, the engines aren't running," he answered. Then I heard a bumping against the side of the ship, and I went into the engine room, and later oiled the steering gear, my regular task.

'Soon after 4 o'clock I turned in again and was soon roused by the chief engineer, who said that all hands were to muster, as the Titanic had sunk. Soon after the engines were started and we put for the wreck. It took us more than two hours to get there, and we recognized the place by the big pool of oil and by many bits of wreckage that floated about.

'I think that Gill would have told me if he had seen rockets. I can't believe that he could see a ship ten miles off if there was one, because the change from the engine room to the deck partly blinds a man, and besides, that night it would have been easy to take fixed stars for vessels' lights and shooting stars for rockets.'

'Yesterday afternoon, the barman from a Marginal Street saloon came to me and said I was wanted at the "pub". I went over and when I got there, the bartender said to me, "You're not the fellow. Where's the chap that was with you yesterday with a brown suit on?" I knew that was Gill, so went back and told him. He went away then without telling me where he was going. He came back some time later, didn't say a word to me but soon went ashore again. He must have taken all his dunnage with him, for there isn't any here now.

'Gill was engaged to a girl in England. I can see where the offer of a sum as large as reported in the forecastle would greatly tempt him. He could very

easily set up a small shop in England, or get work in America with a comfortable nest egg in addition' [Boston Herald, April 26, 1912].

In all likelihood, Gill left the engine room just before midnight, went straight
to his bunk and did not get out again until roused the following morning
while the ship was under way. It was up to Senator Smith and Lord Mersey
to subject Gill to a gruelling cross-examination, as they later did with Stone
and Gibson, and confront him with the many absurdities in his story, then
kick him out for contempt of court and have him sued for perjury. They did
not, most probably because they must have felt they already had their man
at that stage of the investigation. The six nautical assessors at the inquiry
were also remarkably conspicuous by their silence. They showed no signs of
uneasiness that Gill's yarn and ignorance of judging distances at sea should
have caused among them.

On more than one occasion during the inquiry, Lord Mersey also displayed his ignorance of maritime matters. This is evidenced amply on page
53 of the official report of the investigation. Lord Mersey had strongly argued
at length with literally all the legal and nautical advisers present in court that
the lights of a ship, apart from emergency lighting, would, of necessity go out
the moment a ship's main engines are stopped. The argument became very
heated and Mersey even browbeat his own nautical advisers. Stubborn to
the last, he remained adamant and, almost with a child's insistence stated: 'At
some time the light which was produced by the main engines did go out'.
Having made this outrageous and contentious statement, Mersey allowed
no further discussion on the subject. There the highly important issue was
allowed to remain, as the questioning of the witnesses continued.

In adopting this stance, Lord Mersey not only displayed, again, his total
lack of maritime experience but, even more importantly, clearly chose to
ignore the sworn affidavits before him, which all categorically stated that at
no time, prior to her foundering, did the lights on the Titanic fail or go out.
Rejecting these facts, it was obviously more important to Lord Mersey that
he be allowed to impose his will on the court. Nevertheless, by his childish
attitude and insistence, Mersey was actually belittling the brave and unselfish acts of the Titanic's engineering staff, who all did their utmost to keep
the lights burning on the doomed vessel and without exception remained
at their posts even though the sea was enveloping them. Despite the fact
that each man knew his only release would be merciful death, not one left
their posts. All thirty-six men, most of them family men, died that night

so that others might have a chance to live. It can only be to Lord Mersey's shame that he so vehemently and offhandedly demeaned the unquestionable courage of these brave men.[1]

If we accept that Gill did in fact see two rockets 'at a considerable distance' to the south, then we must suspect that Gill was, to a certain extent, guilty of dereliction of duty in not reporting the matter immediately to his superiors. By his own admission, he returned to bed. The fact that the rockets were not seen by Mr Stone at this stage may be due to the fact that he was engaged in watching ship X, which was bearing SE (true) and, as a consequence would have had his eyes shielded by the binoculars and therefore missed the two 'flashes' in the distance. This is an interesting aspect and serves to prove without any shadow of doubt that the rockets could not have come from ship X. If they had, then obviously Stone would have observed them.

In view of Groves' determined statement that the lights of ship X appeared to go out when she stopped, and the subsequent stress put on this by Lord Mersey, it may be beneficial to look at Groves' evidence in some detail, as questioned by Mr Rowlatt:

Question 8217	'What makes you fix the time of 11.40 p.m. for her lights going out?' (referring to ship X)
Groves	'Because that it the time we struck one bell to call the middle watch.'
8218	'Do you remember the bell was struck at that time?'
Groves	'Most certainly.'
8219	'Did the steamer continue on her course after that?'
Groves	'No, not as far as I could see.'
8220	'She stopped?'
Groves	'She stopped.'
8221	'Was that at the time when her lights appeared to go out?'
Groves	'That was at the time her lights appeared to go out.'
8222	'Were the lights you saw on her port side or her starboard side?'
Groves	'Port side.'
8223	'I want to ask you a question. Supposing the steamer whose lights you saw turned two points to port at 11.40 p.m., would that account to you for her lights ceasing to be visible to you?'
Groves	'I quite think it would.'

There was a slight deviation from the line of questioning at this stage and a discussion ensued, establishing that the lights had gone out temporarily in a stoke hold of the Titanic, but that all the other lights had remained on:

Commissioner	'Very well. Now I understand it. Those engines (which worked the electric light) would be going on just the same although the signal had come from the Bridge to stop the main engines.'
Mr Rowlatt	'Yes. I have got an answer from the witness which may throw some light upon it. He said that, in his opinion, the turning of the ship …' (interrupted by the Commissioner)
Commissioner	'I heard him. That would be when the order was given to change direction.'
Mr Rowlatt	'Hard-a-starboard; and your Lordship remembers we had evidence that the ship did answer to the extent of two points at once.'
Commissioner	'Yes, she did answer her helm. Very well. Two points. You were saying?'
Mr Rowlatt	'Two points, my Lord. The man at the compass said she altered her course two points.'
Commissioner	'A change of two points to port would conceal the lights in the ship?'
Mr Rowlatt to Groves, Question 8224	'Did you say "would" or "might"? I do not want to put it too high?'
Groves	'In my own private opinion it would.'
8225	'You are speaking of deck lights?'
Groves	'Yes.'
8226	'Lights from the ports and windows?'
Groves	'Yes.'
8227	'Did you continue to see the masthead lights?'
Groves	'Yes.'
8228	'Did you see any navigation lights, side lights?'
Groves	'I saw the red port light.'
Commissioner, 8229	'When did you see that?'
Groves	'As soon as her deck lights disappeared from my view.'

Groves	'Yes, some course to the westward.'
8478	'Does it follow from that that the side which she was showing to you at that time must have been her starboard side?'
Groves	'No, it does not follow at all. If she is steering a direct west course, yes.'
8479	'Did you see her green light at all?'
Groves	'Never.'

Groves obviously made a mistake in his replies to some of these questions. However, in fairness to him, it would appear to have been a genuine, rather than a deliberate, attempt to confuse the issue. In all probability he became somewhat confused by the inexpert line of questioning and lost concentration. Bearing this in mind, he is entitled to the benefit of doubt. It is, however, most curious that he stated that he saw no red light until the other lights disappeared. There is little doubt that this statement should have been, and probably would have been, pursued by Mr Dunlop were he not in the delicate position of acting in the interests of Groves, as well as the rest of the Californian complement. Without doubt it was an unenviable situation and one which obviously required delicate treatment. Nevertheless, it must be said that the evidence of all three, Stone, Gill and Groves, appeared to be seriously contradictory and in many aspects bordering on hostility.

An interesting aspect to this line of questioning and the case in general was published in an article in the Nautical Magazine in 1913 (p. 587):

… As instances of points which should have been followed up we give the following:

1. Mr Stone was not asked how many rockets he reported at 1.15 a.m.

2. Gibson was not questioned as to what the captain said when he closed the chartroom door after giving his report.

3. Other Californian witnesses should have been called, such as the look-out man and the quartermaster on duty.

4. We have placed Z NW of the Titanic on the evidence of quartermaster Rowe, who was the only witness asked who knew how the Titanic was heading after she had turned the two points to port. The officers were asked if she were altering her heading at all but not how she was heading.

5. The time at which the Titanic rockets commenced might have been approximated by further search in the records of the Marconi Company.

6.   Captain Rostron should have been asked if he verified his opinion as to
      the Titanic's position.

7.   The Board of Trade made no attempt to obtain a list of the vessels in the
      neighbourhood on the night of the disaster.

The Force of Circumstances
In dealing with this case it is particularly necessary to consider all the details
in their relation to one another. This is more easily done at leisure than during the stress of a public inquiry. Moreover, the case of the Californian was
only a part of the Titanic Inquiry. Our object is to analyse and not to criticise;
and if the whole of the strange circumstances (which we have discussed) be
reviewed, we think it must be allowed that the fates were singularly unpropi-
tious to a full understanding of the facts. In relation to the disaster a chain
of coincidences undoubtedly pointed to the Californian as being to blame.
Another chain of unfortunate circumstances prevented the captain from
knowing what was taking place. In relation to the Inquiry (1912) we find an
adverse fate mitigating against a full understanding of the circumstances and a
simple case becomes a complex one.

This is undoubtedly hitting the nail on the head. There can be little doubt
that the case should have been very much an 'open and shut' affair but,
because of all the varying circumstances, both coincidental and in many
areas highly suspect, the case became engulfed in absurd bureaucratic
mishandling, malice, hostility, ignorance, dispute and gain. The inevitable
result of this was that the case became an almost intangible mess of gross
speculation, rumour, hearsay and idle gossip and, thanks largely to press
sensationalists, a not insubstantial political football with deep international
connotations. The entire facts of the case were not brought to the fore, and
the central character, Lord, was effectively 'gagged' and had no avenue of
defence or escape left open to him. Over the intervening years, despite petitions and sound arguments in support of Captain Lord, the Board of Trade,
whose duties were later taken over by the Department of Transport, resolutely refused to re-open the case, claiming that to do so would 'serve no
useful purpose'.

Returning to the question of lights, it is now appropriate to introduce
yet another vital aspect into the case: green flares. It was actually the use
of these flares which first gave Captain Rostron of the Carpathia his first
inkling of the position of the lifeboats. The fact that nobody aboard the

Californian reported seeing green flares, once again only serves to reinforce the claim that Lord's ship was nowhere near the disaster site. Indeed, Captain Rostron is quoted as stating that he first saw the flares when he was almost twenty miles away from the area. This distance is probably exaggerated, as flares burn only near the surface and do not soar upwards like rockets and would be unlikely to be seen from so far away. Nevertheless, it still serves to emphasize that the Californian could not have been in close proximity to the disaster area. If she had been, then she too would have undoubtedly observed the flares. Evidence that green flares actually were fired from the lifeboats is also contained in the testimony of the Titanic's fourth officer, Joseph Boxhall:

Question 15448	'In your boat did you also put in some green lights?'
Boxhall	'Yes, there were some green lights lying in the wheelhouse. I told the quartermaster or someone who was around there to put them in the boat …'
15465	'Did you remain in that position, about 200ft away from the ship, until she sank?'
Boxhall	'No, I did not; I turned the boat away and pulled in a north-easterly direction.'
15466	'You mean, you pulled further away from the ship?'
Boxhall	'Yes.'
15467	'How far were you from the ship when she did sink?'
Boxhall	'Approximately, half-a-mile.'
15468	'That means you could not have seen what happened?'
Boxhall	'No, I could not.'
15469	'After she sank, did you hear cries?'
Boxhall	'Yes, I heard cries. I did not know that when the lights went out the ship had sunk. I saw the lights go out, but I did not know whether she had sunk or not, and then I heard the cries. I was showing green lights in the boat then, to try and get the other boats together, trying to keep us all together.'
15482	'I was the first boat picked up on board the Carpathia … He saw our green lights and steamed down for them' [Boxhall].

Captain Rostron also corroborated this incident a little later when he testified:

25394   'At 20 minutes to 3.00 I saw the green flare, which is the White Star Company's night signal, and naturally, knowing I must be at least 20 miles, I thought it was the ship herself. It was showing for just a few seconds and I passed the remark that she must be still afloat. Naturally, before this I had got the wireless message that the engine-room was filling, so I felt it was a case of all up ...'

Rostron, 25401   'At twenty minutes to three I saw a night signal, as I was saying, and it was just about half-a-point on the port bow, practically right ahead. At a quarter to three I saw what we knew was an iceberg by the light from a star – I saw a streak of light right on the iceberg. We saw it, I cannot say the distance off, but some distance – not very far; and from then till four o'clock we were altering course very often to avoid the bergs. At four o'clock I considered I was practically up to the position, and I stopped, at about five minutes after four. In the meantime I had been firing rockets and the company's signals every time we saw this green light again. At five minutes past four I saw the green light again, and I was going to pick the boat up on the port bow, but just as it showed the green light I saw an iceberg right ahead of me. It was very close, so I had to put my helm hard-a-starboard and put her head round quickly and pick up the boat on the starboard side. At ten minutes past four we got alongside.'

While there can be no doubt but that Captain Rostron did observe the first green flare from a considerable distance, his figure of 'about twenty miles' is perhaps, something of an overstatement. Once again we must consider the earth's natural curvature and the fact that the flare was being fired from a point (lifeboat) exceptionally low in the water. Even though the weather conditions prevailing that night and morning, unusually clear and with no cloud, would be most conducive to rockets being seen at a considerable distance, because of the lack of any cloud cover, a flare, obviously, would not be capable of being seen at any great distance due to the fact that it would not have reached the same height as a rocket. Another most important point raised in Captain Rostron's evidence is the fact that he said he had been firing rockets and company's signals every time he saw the green light. Rostron commenced this practice, according to himself, between 'a quarter

to three' and 'about five minutes past four' and the strong possibility cannot be ruled out that it was in fact, Rostron's rockets which the witnesses
on the Californian say they saw. Credence is added to this possibility when
we recall that both Gibson and Stone claimed to have seen three distant
flashes in the sky to the south. These would more or less correspond to the
direction and approximate time that the Carpathia was firing her rockets.
A closer look at the testimony of Stone and Gibson reinforces this very real
possibility:

Stone, 8008	'At about 3.20 a.m., just before half past three, as near as I can approximate, Gibson reported to me that he had seen a white light in the sky to the southward of us, just about on the port beam. We were head- ing about west at that time. I crossed over to the port wing of the bridge and watched its direction with my binoculars. Shortly after, I saw a white light in the sky right ahead on the beam.'
Commissioner, 8009	'How far away?'
Stone	'At a very great distance I should judge.'
8010	'What do you mean by a very great distance?'
Stone	'Such a distance that if it had been much further I should have seen no light at all, merely a faint flash.'
Mr Aspinall, 8011	'Was it the same character of light as the rockets, or something quite different?'
Stone	'It was so far away that it was impossible to judge.'
Commissioner	'And were these lights rockets?'
Stone	'I think not.'

Stone clearly states that the Californian was so far away as to make the lights
in the sky all but invisible. In this respect, the commissioner seemed to be
inclined to doubt the evidence. A little later he questioned Gibson on the
matter:

7591	'Are you quite sure that these three rockets were ever seen by you at all?'
Gibson	'Yes, sir, I saw the first one and reported it to the second officer, and we looked out for more to see if we could see any more - and we saw two more.'

Solicitor general, 7592	'You say you saw the first one?'
Gibson	'Yes.'
7593	'Do you mean you saw it with your naked eye?'
Gibson	'Yes.'
Solicitor general, 7594	'Yes, my Lord, Roman candles. (to the witness) … If it was twenty minutes to four it was not very far off the beginning of dawn, was it?'
Gibson	'No, dawn was just breaking.'
7595	'Had it got any lighter?'
Gibson	'Yes.'
8596	'Could you see when you saw this flash at all how far away you thought it was?'
Gibson	'It was right on the horizon.'
7597	'What sort of a light was it? You called it a rocket. Was it a flash; did you see it go up into the sky?'
Gibson	'Yes.'
7598	'What colour was it?'
Gibson	'White.'
7599	'And you called Mr Stone's attention to it, did you, and then there were two more seen?'
Gibson	'Yes.'

Here again is either a glaring contradiction or yet another display of the qualifications necessary to have conducted such an important inquiry. In either event, it went unchallenged. In reply to the commissioner's question, 'Did any of the boats of the Titanic fire Roman candles?', the solicitor general replied in the affirmative. From this leading response one would almost assume that the solicitor general was himself on board one of the lifeboats – so positive was his reply. In actual fact, in their evidence both Captain Rostron and Mr Boxhall made it abundantly clear that it was green lights or flares which were being burnt by one of the lifeboats, not Roman candles. While this might seem to be a trivial point, such is not the case. Roman candles, of the type used by the White Star Line, threw two green stars to considerable height, while a green light burns for some seconds and does not go up in the air. In other words, the prolonged green light itself remains on the water until it burns itself out. Only the 'stars' of the flare actually go up in the air and, even then, not as high as a rocket would have gone. The obvious solution to this is, apart from the ludicrous possibility that both Gibson and Stone were colour blind, that both men were probably observing the rockets from the Carpathia. If we bear in mind that Captain Rostron, and likewise Gibson and Stone, were somewhat vague about the exact times, both instances would appear to concur with each other.

There is also the important point that if the Titanic's boats had fired any Roman candles, then these candles would have had to reach an enormous height to show green stars at a distance approaching twenty miles or further. By doing a few simple calculations we see that for an object to be seen at a distance of twenty-one miles, at sea, it would have to reach a minimum height of 120ft above sea level. Even then, the person observing it would have to be 40ft above sea level. When we consider that the distance claimed by Lord was in about twenty miles, and that the lifeboat was no more than five or six feet above sea level, to observe any lights or flares would have been a manifestly impossible task.

In hindsight, the entire inquiry would appear to have been a haphazard affair, smitten with many inconsistencies and contradictions. Let us return to Lord Mersey's statement that the Californian was, to use his amended words, 'no more than eight to ten miles distant'. If such were the case, then it must surely follow that the Carpathia would have had to observe the Californian not alone during the hours of darkness, when the Californian was lit up and using her powerful Morse lamp, but also the moment the dawn broke. Yet, in his sworn affidavit, made in New York and read at the British inquiry on 21 June, Rostron clearly states:

> At five o'clock it was light enough to see all around the horizon. We then saw two steamships to the northwards, perhaps seven or eight miles distant. Neither of them was the Californian. The first time I saw the Californian was about eight o'clock on the morning of the 15th of April.

Obviously it would have been quite impossible for Rostron, or anyone in the area, to have seen the Californian, as that ship had been hove to between the hours of 10.20 p.m. until almost 6.00 a.m. on the morning of 15 April.

Still another interesting and debatable point is that in spite of being read-ily available, several members of the Californian's crew were not called upon to give evidence. Was it possible that Lord Mersey was reluctant to call other witnesses who might conceivably demolish his argument and further com-plicate the issue? Apparently so. Most amazingly, though perhaps not, given the circumstances, neither was Mr Lawrence Beesley called to give evidence, in spite of the fact that he would have proved to have been an excellent witness and could have been instrumental in exonerating Lord of any blame. Was it for this very reason that Mr Beesley was not called to the stand? Clearly, Lord Mersey appeared to be satisfied with contradictory evidence of those he had questioned and, as a result of this highly questionable testimony, launched an outrageous attack on Captain Lord. The scapegoat was well and truly ensnared.

As president, Lord Mersey was entitled to accept or reject evidence put before him without giving reason. However, an appeal by Captain Lord, if properly presented, could have embarrassed him. As so many have done, Sir Rufus Isaacs and Lord Mersey were obviously united in their early conclusion that only the Californian and Titanic could possibly have been involved, and that no further time need be wasted in listening to arguments contesting this view. Throughout the British inquiry, there was a clear impression that all concerned had agreed that the Mount Temple was not to be criticised and this attitude could justifiably be called a cover-up.

In his superb 1998 work *The Lusitania Controversies* (Book One) author Gary Gentile describes Lord Mersey as follows:

[His] expertise lay in creating scapegoats and whitewashing events, in which respects he knew no mercy and outbrushed the adventures of Tom Sawyer. Lord Mersey handled [the Titanic and Empress of Ireland] investigations with great incompetence and evident prejudice. In the Titanic case, he completely exonerated Captain E.J. Smith for travelling at full speed … despite repeated warnings of field ice ahead … Mersey blamed the high number of fatalities on the master of the Californian, who had nothing to do with the collision, who was more than twenty miles away when it occurred, and who was wise enough to heave to until morning when he could see how to steer safely through the pack ice which surrounded his ship.

In 1914, he exonerated the Empress of Ireland for turning into the path of the Storstad on a fog-shrouded night in the St Lawrence Seaway…Mersey blamed the Storstad for not getting out of the way of the veering Empress of Ireland.

Mersey was predictable, for everyone knew where his allegiance lay. He was quintessentially British. The purpose for holding the 1915 hearing was to blame Germany for sinking the Lusitania and to absolve British hands of all responsibility for contributory negligence. Lord Mersey saw to it that these goals were achieved – at least in the eyes of loyal British subjects and bitter American citizens.

Mr Gentile is not alone in criticising the way Lord Mersey handled the investigation into the loss of the ill-fated Cunarder. Patrick O'Sullivan, author of *The Lusitania - Unravelling the Mysteries* (1998) states:

> The enquiry was chaired by Lord Mersey ... Two naval and two merchant officers attended as assessors ... Late in the evening of the disaster, 7 May, the Admiralty had already decided to make Captain Turner the scapegoat for the loss of his ship. Fisher, the First Sea Lord, wrote a memorandum to his colleagues before the trial which stated – 'I hope Captain Turner will be arrested immediately after the enquiry, whatever the outcome' ... . Lord Mersey received a private letter from the Admiralty which stated: 'The Government would consider it politically expedient if the captain of the Lusitania were promiscuously blamed for the accident.' ... . Two of the most eminent lawyers of the day, Sir Edward Carson, Attorney General, and F.E. Smith, the solicitor general, defended the Government case. Turner did not stand much chance against their brutal cross examination ... The Admiralty's intention from the start appeared to be one of moving the spotlight away from itself and on to Turner.
>
> Another issue, the second mystery explosion, drew a lot of attention as it was noted by almost every survivor. This was potentially embarrassing as it might lend credence to German claims of exploding munitions in the forward part of the ship. This was explained in the Court, which found that two torpedoes had struck the ship ... Mersey also decreed that no other substance exploded or ignited. Any further questions about the second mystery explosion were thus discouraged. Mersey further found that several U-boats had lain in wait for the Lusitania. In his verdict, Mersey exonerated Captain Turner and the Cunard Company, he heaped the highest of praise on the Admiralty for their diligence in collecting all the information available likely to affect the Lusitania, and praised them for their most anxious care and thoughtfulness throughout the affair ... Mersey's judgement commended the crew for its discipline and competence. The opposite is true, however, in the case of those crew members who were launching the lifeboats, which was a fiasco. Mersey finally decreed the whole blame for the cruel destruction of life in this catastrophe must rest solely with those who plotted and with those who committed the crime. When the verdict was made public, many of the survivors received it in stunned disbelief. Captain Turner left the Court, a bewildered and soon to be despised villain, who was seen to be negligent and reckless in handling his ship. He was just another expendable pawn in

the higher game of cynical chess played out in the corridors of the Admiralty. Like many before him, Turner had learned another of life's cruel lessons: that a court of law is not necessarily a court of justice.

Patrick O'Sullivan's graphic description of the 1915 court proceedings bears a striking resemblance to the events of 1912. If one replaces the names 'Captain Turner' with 'Captain Lord', 'Admiralty' with 'Board of Trade', 'Sir Edward Carson' with 'Sir Rufus Isaacs', 'F.E. Smith' with 'Butler Aspinall', and 'exploding munitions' with an 'acute lack of lifeboats' as the real causes for the tremendous loss of life in the Lusitania and Titanic disasters (2,700 souls in total), one is struck by the similarities of the proceedings in both investigations. Exploding munitions on board the Lusitania that accounted for the second blast from her forward cargo holds and the lack of lifeboats on the Titanic, and on almost any other contemporary British liner, were responsibilities of the government that cropped up inevitably as both disasters unfolded. They were, therefore, extremely delicate issues by their very nature since, under scrutiny, they might reveal forgery of the ship's manifest. Also, they could reveal hopelessly out-of-date safety regulations on the part of the gentlemen in the higher echelons of society that, firstly, had much to lose, as far as their influential positions were concerned, and secondly, showed utter disrespect for human life. It stands to reason that any embarrassing questions about them should therefore be stifled at all cost. Those responsible, the Admiralty and Board of Trade, which had so much at stake, should not under any circumstances be criticised. Given this mindset, it then becomes abundantly plain that Lord Mersey was almost certainly acting under strict instructions from above in both inquiries. Hence, he was very keen on letting the authorities responsible for the safety and safe navigation of a vessel completely off the hook, and put the blame squarely on the shoulders of one single, utterly defenceless human being. Like Captain Turner, Captain Lord had left the court 'a bewildered and soon to be despised villain' three years earlier. Mersey seemed a logical choice for either inquiry. His methods of handling delicate issues obviously satisfied the policy-makers and fooled the uncritical mind of the casual observer with a scapegoat for decades to come. He later commented on the Lusitania affair: 'It was a damned dirty business' and refused to accept his fee.

So, again: the purpose for holding Captain Lord responsible for the 1,500 lives lost in the Titanic tragedy was to exonerate the Board of Trade, which Lord Mersey represented, for having failed to equip the Titanic and other large British passenger liners with sufficient lifeboat accommodation. It is clear that Captain Lord never had the slightest chance at the hands of Lord Mersey and his attorney general, Sir Rufus Isaacs, whose treatment of the master of the Californian was hostile from the very beginning. This policy could be described as a damned dirty business too, with justification. Mersey should have refused his fee in this case as well.

Over the years it had been strongly suggested by several popular and well-known, yet ill-informed writers that when the Californian set off for the reported site of the disaster, a little after 6.00 a.m., she was almost immediately in sight of the Carpathia. Such writers, apparently, conveniently chose to forget that it actually took the Californian more than two and a half hours to reach the area at full steam, in broad daylight. Are they, perhaps, suggesting that Lord's ship simply went around in circles for those two and a half hours? The obvious answer to this, and the other irregularities that abound in this case, is that far too many people, most of whom should know better, are accepting the findings of both inquiries at face value and 'as gospel'.

We now know that there were several other ships in the immediate area of the disaster, both identified and unidentified. This makes it difficult, if not impossible, to reconcile Lord Mersey's and Senator Smith's insistence that no other ships, apart from the Titanic and the Californian, were in the area that night/morning. Indeed, apart from ships X and Z, one of which may have been the sealing ship Samson, at least three other ships were observed by the Californian. Captain Rostron also testified to having seen two unidentified steamers in the region. In spite of this overwhelming evidence, both courts failed to take into their consideration the distinct possibility that other ships would have been bound to have been in this area if only because they were attracted by the rockets, the wireless messages, or, like the Californian, stopped for the night because of the dangerous conditions. They likewise gave no credence to the many tramp steamers and various sailing and fishing boats that usually plied these waters. If the situation was reversed and a witness in their courts asked either Lord Mersey or Senator Smith to accept that only two ships, Titanic and Californian, were the only two vessels in a twenty- to thirty-mile radius in international shipping and fishing waters, that unfortunate witness would have been laughed out of court. However, as it was, those making this outrageous statement apparently thought it was quite acceptable and well within the bounds of reason.

In referring back to the two 'mystery ships', X and Z, a possible reason for these ships repeatedly ignoring radio and Morse signals from the Titanic and the Californian was that they firstly, did not have any wireless apparatus, and secondly, neither ship was equipped with an electrical system necessary to operate the powerful blinker or Morse lights. These, however, are but observations and idle conjecture and do not detract from the possibility that the ships simply did not wish their presence or identity to become known for reasons of their own. Obviously, the reluctance of the sealing ship Samson to disclose herself is quite clear – she was fishing illegally and was wary of American patrols in the area. This, no doubt, is why she beat such a hasty retreat, albeit unaware of the tragedy which was unfolding relatively close to her. The fact that the Samson sailed in these waters with little or no lights, and that she was constantly on the lookout for American patrols, can only suggest that such patrols were normally in this area. However, here again we are indulging in speculation and that has been an aspect of the case which has influenced the courts to a significant degree and, as a consequence, resulted in a rush to judgement.

In view of all the evidence which was available to them, and particularly in view of the evidence they chose to ignore, it seems totally unjustifiable that both Lord Mersey and Senator Smith placed so much emphasis and importance on the questionable evidence of two witnesses who were in effect hostile, and whose stories obviously contradicted each other to the point of absurdity. Nevertheless, it was mainly on this flimsy testimony that Mersey and Smith reached their respective conclusions that Captain Lord was responsible for the deaths of over 1,500 men, women and children. As a result of findings, a human being was effectively turned into a symbol, a thing to be scorned, reviled and castigated for life. A symbol does not bleed if pricked and its heart does not cry out for justice. In this way, conscience is put aside and, certainly in the case of Stanley Lord, one of the profoundest corruptions of our times was committed. It is perhaps difficult, if not impossible, to convey the enormity of this case, and the implications involved, to people who have firmly put up the shutters of their minds and who have arrived at, or allowed themselves to be brought to a decision which, in view of the evidence, must be recognised as an incorrect decision, and to expect those people to now say, 'OK, we were wrong, we were misled, we were misguided'. Human nature does not operate like that. What a boring old world it would be if we all thought exactly the same on every occasion. Nevertheless, there does come a time when the most stubborn will have to accept the facts, often in light of new information, and step down from their pedestals and be counted. Clearly, that time is now.

In his excellent book, *The Titanic and the Californian*, Mr Peter Padfield, in describing the United States inquiry said in conclusion:

> The evidence from this Inquiry examined in the cold light of fifty years afterwards brings out only the undoubted fact about the Californian Incident: Captain Lord was 'framed'. He was 'framed' either consciously or subconsciously for one of three reasons. Either all the leading actors in the construction of the Report (1912) were natural idiots, or the edict had gone out that a scapegoat had to be found and they were doing the best they could to make it plausible, or the very magnitude and shock of the tragedy so unhinged them that they were incapable of examining the evidence with clear minds.

Today, one hundred years after the disaster, the same words can be applied with equal veracity. There can be little doubt that Mr Padfield was correct in his judgment when he said that Lord had been framed. When we carefully examine the evidence, we see that such was apparently the case and that Captain Lord did in fact become a scapegoat. The question that must be asked is, why? Was it to take public outrage away from the White Star Line and the Board of Trade? Such would certainly have seemed to have been the case. We have seen that the American inquiry was hastily convened and opened a little more than a week after the disaster. No sooner had it ended, than Lord Mersey, armed with the findings of the American investigation, promptly opened the British inquiry. It is then quite reasonable to assume that some, if not all the members of the British inquiry, had already made up their minds as to the outcome. Certainly there can have been no doubt that the members of the British inquiry must have been more than slightly influenced by the United States inquiry findings and, as a result, determined to condemn Captain Lord as the culprit of the affair. In this respect, the entire British inquiry can only be described as a purely cosmetic appease-ment to the general public on the one hand, and likewise to the Americans on the other. The involvement of Lord was totally blown out of propor-tion and clearly served to take the multitude of awkward questions, which would undoubtedly have been asked, away from the White Star Line and the Board of Trade. It indicates how much Lord Mersey was in need of a scapegoat to get the Board of Trade, the real culprit, off the hook. Were it not for the highly sensational aspects of the case, a drunken captain leaving more than fifteen hundred people to die, several pertinent and awkward

31 July 1992: Stanley Tutton Lord standing next to a painting of his father.
Exactly eighty years before, Captain Lord was officially blamed for not having gone
to Titanic's plight. Photograph by Rob Kamps

questions might have been asked and the replies could have had the effect
of putting both the owners and the Board of Trade in a very dim light. As it
was, caught up in the dramatic scenario that surrounded Lord, people were
almost willed not to ask such explosive questions, such as why did the Board
of Trade issue a certificate of seaworthiness to a ship which contained such
glaring deficiencies as unsatisfactory bulkheads and an inadequate supply
of lifeboats? Clearly, it was felt that something was needed to draw attention from these awkward questions. Obviously a much more emotive aspect
needed to be introduced to the drama – a scapegoat? Stanley Lord fitted the
bill admirably.

    This hypothesis is considerably strengthened when we note that the care-
ful manipulation of each session of the British Court of Inquiry ensured
that no mention of any charges or blame were ever made in the presence
of Lord. Attending the inquiry only in the capacity of a witness, he only
appeared very briefly, gave his testimony and then left. At no time during
his brief appearances in court did Captain Lord ever hear of any charges or

blame being laid against him. It was only on a day in which Lord was not in Court that the outrageous charge was voiced. In spite of his protestations, Lord was blankly refused again and again any opportunity of defending himself, the reason being given that he was only appearing as a witness in the case. As such, Lord was also denied the right to appeal the findings and the door, effectively, was slammed in his face.

Lord had no legal right to call witnesses on his own behalf or to even question witnesses, such as Gill and Groves, who gave such damning evidence against him. As we have seen, the court only introduced the now infamous question 27, which asked what ships, if any, were in a position to come to the assistance of the Titanic, to which Lord was not allowed to respond or challenge. This virtual 'gagging' of Lord should have shown what the inquiry obviously was – a sheer and utter farce which denied a man his basic and constitutional legal rights, but it apparently did not matter. The scapegoat was ensnared and no amount of wiggling was going to let him slip through the closely-wound net. Both courts saw fit to overlook the fact that British and American legal tradition 'guaranteed' that a person on whom charges may be made is entitled to be made aware of these pending charges and that he is given sufficient time in which to prepare a defence against such charges. This basic and legal right was manifestly denied to Captain Lord and must therefore be seen as a violation of his rights. On this basis alone the findings of both inquiries, in respect of Lord's alleged involvement, should have been declared null and void, and this issue also must stand as a total disgrace which led to an obvious gross miscarriage of justice.

REFERENCES

1   The Dictionary of National Biography was later to record of Lord Mersey: 'As a judge, he showed the ability that was expected of him, though he was inclined to the failings of those whose minds work quickly. Disliking tedious arguments, and full of robust common sense, he often took a short cut'.

SEVEN

Stanley Lord:
Man and Mariner

What sort of man was Stanley Lord? Was he the heartless ogre depicted in countless books and films? This question has been asked many times, and perhaps nobody is better qualified to give a deeper insight into the man than his own son, Stanley Lord Junior, now also deceased. In a reply to a request for information concerning his father, in respect of research for this book, and the affair which was later to become known as the 'Californian Incident', Mr Lord kindly responded:

> April 15th 1990. With regard to your request for information on the Titanic and the Californian affair, there is little if anything, now remaining, that has not been scrutinised and included in one or other of the many books dealing with the incident that have been published during the passage of time. Turning to father's life at sea and later at home, I feel that there is little that would be of sufficient interest to warrant inclusion in your book, but I will mention a few incidents which may be of some use to you.
>
> It has always astonished me why anybody could have the desire to go to sea especially at the time my father set off on his first voyage. He was apprenticed to Walmsley's who were, in those far off days, owners of a large sailing ship fleet based in Liverpool. I remember my father showing me their office, off Chapel Street in Liverpool many years ago. It was all dirty and desolate, the windows which remained intact were covered with the accumulated dirt of many years – from which I got the impression that half the rats in Liverpool had taken up their abode inside the crumbling facade. However, it was not like that when father went there with his parents in May 1891 to start his sea-going career. He was the youngest of the four apprentices at the tender age of 13 years. His ship – the Naiad (which was a small sailing ship) was better known as the 'Diving Belle' of Liverpool, due to her somewhat alarming

ability to ship more of the ocean than was comfortable to have on board. The voyage, I believe, was to Iquique and Valparaiso and, by the time they arrived at Staten Island it was Christmas Eve. They had taken an unfortunate pig named Oscar on board of whom they all became very fond of and, when the poor thing was killed by the cook for their Christmas dinner, the Yuletide feast was not enjoyed by any of the diners.

After encountering tremendous seas in their endeavour to get around the Horn, much to their astonishment they sighted the light on Staten Island again four weeks later. After considerable perseverance and not a little good luck, they achieved their aim and sailed into the tempestuous waters of the Pacific and continued their journey north. On arrival at Valparaiso, more or less intact, the captain of the Naiad found that a friend of his was also there and he paid him a visit – being rowed to the other sailing ship by the four apprentices. Whilst the two old boys were presumably enjoying themselves drinking and chatting, the exhausted rowers were making friends with the apprentices on the host vessel, one of who later became the celebrated explorer, Sir Ernest Shackleton (and, who, ironically enough, was to give evidence to the British Inquiry many years later). The return voyage appears to have been uneventful and they arrived at Liverpool via Swansea after 18 months at sea with, I think certainly with father, the fate of poor Oscar still in their minds.

Father continued in sail for some time until he managed to get a job with the West Indian Pacific Line due to his determination and good luck. It was Christmas and he had been home with his mother in Bolton for the holidays. She, quite naturally I think, wanted him to stay until the New Year but he would not do so as he thought that the prospects of getting a job were much better during the holiday time – which proved to be correct. He came back to Liverpool on Boxing Day and to his great delight found that a post was vacant with the WIPL, who were short of a second mate. As far as I can remember, a first mate's ticket was required for the post and father only had a second mate's. During the interview the Marine Superintendent said to father; 'You look very young you know for this job, and we really wanted somebody older and with the requisite qualifications for it.' Father pointed out that he was getting older every day and that drawback would soon be remedied, to which observation the old boy said; 'Well, as we are unable to get anybody else, I suppose we shall have to take you.' His determination had been successful and that is how he made his debut in steam where he remained. In January 1901, he remained home for his Master's and Extra Master's certificate which he obtained at the early age of 23 years – just a few months short of being at sea for 10 years.

On the night of the disaster, as I expect you will know, the Californian warned the Titanic that they had stopped and were surrounded with ice, only to be told to keep out as they were working Cape Race; a little while after which the Californian's operator – it was only the second voyage that wireless had been installed on the vessel – took off the earphones to have a rest on his bunk. As the Californian was now stationary, and he had been on his feet for something like twenty-four hours, father went into the chartroom for a rest after having told the officer on watch to call him if he thought it was necessary. Once in the warm and comfortable surroundings of the chartroom, and being weary, he quite understandably I think, dozed off. At about 6.00 in the morning he went up to the bridge and sent the apprentice (Gibson) down to the wireless cabin to instruct the operator to see what was going on. He, putting on the earphones, heard that the Titanic had gone down. The Californian was immediately started on the journey to the site of the disaster, a journey which was to take until 8.30 a.m. when passengers on the Carpathia saw her appearing over the horizon.

During the precarious journey through the ice – which could never have been accomplished during the night – the Californian saw a vessel with a pink funnel away to the west which I believe was the Almerian and later came upon the CPR [Canadian Pacific Railway] liner, the Mount Temple, neither of which was showing any interest in what had happened during the night. The Californian went towards the Mount Temple thinking she was the Carpathia – they all had one funnel and four masts, as it seemed most liners in those days had – and, when she realised that the ship was not the Carpathia, the Californian went in search of that vessel leaving the Mount Temple stationary and not making any attempt to be of assistance whatever. The role of the Mount Temple I cannot understand, being so much nearer than the Californian to where the Titanic had sunk and to fail to receive the wireless call for help or to fail to see any rockets seems quite extraordinary and although the passengers said that they had seen rockets, not to have gone to the assistance of the ship.[1]

Regarding the Inquiry, Lord Mersey was, from the beginning, completely hostile and biased and on one occasion turned to Rufus Isaacs and remarked that it was in his mind that the ship seen from the Titanic was the Californian, adding, 'Get it out if you can', which is hardly the remark one would expect from the impartial president of any Inquiry. Another observation which caused my father considerable annoyance was made by Rufus Isaacs when he said that it would not do to enquire too closely into what was going on in the chartroom and captain's cabin that night, the innuendo being of course that they were all drinking. As my father was all but teetotal I think you will appreciate the irritation such a remark caused, so much so, that he wrote to Isaacs drawing his attention to the displeasure the remark occasioned. The reply he received is what you might expect, that Mr Isaacs (he had not then been ennobled) was out of the country and no correspondence was being forwarded. However, Mr Isaacs did not remain out of the country for the rest of his life, but he never bothered to reply to that letter. The mud that was stirred up had stuck and a book was published in Germany about 1922, having a chapter in which it was stated that father and the officers were indulging in whisky drinking in his cabin. I received a letter from America in which the writer expressed his astonishment to learn that father had never been back to sea again as he (the writer) was under the impression that father had gone to London where he lived in the slums – I do not know why he picked on the slums of London as there are plenty much more conveniently situated – where he drank himself to death. This shows the havoc the innuendo contained in a completely irresponsible remark can cause, irreparably, to the reputation of an innocent person. I believe that this remark was made when father was not present to contradict Isaacs, but on his way back from Halifax.

One woman – now dead – said that she saw the Californian sail by so close that she was able to see the passengers walking on the deck, but, when asked how she knew it was the Californian, she said that she recognised it because it had two funnels and two masts. When it was pointed out to her that the Californian only had one funnel and four masts – as did the Mount Temple and the Carpathia – she remarked that it made no difference! It was the Californian. In actual fact, on that particular voyage the Californian had no passengers and if there had been any on board they would hardly have been walking on the deck at midnight in what was a bitterly cold night.

Father was at sea during the whole of World War I, occupied in transporting horses – poor creatures – to Europe for the Army and I have some letters here he received from the Allied Transport Authority congratulating him on the excellent condition the animals were in on arrival and the very low mortality rate among them. Some of course, did succumb – the lucky ones – and were buried at sea. I have here the hoof of one of these which one of the cowboys in charge of the animals mounted on a stand which formed an inkwell, and which he gave to father. On the front of the hoof is carved the poor animal's number which was '53' and I often wonder what that horse looked like.

Sir John Latta often discussed the Titanic affair with father and on one occasion after their talk, remarked; 'Well, Captain, if you had been in command of one of my ships that time, you would not have been sacrificed to public opinion as you were then.' On his retirement from the Nitrate Producers SS Co. – Sir John Latta's firm, with whom he had an excellent association from the very beginning, so much so that Latta, when he brought out his newest and largest ship, the Anglo-Chilean, he gave father command of her, although he was the youngest captain there and also the least senior in service – he played golf which so many retired people do. The idea that is prevalent that his career was ruined after the 1912 affair is not correct and he did very much better with Latta than he would have done had he remained with Leyland's. As for the effect the Titanic disaster had on him personally, I think that it was minimal as the years went along. He never brooded on the assertion that he could have saved the lives of the Titanic's passengers as his conscience was quite clear that, if he had known – which has been suggested he did – but would not risk his ship going through the ice – he would never have been able to reach the stricken liner in time. In all probability, I think, the Californian would have joined the Titanic on the bottom. As for the light that was seen from the Titanic moving towards her and then receding into the night, it could scarcely have been from the Californian stationary some 19 to 20 miles away, and not, as Lord Mersey maintained, just eight miles.

I hope all this will be of some interest to you but there is nothing remaining now of outstanding interest or importance that has not been examined and written about sometimes incorrectly and with exaggeration.

Yours sincerely,
Stanley Lord

At the time of the Titanic-Californian affair, Captain Lord, at thirty-five years of age, had been at sea for a total of twenty-one years and attained his present position of master after a relatively short time, insofar as these responsible and important positions are usually attained. Rated a first-class officer, Lord achieved his Extra Master's Certificate while he was just twenty-three years old, a considerable achievement for one so young. One year later he became a fully-fledged master of a passenger/cargo liner. From day one, Lord was a thorough professional at his job and carried it out to the letter.

Strangely enough, Captain Lord was judged, not only on the highly questionable charges laid against him at the British and American inquiries, but also, amazingly, on the basis of his photograph! It is of course human

A typical sailing vessel making 'heavy going' around the turn of the century.

nature for people to form opinions, usually incorrectly, when judging a photograph of somebody they have never met, and this was yet another aspect drawn upon and utilised by the press sensationalists of the day. Many of the photographs taken of Lord, generally at sea, came across as depicting a very stern-faced individual, with his expression suggesting that he could be bitter and hard. His face generally gave the impression that here was a man who would brook no nonsense from any quarter. A glance at just one of these photographs (p. 188) would seem to confirm this view. However, to actually believe that it is possible to judge a person's character from a photograph is bordering on the absurd. There is no doubt that Hitler and his cohorts often came across as a benign and kind old gentlemen in some of their photographs. All of us, at some stage, have had photographs taken which made us look stern, bitter, austere, foolish or even downright idiotic! Nevertheless, the most uncomplimentary photographs of Lord were used in the press to give added credence to the image of a monster in human clothing.

Captain Lord, Master of the Anglo
Chilean, at sea c.1924. Although it
was twelve years since the Titanic
disaster, this is the photograph most
favoured by the 'sensationalists'.
Courtesy of Stanley Lord Jnr

Stanley Lord's son referred to his father as 'a kind and loving father' and
this he undoubtedly was. He was also a very brave and compassionate person as is instanced by his action aboard the Anglo-Chilean. Frank John
Goodchild was an apprentice aboard that ship when he slipped and fell
many feet into the hold of the vessel. Under normal circumstances a ship's
captain would have detailed somebody to go to the assistance of the injured
man and tend to him. Not so with Captain Lord. He immediately clam-
bered over the side of the gaping hold and lowered himself down to the
injured youth where he lifted him and cradled him in his arms until medical
help arrived. Fortunately the young man survived the accident and both he
and his grateful parents were to become lifelong friends of Captain Lord.

Not only did Senator Smith's and Lord Mersey's irresponsible remarks
cause Lord great personal distress and humiliation, but he was also forced
to give up command of the Californian and resign from the company. In
spite of the fact that his employers, the Leyland Line, supported him fully
and were also convinced of his innocence, it was one of the directors of the
Leyland Line at the London headquarters, Miles Walker Mattinson, K.C.,
who demanded Lord's resignation.

However, Lord's employers did not desert him completely. Just a few months later, thanks to the efforts of some of his former superiors, Lord was once again in command of a medium-sized 4,263-ton ship, the Anglo-Saxon. His new employers were the shipping company of Lawther Latta and, in the person of the chairman of this company, Sir John Latta, Captain Lord found, not only an employer, but a true friend. Such was the confidence and trust that Sir John placed in Lord that when his largest, and last, ship was ready for her maiden voyage, he had no hesitation about appointing Captain Lord as master. It was perhaps, Sir John's way of showing that London director of the Leyland Line that he had faith and confidence in Lord's ability as a responsible ship master.

Serving to reinforce Captain Lord's inbred caution, when the Anglo-Chilean did make her maiden voyage from Sunderland to the Clyde, the First World War had started and the ship, in effect, was about to sail through what could be described as dangerous waters, from the point of view of submarines and mines. Captain Lord wrote to Sir John on this very point and set out the dangers possibly involved in the trip. The reply was typical of a man who has placed every confidence in the ability of another. He told Captain Lord to 'deal with the ship exactly as if she were your own property'. Lord did just that and the ship arrived safely at her destination. Remaining with the company, Lord served throughout the war with great dignity and honour, and continued to do so until his retirement in March of 1927 when he was almost aged fifty. He had spent the preceding thirty-six years at sea, fourteen of them with invaluable service to the Latta Company, who had placed its faith in him when so many others saw fit to castigate him.

Captain Lord was, as we have seen from the letter of his son, devoted to animals, a trait which his son obviously inherited. His compassion in this respect is evidenced by his remarks when his dog, Jerry, Labrador/Airedale cross, had to be put to sleep due to old age. The captain refused to delegate this unenviable task to anybody else and he brought the dog to the vet himself for the final injection. When he returned home he told his family how he had held on to the dog's paw until he was gone. 'I cried a bit then, you know,' he said. The memory of his faithful old companion lingered and when, almost thirty years later, the captain himself was nearing his end, he still recalled his old friend: 'Ah ... dear old Jerry ... he was one of the family.' A few moments later he quietly said, 'I think I will go home now.' Then, settling himself comfortably in the bed, he drifted into his final sleep.

A relaxed Stanley Lord in
New York in 1921. He was
clearly a man with nothing
on his conscience – hardly the
face of an 'uncaring drunkard'
and 'callous murderer'.
Courtesy of Stanley Lord Jnr

No longer would the lies, the slander, the speculation or the innuendos
assail his mind or soul. He died quietly with pride and dignity, confident of
a berth in the great beyond. Such is a fitting reward for a man with no guilt
on his soul.

From the time he retired from the sea in 1927 (Lord had married Miss
Mabel Tutton in Walton-on-the-Hill parish church, Liverpool, on 19 March
1907), Captain Lord did not allow the unfortunate circumstances of his connection with the Titanic to intrude on his life. It was only in 1958, forty-six
years after the disaster, when Lord was over eighty years of age that the ugly
spectre of the disaster reared its head and catapulted him, once again, into
the headlines of the world. The situation came about with the publication
of a book by Walter Lord (no relation) entitled *A Night to Remember*. Later,
a movie bearing the same name was made from the book. Almost immediately, both the book and film were enjoying tremendous popularity with
the general public and, although both accurately depicted the final voyage
and loss of the Titanic, they erroneously depicted Lord as the captain who

slept while his ship, a few miles away from and in full sight of the foundering Titanic, did nothing to assist. The fact that the filmmakers cared little
for accuracy is clearly shown in a segment from the film which has Captain
Lord lying in his bunk, semi-clothed and apparently not putting too much
emphasis on the reports being conveyed to him. In fact, as we have seen,
Captain Lord only laid down on the chartroom settee, fully clothed, for a
brief rest, and he only did this after seeing that he had a competent officer
on duty.

The release of the film so incensed Lord that, in spite of his advancing
years, he went immediately to his old union, the Mercantile Marine Service
Association and addressed its then Secretary, Mr Leslie Harrison, with the
words, 'I'm Lord of the Californian and I want to clear my name'.

The association's council began to study the evidence and testimony of
the case and, after meticulous and careful scrutiny of the facts at hand, the
association unanimously agreed that Captain Lord had been brutally treated
at both inquiries. A long and sometimes frustrating battle began. In February
1965, a petition was presented to the Board of Trade requesting that the case
be re-opened. A short extract from just one of the many statements issued
by the association reads:

> Although since 1958 the MMSA at Captain Lord's request has done all that
> it can to defend him by publishing the true facts of the case, it is now clear
> that so long as the findings of the British and American Inquiries remain on
> record there will be writers who will ignore the evidence in Captain Lord's
> favour, and will continue to publish what are often grossly defamatory attacks
> upon him. In the opinion of the Council of the MMSA the findings cannot
> not be upheld and the failure of the Courts to give him proper legal protec-
> tion constituted a miscarriage of justice which permits the Board of Trade to
> order a rehearing.

Although the petition presented a very strong case on behalf of the late
Captain, the reply from the Board of Trade was a familiar rejection and read:

> Your petition does not suggest that there is any new and important evidence
> which could not have been presented/produced at the formal investigation
> into the loss of the Titanic; and the president has asked me to tell you that,
> having carefully considered your petition, he is satisfied that there is no reason
> to believe that a miscarriage of justice has occurred.

Captain Lord with Chin the peke on his lap, Christmas 1961. He died one month later. Courtesy of Stanley T. Lord

This then, was to be the classic reply from the Board of Trade for many years to come. The wording was to change very little over the intervening years. Many a frustrated writer came to the excusable conclusion that the Board of Trade had a special stock of these letters asking for 'new and important evidence' and simply sent them out as and when requests for a re-opening of the case arose. The term became so favoured by the Board of Trade that it was actually included in the Merchant Shipping Act of 1970. Although it was not recognised at the time by the Board, or if it were it was conveniently brushed aside, the inclusion of this very term represented the first chink in the armour of the Board of Trade. They seemed to forget that there was a whole host of information which, for one reason or another, was not produced at either of the initial formal investigations and that some of this data could therefore be considered as 'new and important information'. Following is an extract from the Merchant Shipping Act of 1970:

Rehearing of an appeal from Inquiries and Investigations

57 - 1. Where an Inquiry or formal investigation has been held under the preceding provisions of this Act the Board of Trade may order the whole or part of the case to be re-heard, and shall do so –

a. If new and important evidence which could not be produced at the Inquiry or investigation has been discovered; or –

b. If there appear to the Board of Trade to be other grounds for suspecting that a miscarriage of justice may have occurred.

2. An order under subsection (1) of this section may provide for the re-hearing to be as follows:

a. If the Inquiry or investigation was held in England, Wales or Northern Ireland, by the persons who held it by a wreck commissioner or by the High Court;

b. If it was held in Scotland, by the persons who held it, by the sheriff or by the Court of Session.

3. Any rehearing under this section which is not held by the High Court or the Court of Session shall be conducted in accordance with rules made under section 58 (1) of this Act; and section 56 of this Act shall apply in relation to a re-hearing of an Investigation by a wreck commissioner or sheriff as it applies in relation to the holding of an investigation.

4. Where the persons holding the Inquiry or investigation have decided to cancel or suspend the certificate of any person or have found any person at fault, then, if no application for an order under subsection (1) of this section has been made or such an application has been refused, that person or any other person who, having an interest in the inquiry or investigation, has appeared at the hearing and is affected by the decision or finding, may appeal to the High Court or the Court of Session, according as the inquiry or investigation was held in England, Wales or Northern Ireland or in Scotland.

What a sad state of affairs that this act was not in force when Captain Lord was being castigated on both sides of the Atlantic.

To conclude, perhaps the final word should go to Captain Lord's son. In a television programme commemorating the 50th anniversary of the loss of the Titanic, he was asked if his father would have gone to the rescue of the

Titanic immediately had he known that she was in trouble. His response would have made the old captain proud of his son: 'My father would have gone to the rescue of a tug-boat if he thought it was in danger.'

REFERENCES

1   Mr Lord was quite obviously confused in this aspect. In actual fact the Mount Temple received the distress call shortly after midnight and immediately turned about and set course for the position given. Her distance from the Titanic disaster site was estimated to have been in the region of fifty miles. Arriving at the scene, and being much too late to render any assistance, the Mount Temple cruised the area for some time before resuming her journey. The Mount Temple, Almerian and the Frankfurt could not have been mistaken for any of the 'mystery ships' due to their different positions over the period of the disaster.

EIGHT

New and Important Evidence

Perhaps this is the favourite term of the Department of Transport, formerly the Board of Trade. To the many hundreds of people who made various representations and presented petitions over the years on Captain Lord's behalf, the standard reply was 'new and important evidence'. The obvious question must be asked, why? Surely enough anomalies had been shown to exist in the case over the years to introduce a shadow of doubt? Why then was the Department of Transport continuing to adhere to its old obsession that to re-open the case, or that section of it dealing with the Californian affair, would 'serve no useful purpose'? Were they afraid that to do so would make their department lose credibility and possibly bring into question the reputation of Lord Mersey? Such would seem to have been the case but why, after almost three quarters of a century had passed and all of the central characters had died, was the Department of Transport so obviously opposed to re-opening the case? Could it be that to do so would have caused embarrassment? Did the Department of Transport have some proverbial skeletons in its cupboard, and were they aware that any reappraisal of the evidence would positively show that both Lord Mersey and Senator Smith had both made a frantic rush to judgement that was, even in 1912, highly questionable? In recent years, the Department of Transport's continued refusal to re-open the case became absurd and also contravened subsection A (1) of the Merchant Shipping Act of 1970, in view of the location of the wreck of the Titanic. In spite of this, and being more than aware of the other irrefutable and conclusive evidence surrounding the case, it still adhered to their decision not to re-open it. Not unlike the play Hamlet, something was decidedly 'rotten in the State of Denmark'. It became quite clear that the Department of Transport had no desire to re-open the case, which would have exonerated Lord from the responsibility of coming to the aid of the Titanic's victims.

To do so would have opened a very large can of worms, worms that bite! The suspicion was that if Captain Lord was to be cleared on the charges, then the distinct possibility would arise that the finger of blame just might be pointed in some other direction, their own, perhaps? In any event, the Department of Transport was obviously quite content with the situation as it stood. After all, Lord, the scapegoat, was dead. How could a dead man defend himself?

Fate, which had dealt Captain Lord such a cruel blow, now did likewise to the Department of Transport and served to shake them out of their complacency. The wreck of the Titanic was finally located and immediately an entirely different complexion was put on the whole affair. When the actual location of the wreck became public knowledge on 6 October 1987, it quickly became clear that the distance between the Titanic and the Californian was, as Lord had claimed, about nineteen to twenty miles. Obviously this meant that firstly, Captain Lord could not have reached the sinking ship in time to have been of any assistance and secondly, the ship seen from the Californian could not have been the Titanic, and vice-versa. These facts immediately belied Lord Mersey's assertion that the ships were no more than eight miles apart at the time of the tragedy. Armed with these irrefutable facts, and several other pertinent points, including the section of the Merchant Shipping Act of 1970, it was brought to the attention of the Department of Transport, by the author and other interested investigators, that the department was now compelled to re-open the case in the light of this new and important evidence. Subsequent replies from the Department of Transport were evasive and totally non-committal. Remaining slow to agree with the barefaced facts of the case, they side-stepped, hedged, and, with a lot of official bunkum, managed to postpone the inevitable day of reckoning. In a reply to a letter from the author, calling for a reappraisal in the light of recent events, the Department of Transport replied:

Thank you for your letter of August 11 enclosing feelings on the locating of the wreck of the Titanic to assist the Department in your representations on behalf of the late Captain Lord.

The Department has carefully considered the evidence, including that provided by the finding of Titanic's wreckage, and its conclusions are that you are probably correct in deducing that Californian was in all probability substantially further from Titanic than Lord Mersey found.

Here then, at last, was a tacit admission from the Department of Transport that Lord was 'substantially further from Titanic than Lord Mersey found'. This was to be the second chink in the armour of the department. It was destined to be some time before any further chinks appeared. I had been conducting intensive research into the case of Stanley Lord for far too many years to begin clapping myself on the back and yelling. It was of course, obvious that the department was going to agree with me that the Californian was further from the Titanic than at first thought. It could hardly disagree with me considering the discovery of the wreck. Having graciously granted me this small concession, the letter, dated 1988, went on to say:

> At the same time however, the Department consider it inescapable that Captain Lord did merit a degree of censure. When all possible allowances are made for the common use of company signals, and for the different circumstances of 76 years ago, the fact remains that signals which could have been signals of distress were seen in an area which Captain Lord himself considered hazardous enough to require him to stop his ship until daylight.
>
> In these circumstances the Department consider that to reopen the case would serve no useful purpose and might indeed do more harm than good, and so do not propose to do so.

So, there it was. In spite of the inescapable fact that the Department of Transport now knew, and admitted, that the Californian was not close enough to the Titanic to be of any assistance, it was still content to let the matter lie and, as a consequence, was quite prepared to allow an innocent man's name continue to be sullied. Two intriguing points fascinated me about this letter from the Department of Transport, apart from the fact that several dozen identical letters were sent out to other investigators. The first concerned the question of 'censure'. If, as the department stated, Captain Lord merited some degree of censure, then he, quite obviously, must also have merited the same degree of censure in 1912. In this context it follows that to have merited censure he should have been charged under section six of the Maritime Convention Act (1911). This Act carried a sentence of two years imprisonment, with possible hard labour. Contrary to this, and several other Acts in force at the time, Lord was never actually charged with any crime. In the weeks and months following on the 1912 inquiries, the Board of Trade seemed most anxious for no charges to be brought against Captain Lord, under section six or any other Act. Were they afraid that to bring such charges would, invariably, give Lord the legal redress he was otherwise denied? Had Lord been given the right to defend himself and to call and question witnesses on his own behalf, then there is no doubt that a totally different complexion would have been put on the case. There is also the strong possibility that several members of the Board of Trade and Marine Department were most anxious that their inaction should not come to the attention of the president. The following extracts from two letters of Sir Walter Howell to Captain Young of the Board of Trade files at the Public Record Office, 5 September 1912 would appear to bear out this hypothesis:

> ... I think there is some confusion about this. All the president has decided is that there should be no prosecution (of Captain Lord) under Section 6 of the Maritime Conventions Act and Section 680 of the Merchant Shipping Act, 1894. The point now is whether you think any other action ought to be taken – e.g. under Sections 470 or 471 of the Act of 1894. I am disposed to think not for we shall have to defend inaction and the president must see ... .

Clearly, moves were afoot in the background to ensure that Captain Lord had no course of redress left open to him. The reply to the letter on 8 September 1912:

> In response to your minute of 5th inst., I have given this matter further consideration and note that the solicitor has advised against proceedings under Section 6 of the Maritime Conventions Act, 1911.
>
>   While agreeing generally with the opinions expressed that Captain Lord's fault carries its own punishment, I also agree with your view that we must be in a position to justify, if need be, our inaction. It appears to me that if the Board consider it desirable to carry the matter further the case must fall into Section 470 (b) of the Merchant Shipping Act, 1894 re 'gross act of misconduct' but I think this point is for the solicitor. On the other hand, should the Board consider it desirable to drop the matter, it would perhaps be a sufficient answer to any eventual criticism that the case had been really or already dealt with by the Titanic Court of Inquiry, when Lord Mersey's strictures on Captain Lord's evidence amounted to a tacit condemnation. All things considered, I am inclined to the opinion that the latter course would be the best one to adopt.

'When Lord Mersey's strictures on Captain Lord's evidence amounted to a tacit condemnation.' How officious this statement is when couched in the bewildering language of the dedicated bureaucrat. Put another way, what Captain Young was saying, in a nutshell, was that Lord Mersey didn't believe Captain Lord's testimony and went on to condemn the man with a plethora of groundless suppositions.

The second part of the letter from the Department of Transport which caught my interest was contained in the final paragraph and stated in part: 'to reopen the case would serve no useful purpose and might indeed do more harm than good'. I consider this a profoundly absurd and inane statement. How in heaven's name could re-opening the case serve no useful purpose? It would have utterly exonerated Stanley Lord, and to my way of thinking that would have served quite a useful purpose. The idea that re-opening the case might 'do more harm than good' had me somewhat puzzled. How could it possibly do more harm than good to Captain Lord? Had not the man been castigated, condemned, maligned and labelled a drunken murderer and coward? How then could re-opening the case possibly cause any further harm to this unfortunate man? … Unless of course, the Department of Transport was not alluding to Stanley Lord, but to Lord Mersey's reputation and the questionable findings of the inquiry. Then the statement began to make sense. Could it be possible that Captain Lord's reputation was being sacrificed, yet again, to protect Lord Mersey and his reputation? Apparently so.

In digressing for a moment, it may be recalled that some members of the British cabinet, though the charge was always rigorously denied, were reputed to have been aware of the Japanese intentions to launch an attack on Pearl Harbour during the Second World War, but, aware that such an outrage would invariably bring America into war on the side of the allies, they remained silent on the matter. This is now of course all history and is an issue which may well be open to reasonable argument from various areas. However, if the allegations were true, then it would appear that history was merely repeating itself in circumstances which were almost identical with a still highly controversial incident that happened in the early stages of the First World War.

When the Cunard liner Lusitania was sunk by a torpedo off the southern Irish coast in 1915, with an appalling loss of life, including Americans, it was rumoured that the Lusitania was not only a passenger ship, but also a clandestine munitions ship, carrying a selection of arms and high-explosives in her holds and in several locked cabins. Indeed, the ship itself would seem to provide several clues to reinforce this theory and a distinct basis for truth

emerges when these are closely examined. In 1960 a series of exploratory
dives on the wreck, which is lying in a mere 300ft of water, revealed a massive gaping hole in the side of the ship with jagged edges pointing outwards.
This naturally suggests that a massive explosion took place inside the ship.
Closer examination of this enormous hole concluded that its actual size and
the jagged edges are not consistent with a torpedo detonating against the
ship's plates, in which case the hole would be much smaller and the jagged
edges would have pointed inward. There is also the fact that the Lusitania
sank in just eighteen minutes, causing utter disbelief, not only to the passengers, but also to the commander of the U-boat that had fired the fatal
shot. This lends weight to the suggestion that an exceptionally big explosion took place inside the ship. As in the case of the Titanic, an investigation
into the disaster was held, just as questionable as the Titanic inquiry (chapter six), and the official findings were that the Lusitania was not carrying
any explosive material or arms. There is ample positive evidence that this
inquiry was a rush to judgement as well. The similarities of the proceedings in both inquiries were absolutely striking. It came as no surprise that
the man who conducted this particular inquiry was none other than Sir J.
Charles Bigham, otherwise known as Lord Mersey.

There were many anomalies involved in this inquiry, and the allegation
has frequently been made that Captain Turner of the Lusitania was, among
others, effectively gagged by the Official Secrets Act. Whatever did or did
not occur during the case is of little importance to the matter at hand, but it
is interesting that after the inquiry ended, Lord Mersey, in a private capacity,
declared that the entire affair was 'a damned dirty business' and declined to
accept his fee for the job (see pp. 174-177).

Adding yet further weight to the speculation that the British government had something to hide in the case of the Lusitania is an extract from
the soundtrack of a film which was in the process of being made by an
American television programme called *20/20* in 1982:

> ... To continue the conspiracy theory, when Winston Churchill came back
> to power in the early 1950s, the Admiralty (British Admiralty) commissioned
> several dives in this area. The Royal Navy salvage vessel Reclaim was seen over
> the wreck. The theory goes that the Admiralty either removed or destroyed
> evidence that might have been embarrassing to Winston Churchill or the
> Admiralty or the British Government. The Admiralty denies that scenario,
> but after Oceaneering's survey vessel (an American company) anchored over

the wreck last month, something happened to make the conspiracy theory even more credible. The company's British office received a telex, sent on behalf of the British Ministry of Defence, advising the company to stop its operations. The telex said in part that 'It would be imprudent not to point out the obvious but real danger inherent if explosives did happen to be present. In that unlikely event, you are strongly advised to stop operations and consider your position most carefully.' The telex added: 'The Ministry does not know of any evidence whatsoever that might substantiate rumour of other explosives.' It was the sort of warning [the soundtrack continued] that adds rather than detracts from the suspicion that the British Government had something to hide. And the warning didn't work. This weekend Oceaneering is launching a second more thorough operation, one that will make a complete public search of the ship that helped get America into World War One. They hope their next operation will solve the mystery of the Lusitania once and for all. So, will more evidence be coming up out of the depths?

Whether or not any further evidence ever 'came up out of the depths' was destined to remain a mystery. For some reason not published, there were no more broadcasts from the site of the wreck and all exploratory work stopped abruptly. Had pressure been put on the Oceaneering Company? Did the British Ministry of Defence, or some other government agency, notwithstanding the fact that the wreck was in Irish waters, manage to put a stop to all further operations? To date, these queries are met with a blank wall of silence and disavowal of any knowledge of the incident. Only one thing is apparent at this stage. Clearly the British government was most reluctant to allow people to go poking about in the area. This can only prompt one question – if the British government was afraid of what might be found in the way of evidence in the wreck, would not this fact, assuming that something was found, clearly point to the near certainty that Lord Mersey was under orders to bring in the decision he did? Indeed, food for thought.

There can be little doubt that if it were to be proved that the Lusitania was indeed set up in order to bring the United States into war, the claims against the British government would be staggering. It naturally follows that in such an event it would be reasonable to expect the British government to deny any such knowledge and to keep as low a profile as possible. Indeed, could this be the reason behind the Department of Transport's obvious insistence that no attention should attach itself to Lord Mersey himself in a manner which might bring into the open matters of international controversy? Could this have been the main reason why the department was so reluctant to re-open the case of the Titanic for so many years? Obviously it must have been apparent that to resurrect the case would have the effect of bringing Lord Mersey to the attention of the world once again and possibly instill in somebody, like myself, the necessity to examine the entire circumstances of the sinking of the Lusitania in thorough detail. Was this then the reason for the veiled and rather obscure statement that to re-open the files on Captain Lord might 'do more harm than good'? Such would appear to be the case. It would also appear that the Department of Transport have only succeeded in putting themselves, and as a consequence the British government, into a situation from which it will be difficult, if not impossible, to extricate themselves. An old adage immediately springs to mind: 'Oh, what a tangled web we weave, when first we practice to deceive'.

As if the mountain of circumstantial and outrageous evidence against Lord were not enough for those who sought to condemn him, yet another major discrepancy arose and, like many other points that might have favoured the captain, were totally ignored. In the first instance, the blame for allowing the charge to be laid against Lord must rest with the Board of Trade, not only because it was they who set up the inquiry, but because it was also they who were charged with enforcing the Merchant Shipping Act of 1894. This Act provided safeguards for any shipmaster against whom adverse findings might be recorded by a court of inquiry into a marine casualty. Clearly, in the case of Stanley Lord, these safeguards were not only totally and blatantly ignored, which amounted to an infringement of the captain's legal and democratic rights, but were not even considered by the court in their findings. Again, on this point alone, Lord should have had the charges against him declared null and void.

Subsequent attempts to persuade the Board of Trade to implement these very safeguards were consistently refused, despite forceful and strong arguments by the Mercantile Marine Service Association in 1912, 1913, 1965 and in 1968. Also rejected by the Board of Trade were countless private requests from concerned investigators to have the case re-opened. It soon became evident that the Board of Trade was hedging and had absolutely no intention of becoming involved in a public hearing, which, considering the possible implications involved, could turn into a crisis that might rock the British government to its very foundations. Over the intervening years, two camps of supporters sprung up in connection with the case of Stanley Lord:

The 'Lordites', so called because they firmly believed in the innocence of the captain, and the 'anti-Lordites' who were of the opinion that the original inquiry findings were correct and that Lord was the culprit. As both of these camps numbered several thousands of people, many of them highly placed and influential, the Department of Transport soon found themselves in something of a quandary. Who to please? Ironic to think that all Captain Lord ever wanted was a public statement in the Houses of Parliament to the effect that he was not responsible for the deaths of more than 1,500 people in the Titanic tragedy.

Apparently it never occurred to any of the anti-Lordites, who were so determined to prove Lord guilty, that his actions on that fateful night and morning were consistent with what any responsible ship master would do under the same circumstances. To blame him for inaction is nonsense. He had, as far as he was concerned, a fully competent officer on watch and was receiving reports from him regarding the ship they had observed. He had instructed the officer to try to raise this other ship with the Morse light and, although he received no reply, told his officer to continue with the signals and to let him know if any change occurred. The fact that he lay down on the chartroom settee, fully clothed, for a rest, after almost twenty-four hours on his feet, is something of a moot point. If this were to be given as a cause for the loss of the lives on the Titanic, then the entire ship's officers must also share the blame for 'inaction'. There is also the inescapable fact, as yet not explained by anyone, that if the Titanic was flashing her powerful Morse lamp in an effort to contact the ship she could see some few miles off, and the Californian was doing likewise with her Morse lamp, then how is it that neither saw the other's signals? And this on a night that was reputedly one of the clearest and calmest that many sailors could recall. The reason of course was that the two ships were not in close proximity to each other.

To appreciate the overwhelming odds stacked against Lord at the British inquiry, it is necessary to take a brief look at the formidable selection of solicitors, barristers and counsels who attended. Appearing as the Board of Trade's counsel was Attorney General Rufus Isaacs; KC, the solicitor general, Sir John Simon; KC, Mr Butler Aspinall; KC, Mr S.T. Rowlatt and Mr Raymond Asquith. The legal counsel, representing the White Star Line was, if anything, even a more impressive line-up. Headed by the Right Honourable Sir Robert Finlay; KC, MP, it included Mr Norman Raeburn, Mr F. Laing; KC, and Mr Maurice Hill; KC., all instructed by the firm of Messrs Hill, Dickenson & Co. Mr Thomas Scanlan;

MP, appeared for the National Sailors' and Firemen's Union; Mr Clement Edwards for the Dockers' Union and, finally, and most significantly, Mr C. Robertson Dunlop was allowed only to watch the proceedings in an advisory capacity on behalf of the Californian's owners, master and officers. It would be something of an understatement to say that Lord was sufficiently represented or given much opportunity of defending himself.

Early in the British inquiry it became obvious that something would be required to deflect public opinion and anger away from the Board of Trade and the White Star Line. In this respect, Rufus Isaacs diligently applied his efforts. When the Order for Formal Investigation was read at the inquiry, Isaacs summarised the questions by reading them to Lord Mersey, and yet another blatant and quite successful attempt to blame Captain Lord can quite easily be seen on page 261:

> The questions 1 to 8 inclusive relate to what happened before the casualty and before there is any suggestion or question of a warning that Titanic was approaching ice.
>
> Questions 9 to 14 relate to the suggestion of warning given to the Titanic and ask what was done with regard to lookout or other precautions before the casualty; that is to say, it is suggested by those questions that those responsible for the navigation of the Titanic were warned that they were approaching ice; and then the questions are put in order to ascertain what was done and the Court may answer what it finds as a fact was done by those responsible for the Titanic after they received such warning, if they did receive it.
>
> Then, my Lord, Question 15 is a question relating to the casualty itself.
>
> Questions 16 to 24 relate to the events after the casualty, as to what steps were taken either to save the vessel or to save life.
>
> Then there is a general question, 25, which relates to the construction and equipment of the Titanic as a passenger steamer and emigrant ship for the Atlantic service.
>
> Question 26 relates to the rules and regulations under the Merchant Shipping Acts and the administration of those Acts and the rules and regulations, invites such recommendations or suggestions as the Court may think fit to make with a view to promoting the safety of vessels and persons at sea.

While the foregoing may appear straightforward, our attention is drawn to question twenty four, which states, almost casually, what steps were taken either to save the vessel or to save life. The word 'casually' is used here to

emphasise the seemingly innocent manner in which Rufus Isaacs summarised the questions, and in particular question twenty four. In the written
version this question actually read:

> What was the cause of the loss of the Titanic and of the loss of life which
> thereby ensued or occurred? Was the construction of the vessel and its
> arrangements such as to make it difficult for any class of passengers or any
> portion of the crew to take full advantage of any of the existing provisions for
> safety?

Evidently this question was a bit too specific for comfort and could have
serious implications for both the Board of Trade and the White Star Line. A
little rearranging was called for and duly took place. On 24 June Attorney
General Isaacs proposed a new sentence for insertion between sentences
one and three of question twenty four. The addition to the question read:

> What vessels had the opportunity of rendering assistance to the Titanic, and,
> if any, how was it that assistance did not reach the Titanic before the steam-
> ship Carpathia arrived?

So, effectively, with one stroke of the pen, the attorney general transferred
the blame from the Board of Trade and the White Star Line to Captain Lord
and the Californian. We have seen how this new sentence, and all that it
implied, was introduced to the court on a day when neither Lord, his officers, owners or legal adviser were present. Clearly the wedge was driven in
deeper and the scapegoat was not about to be allowed escape. In order to
lessen the obvious objections from Lord and the owners of the Californian,
the proposed inclusion of this new sentence was brought to the attention of
Mr Robertson Dunlop but he was not informed as to when it would actually be introduced to the court. The ploy had quite clearly been planned
with great care and deliberation and the sentence was duly introduced to
the Court without any fear of objections.

The subsequent findings of the inquiry, almost a carbon copy of the
American investigation was, thanks mainly to the inclusion of the new
sentence and the contradictory evidence of donkeyman Ernest Gill, who,
incidentally was the only rating to give evidence, almost a foregone conclusion. Captain Lord, upon hearing the charges against him immediately
wrote several times to the secretary of the Board of Trade, Walter J. Howell

and asked for his assistance in bringing the truth before the general public. In his letters, Lord pointed out that he had never been officially named as a defendant in the case and, as such, had no effective legal redress. His requests were consistently denied, and it was continuously pointed out to him that because he only appeared as a witness in the case and was not a named defendant, he was therefore not entitled to a hearing of his case. Sadly, the advice given to Lord, by those whose judgement he respected, in 1912 did not cover the initiation of legal action by way of counters to libel or slander. Once the Board of Trade had refused his appeal, the way was effectively barred to instigate any further action by Lord. There is no doubt but that had he been a wealthy man, Captain Lord could have brought a private action against his accusers. As it was, having lost his job, but obtaining another at £20 a month, his financial situation was such that he could not afford to seek legal help. When he was offered a job with the Lawther Latta Line, in early 1913, Lord found it too expensive to make the trip to London where he was required for an interview for the job. Mr Latta volunteered to pay his expenses in the event he was rejected and Lord had to be content with accepting the post by letter. The year of 1912 had been a black one indeed for Stanley Lord and his family, and was but to be the forerunner of many dark and frustrating years.

And so, all avenues of appeal and escape were effectively blocked by the Board of Trade's legal advisers. The situation was to remain that way for almost exactly three-quarters of a century. As we have seen, the many and varied petitions and requests for a re-opening the case were consistently denied, and the Board of Trade resolutely stuck to their decision that the case was absolutely and positively closed. Over the years the case has become both complicated and confused, as fact was liberally mixed with fiction. A whole host of books, films, and press stories, invariably resurrected the tragedy every now and then and gave the matter some imagined embellishments to make it more appealing to the general public. As we have seen, feelings ran so high that two separate camps evolved and often unhealthy rivalry grew to alarming proportions. The observation was made at one stage that the case of the Titanic and the Californian must rate as one of the most controversial and commercially exploited non-events in maritime history.

It now became apparent to the Department of Transport that, since the wreck of the Titanic was located, the supporters of Captain Lord were not just going to go away. In a renewed show of solidarity with Lord, the Department of Transport was once again deluged with requests and demands to re-open the case and, in spite of the fact that the finding of the Titanic's wreck constituted the required 'new and important evidence', the Department of Transport still saw fit to turn down all requests. Nevertheless, undeterred by the unreasonable attitude of the Department of Transport, old stalwarts of the case for Lord continued to assail the relevant offices with mountains of literature and pertinent reasons why the case should be reopened.

It was destined to be almost five long years before yet another chink showed in the armour of the Department of Transport. In the interim, various letters had been sent back and forth with the self-same results. Finally, a lengthy letter sent to the Marine Accident Investigation Branch at the Department of Transport in late April 1990 produced a reply from Deputy Chief Inspector Captain J. de Coverly of Marine Accidents.

We see that while the foregoing letter is almost a carbon copy of the previous letter of 11 August 1988, the department still insists that Lord should merit a degree of censure, the content now seemed to be a little less adamant and even conceded the presence of the sealing ship Samson in the area, as well as even suggesting that the Californian was probably in the order of twenty miles away from the Titanic. This little victory was, in itself, quite heartening, despite the fact that there were still no plans to re-open the case. Acting on this concession from the department's investigation branch, further critical approaches were made, and stepped up. Among the 'new and important evidence' supplied, reference was made to the fact that to warrant 'censure', particularly at the formal investigation in 1912, Captain Lord should have been charged under section six of the Maritime Conventions Act. In addition to this, the second critical approach to the Marine Accident Investigation Branch pointed out the position of the Titanic wreck in relation to the position of the Californian and also raised various anomalies in the formal investigation of 1912, including the lack of effective legal representation for Lord. The point was also emphasised to the chief inspector that the apparent uncompromising attitude of the department would avail them nothing and the problem, now gaining momentum, was highly unlikely to disappear. A similar letter and contents were forwarded to the then secretary of state, The Right Honourable Cecil Parkinson, MP. He too was made aware of the growing support for re-opening the case.

Two weeks passed and finally a brief note arrived from the Marine Accident Investigation Branch of the Department of Transport. It merely acknowledged receipt of my representations and stated that 'the various points you raise are under consideration'. In the interim, further letters of a similar content were forwarded to the American senate pointing out the various facts which the British Department of Transport now, apparently, accepted. Not surprisingly perhaps, the reply from the American senate was a deafening silence. Not even so much as the common courtesy of an acknowledgement was received. Undeterred, yet another letter was sent to the American embassy in Dublin and, eventually, a brief note arrived which completely ignored the contents of the letter they had received and which contained the addresses of two Titanic societies in America. Clearly the Americans just weren't interested. Stubborn to the last, yet another letter was sent off to Dr Robert Ballard for his remarks, despite the fact that Dr Ballard found the wreck and was still of the opinion that Lord was guilty, and, again, no reply. It was on 20 June 1990, in a letter from the Marine Accident Investigation Branch, that the long-awaited breakthrough finally came.

So, at long last the almost unbelievable had happened and the long-awaited re-opening of the case was about to become reality. Almost overnight, the long and frustrating years seemed to melt away and uncertainty became a thing of the past. The almost countless files, documents, and other reams of literature concerning the case, and which took up one whole room, at last appeared to have served their purpose. It had been a long and often thankless battle, but at last the seeds of many years' work were about to bear fruit. I was aware that even though the Department of Transport did not see fit to give a reason for their apparent 'volte face' on the matter, it was, no doubt, all due to the relentless pressure brought to bear over numerous years by countless investigators whose magnificent support of the captain finally brought about this overdue situation.

Even more encouraging was the fact that the reappraisal was not to be conducted by a politician, who might be ignorant of maritime matters, but by a man who had recently retired from the highly prestigious position of Principal Nautical Surveyor with the Marine Department. A retired mariner himself, Captain Barnett duly impressed me with his practical approach to the new hearing and certainly did not give the impression that he would rush to judgement but deal with the case in a thorough and meticulous way. Justice, it seemed, was almost in sight for Captain Lord. News of the breakthrough spread quickly and the desk of this humble merchant of words soon began to resemble a clearing-house for official documents. Enquiries came from as far away as Sydney in Australia, America, Sweden, Germany, England, Italy and Scotland, to name but a few. Radio, press and television suddenly began to take note of this determined Irishman. I accepted invitations to appear on BBC television, as well as various radio programmes, both at home and abroad. Suddenly, after what seemed like a lifetime of literary obscurity, I was the 'flavour of the month', and, being only human, I must say that the sudden attention was very much to my liking!

Upon initially receiving news of the reappraisal, I immediately contacted Mr Stanley T. Lord and extended to him my congratulations. It was the first enjoyable aspect of the affair that I had enjoyed for many years. I added a postscript to the letter to the effect that I was about to award myself a very large brandy to celebrate the welcome news. The reply from Mr Lord was both complimentary and humorous. It read, in part: 'I was glad to see that you intended to celebrate the news by having several large brandies after which I hope you were able to remain on an even keel. I joined in the fun by drinking some extra cups of coffee.' Just six days later, 26 June, the expected letter from Captain Barnett arrived. Upon reading the letter from Captain de Coverly, I became slightly apprehensive to note that the captain clearly stated that, amazingly, he knew very little about the Titanic tragedy and that he intended to refer to source material to assist him in his work. This, to my mind, could well have proved a disaster to the case. I immediately wrote to Captain Barnett and brought some pertinent points to his attention:

July 5th, 1990
Dear Captain Barnett,

I would at the outset like to express my deep satisfaction that the evidence surrounding the late Captain Stanley Lord is to be finally reappraised. I take this opportunity of introducing myself to you and of looking forward to a mutually successful outcome to the impending investigation.
Suffice it to say that I have been conducting extensive research into the case of Captain Lord for quite some considerable time and, to date, I have amassed a substantial quantity of relevant literature which I shall be only too pleased to put at your disposal.
I enclose, as requested, a copy of the Henrick B. Naess statement concerning the sealing ship, Samson.
Initially, I should inform you that the Department of Transport – as per their letter to myself, via Captain de Coverly, on May 14th 1990 – now accept

the presence of the Samson in the area of the Titanic on the night, and/
or morning of April 14/15 1912. Likewise, the Department now also accept
that the Californian was 'Substantially further from Titanic than Lord Mersey
found – probably of the order of 20 miles'. I feel that these are two highly
important points which you bear in mind while conducting your investigation.

In view of these two points, which clearly refute Lord Mersey's assertion
that the Californian was within 5 to 8 miles of the Titanic, I must point out
to you that this is an admission by the Department of Transport that, in fact,
Captain Lord could not have come to the rescue of the Titanic or its passengers and crew in the 55 minutes available to him between being informed of
the rockets and the ship subsequently foundering. This, as you will no doubt
appreciate, would have been a human impossibility.

My reason for alluding to these points is that I note you shall be referring
to the Wreck Commissioner's Court Minutes of Evidence and the Report of
the Formal Investigation. It is widely held that the aforementioned sources
may be considered both unfair and unconscionable and in this respect I
would strongly and respectfully urge extreme caution in referring to these
documents.

During the coming weeks I shall be referring to your terms of reference on
a point-by-point basis and would advise you of this fact at the outset. I shall (a)
be sending you the position of the Titanic when that ship struck the iceberg
(the stated position and the actual position of impact) and, (b) the position of
the Californian on the dates in question. This information will enable you to
form an opinion as to the actual distance that existed between both ships.

I shall prove beyond all reasonable doubt that the Titanic could not have
been seen from the Californian and vice-versa.

With regard to the question of 'distress signals', I would respectfully offer
a word of caution and advise that when approaching this particular aspect of
the case, it will be necessary to view rockets/distress signals through the eyes
of 1912 (when such rockets/signals had many and varied meanings) rather
than through the eyes of the present day. I shall be sending you a brief note on
the colours and various uses of these rockets/signals as operated in 1912.

I am of the opinion – and shall prove – that the action taken by Captain
Lord during the times specified and indeed, at all other times, was highly
regarded and was in keeping with the action of a competent mariner. I may
also add that in spite of this unfortunate incident, Captain Lord remained to
be highly regarded as an officer and a gentleman.

While the foregoing are but a few of the points I may wish to bring to your attention in the future, I would greatly appreciate it if you would kindly keep me informed of your progress and arrange to let me have a copy of your report when you have completed your investigation.

In the interim I shall wish you every success with your undertaking and look forward to seeing justice being carried out at long last.

I shall look forward to hearing from you in due course.

Yours sincerely,
Thomas B. Williams

A little under three weeks later I received a brief acknowledgement from Captain Barnett.

Other pertinent papers and documents were duly forwarded to Captain Barnett. I also informed him of my further intention of sending him a rather bulky file which would, invariably, take time to read and absorb. The Captain duly acknowledged receipt of this data on 9 August and, in reply to a query concerning the possible duration of the investigation, said that he was unable at that time to give any indication of when the reappraisal would be completed. I had more or less thrown in this question to see if it was the intention of the captain to merely 'go through the motions' of a reappraisal in order to appease public interest. His reply satisfied me that he was undertaking a thorough investigation of the case and that he would not be rushed into making his final decisions. There was no more for me to do but sit down and await the verdict. Time would tell all.

The re-opening of the case naturally sparked off renewed interest in the whole affair and almost overnight articles began to appear both in favour of, and against Captain Lord. On many a publication the allegation was made that a researcher could prove anything he wants by merely selecting his facts carefully and ignoring those which do not suit his purpose. While this observation would appear to be an honest comment, the point is that it works equally well for those in opposition as well.

Apparently, in the case of the anti-Lordites, many writers simply chose to 'forget' the basic facts of the case and likewise the evidence. To this day, not one supporter of Lord's alleged guilt has been able to answer just this one question truthfully: If , as stated by Lord Mersey and Senator Smith, there were only two ships involved in the affair, the Titanic and Californian, and if, as also stated by these gentlemen, the ships were in reasonable proximity to each other, why then didn't they see each other's Morse signals? Of all the points raised in the case of the Titanic and the Californian, if this one single question cannot be answered truthfully, then any future literature concerning Lord's involvement with the White Star liner must surely see the captain for what he undoubtedly was – a scapegoat and a pawn in the world of big business and dirty politics.

Among the many letters which reached me in the weeks after the news had become public was one from a member of the British Titanic Society. The writer, expressing a personal opinion, was outraged that any reappraisal at all had been sanctioned. His furious letter read, in part: 'Personally, whatever the outcome or findings of the inquiry, I think that Captain Lord was a disgrace to British seamanship, and his activities, or rather, inactivity was unforgivable.' This gentleman had obviously made up his mind as to Captain Lord's guilt and it was clear that no amount of hard evidence or cold facts was about to alter his opinion or bring about a change of mind. This man's stance on the matter only served to exemplify the attitude of countless other like-minded people who had put up the shutters in their minds. In many cases this attitude arrives by too little knowledge of the affair and, in others, by an often childish stubbornness to alter a long-held belief.

While the interested parties awaited the results of the new inquiry, speculation and conjecture began to mount. The entire case was regurgitated once again in the press and on television, and more than a few experts gave their views on the possible outcome of the case. For myself, I had but one view, arrived at after years of painstaking research and careful attention to the minutest detail, that Lord would be exonerated. Considering the wealth of evidence in his favour, there was absolutely no doubt of this in my mind. Nevertheless, the waiting became nerve-racking and the many and frequent letters arriving from people of opposing beliefs did nothing to soothe my rising impatience. I had spent years on the case, and writing about the Titanic in general, and I was anxious to move on to something else. Weeks began to turn into months. The only information emanating from the Marine Accident Investigation Branch of the Department of Transport was a series of brief notes explaining that it would be some time before the findings were released to the public. 'Pressure of work' became the most commonly used reason, and it soon became apparent that all I could do was wait, and wait and wait. It was destined to be a long wait. More than a year passed and still no word came from the Department of Transport. Time dragged on and was now approaching the second year mark.

My approaches to the Marine Accident Investigation Branch now took on a more forceful import. It soon became obvious to me that the delay was quite deliberate, and I was not alone in this opinion. Even Captain Lord's son voiced his displeasure at the inordinate delay and, like myself, was of the opinion that the delay was indeed deliberate. At one stage, the impression was given that the results were to be indefinitely postponed, as it had been almost two years since the case was re-opened. A respectable-sized World War had started and ended. The secretary of state had been replaced. The leadership of the Conservative Party had changed hands, and still the fate of Captain Lord's reputation hung in the balance. Towards the end of February 1992, I had been informed unofficially by one of my sources, who was usually reliable, that the expected date for publication of the new findings was to be in mid-May, after the 80th anniversary of the tragedy.

I had myself reconciled to this date when out of the blue, on 31 March, I received an urgent telephone call from Granada Television to the effect that the findings of the inquiry were due to be released on the following Thursday, 2 April. The news of the impending release had obviously been leaked to the media as, a little over an hour later, I received an invitation to attend at the RTE radio studios on the day in question and take part in an interview about the affair, an invitation I accepted with alacrity.

For the next two days the telephone did not stop ringing. I was bombarded with a multitude of questions, some of them ridiculous, and asked if I was absolutely certain that Lord would be found not guilty of the charge against him. Indeed, on this very point I began to have reservations, in as far as the Department of Transport's Marine Accident Investigation Branch might couch their wording of the findings. In spite of the fact that I remained resolutely confident of Lord's innocence, I worried that something unforeseen might happen and cause all sorts of complications. I continually reminded myself that having conceded that the Californian was about twenty miles from the Titanic, then the Department of Transport could not condemn Captain Lord or blame him for the deaths of all those people. Yet I was worried. I was only too aware that the Department of Transport did not wish to antagonise either the Lordites or the anti-Lordites by their decision. I then suspected that their report would attempt to appease both factions. Nevertheless having arrived at this conclusion, I began to wonder exactly how they would arrive at a fair conclusion and still be seen to be impartial. Why was the publication date brought forward by almost six weeks? Could it possibly have anything to do with catching a few extra votes (the British were in the middle of a general election) or was it an effort to have the report published, and for sale, in time for the 80th anniversary of the sinking? Obviously the forthcoming anniversary would be attended by several hundreds, if not thousands, of people. If the report was available, then it would clearly be snapped-up like hot cakes at £7.50 a time.

I didn't sleep much during the next two nights. I began to fret and worry. Something was going to go wrong. I knew it! Everything was just too pat, too smooth. There were bound to be complications. Nothing ever worked out exactly as we wanted it. My brain was assailed with doubts and agitation. I could hardly wait for Thursday. I had spent the past year nursing my terminally-ill wife in her fight against cancer and, after her untimely death, had been desperately attempting to get life back to some semblance of normality for my five children and myself. Being so involved, emotionally and otherwise, was there some vital piece of evidence that I had omitted to include in my representations to the Marine Accident Investigation's inspector? I mentally began to run through the case and finally declared myself satisfied that I had forgotten nothing. Now all I could do was wait. The next forty-eight hours would tell all.

On Thursday morning, 2 April, I sat, on tenterhooks, in the RTE studios awaiting a fax on the report. When it finally came my worst fears were realised, as my instinct and convictions proved to have been correct. The report was, to say the least, ambiguous. Although Captain Lord had been effectively exonerated, it was evident that the findings of the inquiry were seriously divided on the issue. The department had, not surprisingly, chosen to sit on the fence. On the one hand, the investigation found that the Titanic's distress signals were seen and that no proper action was taken. This, I realised, would probably satisfy the anti-Lordites and give them scope for further attacks on Lord. But on the other hand, the department went on to say that any reasonable action by Captain Lord would not have led to a different outcome to the tragedy, as the Californian would have arrived on the scene well after the Titanic had sunk. This section of the report was, clearly, a very begrudging exoneration of Captain Lord, but it did acknowledge the fact that he could not be held responsible for the deaths of the victims. In view of this admission, I felt that this section of the report automatically invalidated the previous statement that no action had been taken. Clearly, if Lord could not have altered the outcome of the disaster by any actions of his, then the reference to 'no action' was something of a moot point. So why include it in the report? Pointing out this aspect in the subsequent radio interview, I declared myself to be 'reasonably satisfied' with the outcome. I had, after all, succeeded in proving that Lord was not responsible for the deaths of the victims of the disaster, and this was all that the captain himself ever wanted to establish. (See summarized text (fax) on pp. 128-129).

It was to be a little over a week later when, courtesy of Captain Marriott, chief inspector of the Marine Accident Investigation Branch, that I received a complimentary copy of the full report. I was absolutely amazed to read that even in this supposedly impartial document, the inspector appointed (Captain Barnett) by the MAIB to study the evidence, and who, we will recall, stated that he knew very little about the Titanic tragedy, actually stated that the formal investigation report of 1912 was correct in deducing that the Californian and the Titanic were no more than between five and seven miles apart. In view of this almost unbelievable deduction, I formed the conclusion that Captain Barnett, like so many others, had swallowed the assertions of Lord Mersey and Senator Smith in their entirety. How anyone, much less a highly experienced mariner, could arrive at this conclusion in view of the facts was quite beyond me. Apparently, the chief inspector and the deputy chief inspector agreed with my conclusions and both stated that the Californian was in the region of seventeen to twenty miles away from the Titanic when she foundered. On this point, the chief inspector found it necessary to inform the secretary of state of the varying views relating to the case (copy of letter on page 125 (bottom)), and the differences of opinion were included in the full twenty-page report.

The results of the inquiry were given quite different connotations by the newsreaders on television. Some stations took the outlook that the 1912 findings had been upheld, while others declared that Lord had been exonerated. Obviously, the confusion had resulted in the paragraph which first stated that 'no action' had been taken, and then had gone on to say that Lord could not have arrived in time anyway. However, I was able to point out, in the radio studios, the fact that Captain Lord had been exonerated of any blame in connection with the deaths of 1,500 people and, as a consequence, the Irish newsreaders couched their reports in the correct manner.

Needless to say, the ensuing years saw a considerable amount of discussion and controversy arising as a result of this case. Nevertheless, one inescapable fact remains – Stanley Lord was found not guilty of the charge of leaving 1,500 people to die. Many more questions were raised in connection with Lord's actions that night. Why, for example, when he was told about the rockets, did he not rouse his wireless operator and ascertain what was going on? Had he done so, would it have made any difference to the outcome? Apparently not, considering the distance involved and the prevailing conditions of darkness and ice. As to exactly why Lord did not see fit to call his wireless operator that morning, we can only use conjecture and that would avail us nothing. We will simply have to accept Lord's insistence that he had a competent officer in charge and that he was continually attempting to raise the other ship by Morse lamp. The main implications of the reappraisal were that Captain Lord had been publicly exonerated from any complicity in the deaths of the unfortunate victims of the Titanic tragedy and the open wounds of eighty years were from then on allowed to heal for all time, at least officially.

Marine Accident Investigation Branch
Department of Transport
5/7 Brunswick Place
Southampton
Hants So1 2AN

12 March 1992

The Right Honourable Malcolm Rifkind QC MP
Secretary of State for Transport

Sir,
Your predecessor, The Right Honourable Cecil Parkinson MP, determined that MAIB should carry out a reappraisal of the role played by SS Californian at the time RMS Titanic was lost in 1912.

Clearly, the case was somewhat outside the ordinary run of MAIB investigations and, in order to avoid its clashing with our main work, an Inspector from outside the Branch was appointed to study the evidence and advise me of his conclusions, after which a Report would be prepared. The Officer appointed to this task had recently retired from a post as Principal Nautical Surveyor in the Department of Transport Marine Survey Service and is a very experienced Master Mariner. I do not fully agree with all the Inspector's findings but this does not mean that I have any doubt at all as to either the thoroughness of his enquiries or the fair-mindedness of his approach. It rather serves to emphasize the difficulty of the task he was set and of reaching absolute conclusions.

However, I considered that some further examination was required and I instructed the Deputy Chief Inspector of Marine Accidents to undertake this and report to me. His report, which follows, incorporates his conclusions and those of the appointed Inspector.

I fully endorse the Deputy Chief Inspector's report and conclusions.

I am, Sir,
Your obedient servant

Captain P.B. Marriott
Chief Inspector of Marine Accidents

The fact that it took eighty years for justice to prevail in the case of Stanley Lord is, needless to say, to be deplored, in the context that the case should have been re-opened many years ago. The fact that an innocent man was made to suffer the agony and humiliation of a common criminal all the remaining days of his life is something for which those responsible should forever be ashamed. The guilt for condemning this man must also reach out and touch the governments of America and Norway, whose representatives effectively initiated the lifetime of misery and castigation for Captain Lord.

Although the battle on this side of the Atlantic was won, the fight will continue until Stanley Lord is exonerated in the eyes of the American people and they too accept the fact that Captain Lord was as much a victim of the Titanic tragedy as the unfortunates who lost their lives.

In concluding, this book it would be amiss not to make reference to the other second 'mystery ship' in the saga. After many years of painstaking and meticulous research into this aspect, I am now totally satisfied that the identity of this ship is to be found in the two and a half miles of maritime files on the eastern seaboard of North America. I was not allowed access to them. Even if X's and Z's logbooks are kept there, they, like the Californian's, may not mention anything. The question was put to Mr Leslie Harrison why the Californian's logbook did not have any mention of the rockets. The gist of the reply was that as Californian had not responded there was no legal reason for such an entry and that it was optional in the 'remarks' area. Second Officer Stone may well have noted something in the scrap log but presumably because of the above Chief Officer Stewart did not transfer it to the fair copy.

It may be necessary to advise the American senate to remind themselves of the words of their own constitution, which relate to justice, and also to remind them, and the world at large, that there is no worse form of injustice than pretended justice.

Captain Stanley Lord has long ago thrown off the ties that bound him to this mortal coil and, like the 1,500 men, women and children who perished in the depths of the North Atlantic, he too, at long last, may rest in peace. He has waited long enough.

In their closing paragraph of the 1992 reappraisal report, the Marine Accident Investigation Branch state that 'there are no villains in the story: just human beings with human characteristics' ... I disagree!

I must go down to the seas again, to the vagrant gipsy life,
To the hull's way and the whale's way where the wind's like a
whetted knife;
and all I ask is a merry yarn from a laughing fellow rover,
and quiet sleep and a sweet dream, when the long trick's over.

John Masefield
Sea Fever

Titanic List of Officers, Crew and Subcontracted Employees

The names of the survivors are in CAPITAL LETTERS and have the letter S in brackets. All are in alphabetical order. All addresses are in Southampton unless otherwise stated.

A

Abbot, E.; Pantryman (Lounge), 98 Northumberland Rd/ Abrams, C.; Fireman, 3 Charles St/ Adams, R.; Fireman, 168 Romsey St/ Ahier, P.; Saloon Steward, 136 Northumberland Rd/ Akerman, A.; Steward, 25 Rochester St/ Akerman, J.; Asst Pantryman, Rochester St/ Allaria, B.; Asst Waiter, 9 Orchard Pl./ Allen, G.; Scullion, 32 Grove St/ ALLEN, E. (S); Trimmer, 9 Short St/ Allen, F.; Lift Attendant, Short St/ Allen, H.; Fireman, 3 French St/ Allen, R.; Bedroom Steward, Charlton Rd/ Allsop, F.; Saloon Steward, 73 Obelisk Rd/ Alsopp, A.S.; Jr Electrician, 134 Malmesbury Rd/ ANDERSON, J. (S); Able Seaman, 1 Couzens Court/ Anderson, W.J.; Bedroom Steward, Queen's Tce/ ANDREWS, C.E. (S); Officers' Steward, 145 Millbrook Rd/ ARCHER, E. (S); Able Seaman, 59 Porchester Rd/ Ashe, H.W.; G.H. Steward, 15 Wyresdale Rd, Liverpool/ Ashcroft, A.; Clerk, 28 Canterbury Rd, Seacombe, Cheshire/ Aspilagi, G.; Asst Plateman, 79 St Paul's Rd, London/ AVERY, J. (S); Trimmer, 122 Hills Rd/ Ayling, G.; Asst Vegetable Cook, 22 Wilton St

B

Back, C.F.; Asst Lounge Steward, Weymouth Tce/ Bagley, E.; Saloon Steward, 183 Priory Rd/ BAGGOT, A.M. (S); Saloon Steward, 106 Park Rd/ Bailey, G.F.; Saloon Steward, Brooklands, Shepperton/ Bailey, G.W.; Fireman; 16 Brook St/ BAILEY, H. (S); Master at Arms, 377 Portswood Rd/ Baines, R.; Greaser, 9 Union Pl./ BALL, P. (S); Platewasher, 7 Windsor Tce/ Ball, W.; Fireman, 51 Brintons Rd/ Banfi, U.; Waiter, 33 Aubert Prk, Highbury H1/ Bannon, J.; Greaser, 9 St George's St/ Barker, E.T.; Saloon Steward, 4 Grand Parade, Harringay/ Barker, R.L.; 2nd Purser, Maybush/ Barker, H.; Asst Baker, Kingsworthy, Winchester/ Barker, T.; Asst Butcher, 20 Upper Bugle St/ Barlow, C.; Fireman, 10 St Mary's Rd/ Barlow, G.: Bedroom Steward, Foundry Lane/ Barnes, C.; Fireman, 45 York Rd/ Barnes, F.; Asst Baker, 25 Parsonage Rd/ Barnes, J.; Fireman, Woodley Rd/ Barrett, A.; Bell Boy, 164 Northumberland Rd/ BARRETT, F. (S); Leading Fireman, 24 King St/ Barrett, W.; Fireman, 24 Bevois St/ Barringer, A.W.; Saloon Steward, 52 Padwell St/ Barrow, H.; Asst Butcher, 17 Derby Rd/ Barrows, W.; Saloon Steward, Hanover St, London/ Barton, S.J.; Steward, 85 College St/ Basilico, G.; Waiter, 27 Old Compton St, London/ Baxter, H.R.; Bedroom Steward, 110 Shirley St/ Baxter, T.F.;

Linen Keeper, 81 Atherley Rd/ Bazzi, N.; Waiter, 21 Great Chapel St, London/ Beattie, F.; Greaser, 3 Isthmus St, Belfast/ BEAUCHAMP, G.W. (S); Fireman, Redbridge Rd/ Beaux, D.; Asst Waiter (R), 5 Beauchamp Pl., London/ Beedem, G.; Steward, 81 Shrewsbury Rd, Harlesden/ Beere, W.; Kitchen Porter, 2 Avenue Cottage/ Belford, W.; Chief Night Baker, 163 Manor Rd, Itchen/ Bell, W.J.; Chief Engineer, 34 Canute Rd/ Bellows, J.; Trimmer, 28 Bell St/ Bendell, T.; Fireman, 26 Woolley Rd/ Benham, F.; Saloon Steward, 61 Peach St, Wokingham/ Bennett, G.; Fireman, 3 Deal St/ BENNETT, M. MRS (S), Stewardess, 29 Cranbury Ave/ Bernardi, B.; Asst Waiter, 113 High St, Notting Hill Gate, London/ Benville, E.; Fireman, 4 Orchard Lane/ Bessant, E.; Baggage Steward, 3 Shirley Park Rd/ Bessant, W.; Fireman, 36 Henry Rd/ Bevis, J.; 171 Empress Rd/ Trimmer/ Bietrix, G.; Sauce Cook, 22 Albert Mansions, London/ Best, E.; Saloon Steward, 87 Malmesbury Rd/Biddlecombe, C.; Fireman, 42 Kentish Rd/ Biggs, E.; Fireman, 65 College St/ BINSTEAD, W. (S); Trimmer, 49 Endle St/ Bishop, W.; Bedroom Steward, 17 High St, Itchen/ Black, A.; Fireman, 6 Briton St/ Black, D.; Fireman, Sailor's Home, Southampton/ Blackman, H.; Fireman, 58 College St/ BLAKE, P. (S); Trimmer, 18 Endle St/ Blake, S.; Mess Steward, Engine Dept, Holyrood House/ Blake, T.; Fireman, 35 Peel St/ Blaney, J.; Fireman, Sailor's Home, Southampton/ Blann, E.; Fireman, 99 Pound St/ BLISS, E. MISS (S); Stewardess, 56 Upper Park Rd, New Southgate/ Blumet, J.; Plateman, 26 Richmond St/ Bogie, L.; Bedroom Steward, 100 Crescent, Eastleigh/ Bochetez, J.; Asst Chef, 29 Oakbank Rd/ Bollin, H.; Larder Cook, 37 Orchard Pl./ Bond, W.; Bedroom Steward, 20 Hanley Rd/ Boothby, W.; Bedroom Steward, 31 Winchester Rd/ Boston, W.; Asst Deck Steward, 1 Hanley Rd/ Bott, W.; Greaser, 6 Nichols Rd/ Bouchet, G.; 2nd Head Waiter, Mercer St/ Boughton, B.; Saloon Steward, 10 Richmond Rd/ BOWKER, R. MISS (S); First Cashier, The Cottage, Little Sutton, Cheshire/ Boxhall, J.G. (S); Westbourne Ave, Hull; 4th Officer (Joseph Grove Boxhall was the last surviving officer of the Titanic. As per his last request, his ashes were scattered on the sea on 12 June 1967 over the – incorrect! – position of the wreck)/ Boyd, J.; Saloon Steward, 52 Cranbury Ave/ Boyes, J.H.; Saloon Steward, 106 Clovelly Rd/ Bradley, F.; Able Seaman, 25 Threefield Lane/ Bradley, P.; Fireman, 4 Green's Court/ Bradshaw, J.A.; Platewasher, 2 Portland St/ Brailey, T.; Orchestra (Pianist), 71 Lancaster Rd, Ladbrook Grove, London/ Brewer, H.; Trimmer (Deserted April 10, 1912), 27 Palmerston Rd/ Brewster, G.H.; Bedroom Steward, 5 Carlton Place/ BRICE, W. (S); Able Seaman, 11 Lower Canal Walk/ Bricoux, R. ; Orchestra (Cellist), Place Du Lion D'or, Lille, France/ BRIDE, H.S. (S); Jnr Marconi Operator, Bannister's Hotel/ BRIGHT, A. J. (S); Quartermaster, 105 Firgrove Rd/ Bristow, H.; Saloon Steward, Shortlands, Kent/ Bristow, R.C.; Steward, 49 West Ridge Rd/ Brookman, J.; Steward, 34 Richmond St/ Brooks, J.; Trimmer, 128 Lyons St/ Broom, H.; ; Bath Steward, 2 High St, East Cowes/ Broome, A. T.; Asst Veranda Café Steward, White Lodge Bitterne Park/ BROWN, E. (S); Saloon Steward, 43 Suffolk Rd/ Brown, J.; Fireman, 237 Desborough Rd, Eastleigh/ Brown, J.; Fireman, 2 Russell St/ Brown, W.; Saloon Steward, Hillside Ave/ Brugge, W.; Fireman, Sailor's Home, Southampton/ Burton, H.; Steward, St Andrew's Rd/ Buckley, H.; Asst Vegetable Cook, 7 Brunswick Sq./ BULEY, E.J. (S); Able Seaman, 10 Cliff Rd/ Bull, W.; Scullion, 27 Chandall St/ Bulley, H.; Boots, 31 Carleton Crescent/ Bunnell, W.; Plate Washer, 212 Bedford Rd, Liverpool/ BURGESS, C. (S); Extra 3rd Baker (Charles Burgess was the last Titanic crewman on active sea service), 65 Bridge St/ Burke, R.E.; Lounge Attendant, 26 Southampton Rd, Chandlers Ford/ BURKE, W. (S); 2nd Saloon Steward, 57 Bridge St/ Burr, E.; Saloon Steward, 34 Victoria Rd/ BURRAGE, A. (S); Plates, 9 Elmsworth Rd/ Burroughs, A.; Fireman, 73 Adelaide Rd/ Burrows, W.; Fireman (Left by consent on April 10th, 1912),

Elm St/ Burton, E.; Fireman, 24 Chapel St/ Butt, R.; Saloon Steward, 6 Cawte St/ Butt,
W.; Fireman, 6 Cawte Rd/ Butterworth, J.; Saloon Steward, 270 Priory Rd/ Byrne, J.;
Bedroom Steward, 18 Balfour Rd, Ilford, Essex

C
Calderwood, H.; Trimmer, Sailor's Home/ Cambell, D.S.; White Star Line Clerk
(Kitchen)/ Cambell, W.; Joiner Apprentice, Employee of Harland & Wolff, Belfast/ Carney,
W.; Lift Attendant, 11 Cairo St, West Derby Rd, Liverpool/ Carr, R.; Trimmer, Welham
Cottage, Winchester Rd/ Cartwright, J.E.; Saloon Steward, 77 Gossett St, London/ Casali,
G.; Waiter, 50 Greek St, London/ Casey, T.; Trimmer, Sailor's Home/ Casswill, C.; Saloon
Steward, 81 Melbourne St/ Castleman, E.; Greaser, 37 North Rd/ CATON, A. MISS (S);
Turkish Bath Attendant, 50 Highbury Hill, London/ Cecil, C.; Steward, 194 Millbrook
Rd/ Caunt, W.; Grill Cook, 55 Sidney Rd/ Cave, H.; Saloon Steward, 17 Shirley Park
Rd, London/ CAVELL, G. (S); Trimmer, Lower East Rd/ CHAPMAN; J. (S); Boots,
31 Bellevue Rd/ Charboisson, A.; Roast Cook, 19 Kensington Park Gardens, London/
Charman, J.; Saloon Steward, Malden Hill House, Lewisham/ Cherrett, W.; Fireman, 13
Nelson Rd/ Chisolm, R.; Ship's Draughtsman (Designed Titanic's Lifeboats), Harland
& Wolff, Belfast/ Chiswall, G.A., Snr Boiler Maker, 53 High St/ Chitty, G.; Asst Baker,
Newtown Rd/ Chiverton, W.F.; Saloon Steward (Body found on June 8th, 1912 at 49°
06'N, 42° 51'W, by ship Ilford. The remains were recommitted to the deep), Mill St,
Newport/ Chorley, J.; Fireman, 2 Regent St/ Christmas, H.; Asst Steward, 4 Brintons
Rd/ CLARK, T. (S); Bedroom Steward, Hillside Ave/ Clarke, J.F.; Orchestra (Bass), 22
Tunstall St, Smithdown Rd, Liverpool/ Clark, W.; Fireman, 30 Paget St/ CLENCH, F. (S);
Able Seaman, Chantry Rd/ Clench, G.; Able Seaman, Chantry Rd/ Coe, H.; Trimmer,
10 Cross Court/ COFFEY, J. (S); Fireman (Deserted at Queenstown), Sherbourne Tce/
Coleman, A.; Saloon Steward, Oaktree Rd/ Coleman, J., Mess Steward, Engine Dept,
Mortimer Rd/ COLGAN, J. (S); Scullion, 27 West St/ COLLINS, J. (S); Scullion, 65
Ballycarry Rd, Belfast/ COLLINS, S. (S); Fireman, Sailor's Home/ Conner, J.; Fireman,
17 Shamrock Rd/ Conraire, M.; Asst Roast Cook, 15 Trafalgar Sq., London/ Contin,
A.; Entrée Cook, 37 Orchard Pl./ Conway, P.W.; Saloon Steward, 25 South Front,
Hackney/ Cook, C.; Steward, Chantry Rd/ Cook, G.; Saloon Steward, 13 Franklin Rd/
COOMBES, G. (S); Fireman, 45 Coleman St/ Coombs, C.; Asst Cook, 78 Dykes Rd/
Cooper, H.; Fireman, 9 St George's St/ Cooper, J.; Trimmer, 27 Pound St/ Copperthwaite,
B.; Fireman, 39 Mount St/ Corben, E.T.; Asst Printer, 58 Floating Bridge Rd/ Corcora,
D.; Fireman, Sailor's Home/ Cotton, A.; Fireman, Shore Cottages, Hythe/ Couch, F.;
Able Seaman, Port Isaac, Cornwall/ Couch, J.; Greaser, 42 Canton St/ COUPER, R.
(S); Fireman, 101 Duke St/ Cox, W.D.; Steward, 110 Shirley Rd/ Coy, F.E.G.; Jnr 3rd Asst
engineer, 134 Portswood Rd/ Crabb, H.; Trimmer, 101 Firgrove Rd/ CRAFTER, F. (S);
Saloon Steward, 143 Albert Rd/ CRAWFORD, A. (S); Bedroom Steward, 22 Cranbury
Ave/ Creese, H.P.; Deck Engineer, 2 Enfield Grove/ CRIMMINS, J. (S); Fireman, 7
King St/ Crisp, H.; Saloon Steward, 36 Macnaughten Rd/ Crispin, W.; G.H. Steward,
Sanfoin Villa, Eastleigh/ Crosbie, J.B.; Turkish Bath Attendant, 47 St Dunstan's Rd/
Cross, W.; Fireman, 97 Ludlow Rd/ Grovelle, L.; Asst Waiter, 5 Orchard Pl./ CROWE,
G.F. (S); Saloon Steward, 89 Milton Rd/ Crumplin, C.; Bedroom Steward, Anchor
& Hope, Threefield Lane/ CULLEN, C. (S); Bedroom Steward, 24 Warberton Rd,
Liverpool/ Cunningham, A.; Fitter Apprentice, Employee of Harland & Wolff, Belfast./
CUNNINGHAM, A. (S); Bedroom Steward, 60 Charlton Rd/ Cunningham, B.; Fireman,
6 Briton St/ Curtis, A.; Fireman, 55 Kingsley Rd

D

DANIELS, S.E. (S); Steward, 119 Albert Rd, Southsea/ Dashwood, W.G.; Saloon Steward, Sailor's Home/ Davies, G.; Bedroom Steward, Hillside Ave/ Davies, J.J.; Extra 2nd Baker, 19 Eastfield Rd/ Davies, R.J.; Saloon Steward, 12 The Polygon/ Davies, T.; Leading Fireman, 2 Church Lane/ Davis, S.J.; Able Seaman, 42 Duncan St, Portsmouth/ Dawes, W.W.; Steward (Discharged April 10th, 1912), Nelson Rd/ Dawson, J.; Trimmer, 70 Briton St/ Dean, G.H.; Asst Steward, King Edward Ave, London/ Debreuca, M.; Asst Waiter, 12 Meade St, London/ Deeble, A.; Saloon Steward, 81 Atherley Rd/ Denarcissio, ----; Asst Waiter, 20 Church St, London/ Deslands, F.; Saloon Steward, 405 Portswood Rd/ Derrett, A.; Saloon Steward, Hillside Ave/ Desornini, L.; Asst Pastry Cook, 4 Queen's Park Tce/ DIAPER, J. (S); Fireman, 102 Derby Rd/ Dickson, W.; Trimmer, 10 Oriental Tce/ DILLEY, J. (S); Fireman, 44 Threefield Lane/ DILLON, T.P. (S); Trimmer, Sailor's Home/ DiMartino, G.; c/o Gatti; Asst Waiter/ Dimenage, J.K.; Saloon Steward, 4 Cawte Rd/ Dodd, E.C.; Jnr 3rd Engineer, 26 Queen's Parade/ Dodd, G.; Chief 2nd Steward, 57 Morris Rd/ Dodds, R.W.; Jnr 4th Asst Engineer, 12 Queen's Park Tce/ DOEL, F. (S); Fireman, 20 Richmond St/ Dolby, J.; Reception Room Attendant, 12 Devonshire Rd/ Donati, I.; Asst Waiter, 3 Whitefield St, Tottenham Court Rd, London/ Donoghue, T.; Bedroom Steward, 60 Ludlow Rd/ DORE, A. (S); Trimmer, 9 Mount St/ Dornier, L.; Asst Fish Cook, 3 Orchard Pl./ Doughty, N.; Saloon Steward, 30 Queen Sq., London/ Doyle, L.; Fireman, 10 Orchard Pl./ Dubb, A.; Steward, 81 Atherley Rd/ Duffy, W.; Clerk (Engineering Dept), 11 Garton Rd, Itchen/ Dunford, W.; Hospital Steward, 16 Bridge St/ Dyer, H.R.; Snr Asst 4th Engineer, 53 Middle St/ Dyer, W.; Saloon Steward, 46 Stafford Rd/ DYMOND, P. (S); Fireman, 2 Farmer's Court

E

Eagle, A.J.; Trimmer, 13 Lyon St/ Eastman, C.; Greaser, 17 Cecil Ave/ EDBROOKE, F. (S); Steward, 99 Lake Rd, Portsmouth/ Ede, G.B.; Steward, Manor Farm Rd/ Edge, T.W.; Deck Steward, 28 Clovelly Rd/ Edwards, C.; Asst Pantryman, 7 Brunswick Sq./ Egg, W.H.; Steward, 1-A Trent Rd, Brixton/ Elliott, B. E.; Trimmer, 11 Wilmington St, London/ ELLIS, J.R. (S); Asst Veg. Cook, 40 Dukes St/ Ennis, W.; Turkish Bath Attendant, 141 Bedford Rd, Southport./ Ervine, A.; Asst Electr., Maryfield, Belfast/ ETCHES, H.S. (S); Bedroom Steward, 23 - A Gordon Ave/ EVANS, A.F. (S); Look-Out-Man, 20 Deal St/ EVANS, F.O. (S); Able Seaman, 14 Bond St/ Evans, G.; Steward, 2 Nightingale Gardens/ Evans, G.; Saloon Steward, 46 Richmond Rd/ Evans, W.; Trimmer, 11 Ryde Tce, Itchen

F

Fairall, H.; Saloon Steward, 31 Surrey St, Ryde, I.O.W./ Farenden, E.; Confectioner, 23 South St, Emsworth/ Farquharson, W.E.; Snr 2nd Engineer, 94 Wilton Ave/ FAULKNER, W.S. (S); Bedroom Steward, 16 Malmesbury Road/ Fay, P.; Greaser, 31 Stamford St/ Fei, C.; Sculleryman, 26 Anne's Court, London/ Fellowes, A.; Asst Boots, 51 Bridge St/ Feltham, G.; Vienna Baker, 64 St Denys Rd/ Fenton, P.; Saloon Steward, 19 Middle Rd/ Ferrary, A.; Trimmer, 38 St Mary's Pl./ Ferris, W.; Leading Fireman, 5 Hanover Buildings/ Finch. H.; Steward, 32 French St/ FITZPATRICK, C.W.N. (S); Mess Steward, Engin. Dept, 93 Millbrook Rd/ Fitzpatrick, H.; Jnr Boiler Maker, 169 Nelson St Belfast/ FLARTY, B. (S); Fireman, 21 Stamford St/ FLEET. F.; (S); Look-Out-Man, 9 Norman Rd/ Fletcher, P.W.; Ship's Bugler, 13 Strathville Rd, Southfields, London/ FOLEY, J. (S); Storekeeper, 2 Queen's Rd/ FOLEY, W.C. (S); Steward, 15 Monsons Rd/ Ford, E.; Steward, 100 Brintons Rd/ Ford, F.; Bedroom Steward, 66 Oxford St/ Ford, H.; Trimmer,

Royal Oak/ Ford, T.; Leading Fireman, 36 Russell St, Liverpool/ FORWARD, J. (S); Able
Seaman, Sailor's Home/ Foster, A.; Storekeeper, 38 North Front/ Fox, W.T.; Steward,
Polhawn, Springfield Rd, London/ Franklin, A.; Saloon Steward, Egremont, Newton
Rd/ Fraser, J.; Jnr Asst 3rd. Engineer, 54 Tennyson Rd/ Fraser, J.; Fireman, Sailor's Home/
FREDERICKS, W. (S); Trimmer, 6 Elm Rd/ Freeman, E.E.S.; Chief Deck Steward
(Although officially listed as a crew member, Freeman was in fact secretary to Jnr Bruce
Ismay), 5 Hanley Rd/ FROPPER, R.P.; Saloon Steward, Washington Tce/ Frost, A.W.,
Outside Foreman Engineer, Employee of Harland & Wolff, Belfast/ Frost, A.; Head of
Guarantee Group, Employee of Harland & Wolff, Belfast/ FRYER, A. (S); Trimmer, 1
Charlotte Place

G

Gallop, F.; Asst Cook, 27 Briton St/ Gardener. F.; Greaser, Totton/ Gatti, L.; Manager of
Ritz Restnt., Montalto, Harborough Rd/ Gear, A.; Fireman, 2 Stamford St/ Geddes,
R.; Bedroom Steward, 80 Grove Rd/ GIBBONS, J.W. (S); Saloon Steward, Harbour
View, Studland Bay/ Gilardino, V.; Waiter, 15 Bellevue Rd/ Giles, J.; 2nd Baker, 104 Lyon
St/ Gill, P.; Ship's Cook, 24 Waverley Rd/ Gill, J.S.; Bedroom Steward, 17 Suffolk Ave/
GODLEY, G. (S); Fireman, 17 Mount St/ Godwin, F.; Greaser, Totton/ GOLD, K. MRS
(S); Stewardess, Glenthorne, Bassett/ Golder, M.W.; Fireman, 15 Landsdowne Rd/
Gordon, J.; Trimmer, Sailor's Home/ Goree, F.; Greaser, 5 Belvedere Tce/ Goshawk. A.J.;
3rd Saloon Steward, 6 Coventry Rd/ Gosling, B.; Trimmer, 11 Lower York St/ Gosling,
S.; Trimmer, 17 French St/ GRAHAM, T. (S); Fireman, 28 Downpatrick St, Belfast/
Graves, S.; Fireman, 8 North Front Strand/ Gregory, D.; Greaser, 30 Floating Bridge Rd/
GREGSON, M. MISS (S); Stewardess, 28 Lorne R.d., Portswood/ Green, G.; Trimmer, 57
Howards Grove/ Grodidge, E.; Fireman, 41 Redcliff St/ Grosclaude, G.; Asst Coffee Man,
8 Lumber Court, London/ Gunn, J.T.; Asst Steward, 23 Bridge Rd/ Gumery, G.; Mess
Steward, Engine Dept, 24 Canute Rd/ GUY, E.J. (S); Asst Boots., 5 College Tee, Milton
Abbas/ Gwinn, W.H.L.; Brooklin, Clerk (Post Office), New York

H

HAGGAN, J. (S); Fireman, Sailor's Home/ HAINES, A. (S); Boatswain's Mate, 52 Grove
St/ HALFORD, R. (S); 3rd Class Steward, 2 Latimer St/ Hall, F.A.J.; Scullion, 70 Sidney
Rd/ Hall, J.; Fireman, 2 Westgate St/ Hallet, G.; Fireman, 101 Church St/ Hamblyn,
E.W.; Bedroom Steward, 2 Norman Villas, Dyer Rd/ Hamilton, E.; Asst Smoke-Rm
Steward, 5 Shirley Rd/ Hands, B.; Fireman, St Michael's House/ Hannan, G.; Fireman,
1 Oxford Tce/ HARDER, W. (S); Window Cleaner, 46 Winton St/ Harding, A.; Asst
Pantry Steward, Station Cottages, Swaythling/ HARDWICKE, R. (S); Kitchen Porter, 4
Heysham Rd/ HARDY, J. (S); Chief 2nd Class Steward, Oakleigh, Highfield/ Harris, C.H.;
Bell Boy, 14 Short St/ Harris, C.W.; Saloon Steward, 14 Short St/ Harris, E.; Fireman,
83 Belgrade Rd/ Harris, E.; Asst Pantryman, 13 Greenhill Ave, Winchester/ HARRIS, F.
(S); Fireman, 57 Melville Rd, Gosport/ Harris, F.; Trimmer, 12 Wilton St/ HARRISON,
A.D. (S); Saloon Steward, 131 Oakley Rd/ Harrison, N.; Jnr 2nd Engineer, 30 Coventry
Rd/ HART, J.E. (S); 3rd Class Steward, Aberdeen, Foundry Lane/ Hart, T.; Fireman (Hart's
discharge book was stolen by somebody who signed on in his name and was lost. Hart
himself reappeared at Southampton May 8th, per his Mother), 51 College St/ Hartley,
W.H.; Orchestra Leader, Surreyside West Park St, Dewsbury/ HARTNELL, F. (S); Saloon
Steward, 25 Argyle Rd/ Harvey, H.G.; Jnr Asst 2nd Engineer, 40 Obelisk Rd/ Hasgood,
R.; Fireman, 19 Woodley Rd/ Hasketh, J.H.; Jnr 2nd Engineer, 80 Garrett Ave, Liverpool/

Haslin, J.; Trimmer, Sailor's Home/ Hatch, J.; Scullion, 446 Portswood Rd/ Haveling, A.;
Jnr Asst 4th Engineer (transferred April 10th, 1912), South Front/ Hawkesworth, J.; Saloon
Steward, 18 Wilton Rd/ Hawkesworth, W.; Asst Deck Steward, Lemon Rd/ Hayter, A.;
Bedroom Steward, 10 Mayflower Rd/ Head. A.; Fireman, 19 Russell St/ HEBB, A. (S);
Trimmer, 5 Bell's Court/ Heinen, J.; Saloon Steward, Norden Hill House, Lewisham/
HEMMING, S. (S); Lamp Trimmer, 31 Kingsley Rd/ HENDRICKSON, C. (S); Leading
Fireman, 255 Northumberland Rd/ Hendy, E.; Saloon Steward, 21 Paynes Rd/ Henry, W.;
Asst Boots., 27 Romsey Rd/ Hensford, H.G.; Asst Butcher, 132 Malmesbury Rd/ Hewett,
T.; Bedroom Steward, 94 Devonfield Rd, Aintree/ Hill, H.P.; Steward, 66 Oxford St/ Hill,
J.C.; Bedroom Steward, 64 Padwell Rd/ Hill, J.; Trimmer, 10 Kingsland Square/ Hinckley,
G.; Hospital Attendant, 2 Oxford St/ Hine, G.; 3rd Baker, Bridge St, Buckley/ Hinton, W.;
Trimmer, 26 Cumberland St/ Hiscock, S.; Plate Washer, 19 Palmerston Rd/ HITCHINS,
R. (S); Quartermaster, 43 James St/ Hoare, L.; Saloon Steward, 108 Lyon St/ Hogg, C.;
Bedroom Steward, 24 Bulwer St, Liverpool/ Hodges, W.; Fireman, 6 Britannia Rd/
Hodge, C.; Snr Asst 3rd Enginr., 6 Ivy Rd/ Hodgkinson, L; Sr, 4th Engineer, 67 Arthur Rd/
HOGG, G. A. (S); Look-Out-Man, 44 High St/ Hogue, E.; Plate Washer, Alison Gardens,
Dulwich/ Holden, F.; Fireman, Albany Rd (Deserted April 10th, 1912)/ Holland, T.; Asst
Reception Room Steward, 38 Walton Vale, Liverpool/ Holloway, S.; Asst Clothes Presser,
60 Hartington Rd/ Holman, H.; Able Seaman, Britannia Rd/ Hopgood, R.; Fireman,
81 Ramsey Rd/ Hopkins, F.; Plate Washer, 14 Fanshawe St/ HOPKINS, R. (S); Able
Seaman, 4 Woodstock Rd, Belfast/ HORSWILL, A.E.J. (S); Able Seaman, 44 Derby Rd/
Hosking, G.P.; Snr 3rd Engineer, 28 Avenue Rd/ House, W.; Saloon Steward, 44 Derby
Rd/ Howell, A.A. ; Saloon Steward, 12 Cliff Rd/ Hughes, H.; Asst Chief 2nd Steward, Ivy
Bank, Dyer Rd/ Humby, F.; Plate Steward, 2 Golden Grove/ Hume, J.L. (Jock); Orchestra
(violin), 42 George S., Dumfries/ Humphreys, H.; Steward, 9 Plaswell Lane, Dolgelly/
HUMPHREYS, J. (S); Quartermaster, 113 Dukes Rd/ HUNT, A. (S); Trimmer, 1 French
St/ Hunt, T.; Fireman, 2 Queen St/ Hurst, C.J.; Fireman, Laundry Rd/ HURST, W. (S);
Fireman, 15 Chapel Rd/ Hutchinson, J.; Vegetable Cook, 91 Woodcroft Rd, Liverpool/
Hutchinson, J. H.; Joiner & Carpenter, 40 Onslow Rd/ HYLAND, L.J. (S); Steward, 55
Orchard Pl.

I
Ide, T. C.; Bedroom Steward, 114 Lyon St/ Ingram, C.; Trimmer, 18 Lower Canal Walk/
Inge, W.; Scullion, 45 Stratton Rd/ Ingrouville, H.; Steward, 15 Floating Bridge Rd/
Instance, T.; Fireman, 12 Guillaume Tce

J
Jackson, C.; Asst Boots., 22 Graham Rd/ Jacobson, J.; Fireman, 97 Dukes Rd/ Jago, J.;
Greaser, 47 Millbank St/ Jaillet, H.; Pastry Cook, Jamison St, London/ James, T.; Fireman,
27 College St/ Janaway, W.P.; Bedroom Steward, Alpha House, Richmond St/ Janin, C.;
Soup Cook, 56 Seddlescombe Rd, London/ Jarvids, W.; Fireman, 29 Canal Walk/ Jeffrey,
W.A.; Controller, 2 Church Lane, Highfield/ Jenner, H.; Saloon Steward, 3 Bellevue Rd/
Jensen, C.V.; Saloon Steward, 17 Morris Rd/ JESSOP, V. (S); Stewardess, 71 Shirley Rd,
Bedford Park, London/ JEWELL, A. (S); Look-Out-Man, 32 College St/ JOHNSON,
J. (S); Night Watchman, Sailor's Home/ Johnson, H.; Asst Ship's Cook, 183 Albert Rd/
Jones, A.; Plates, 22 Ludlow Rd/ Jones, A.E.; Saloon Steward, Carlton Rd, Woodfield/
Jones, H.; Roast Cook, Broad St, Alresford/ Jones, R.V.; Saloon Steward, 7 Portland
Tce/ JONES, T. (S); Able Seaman, 68 Nesfield St, Liverpool/ Jouanwault, G.; Asst Sauce

Cook, 3 Orchard Pl.; JOUGHIN, C. (S); Chief Baker, Leighton Rd, Elmhurst/ JUDD, C. (S); Fireman, 98 Derby Rd/ Jukes, J.; Greaser, Moor Green, West End/ Jupe, H.; Asst Electrician, 79 Bullar Rd.

K

KASPER, F. (S); Fireman, 6 Brunswick Sq./ Kearl, C.; Greaser, 17 Chantry Rd/ Kearl, G.; Trimmer, 31 Bay Rd/ Keegan, J.; Leading Fireman, 2 Cross House Rd/ KEENE, P. (S); Saloon Steward, 14 Rigby Rd/ Kelland, T.; Library Steward, Commercial St/ Kelly, J.; Greaser, 12 Woodleigh Rd/ Kelly, W.; Asst Electrician, 1 Claude Rd, Dublin/ KEMISH, G. (S); Fireman, 238 Shirley Rd/ Kemp, T.; Extra Asst 4th Engineer, 11 Cedar Rd/ Kenchenten, F.; Greaser, 9 Latimer Rd/ Kenzler, A.; Storekeeper (Engineering Dept), 21 Blechynden Tce/ Kennell, C.; Hebrew Cook, 6 Park View/ Kerby, W.T.; Asst Steward, Woodminton Cottages, Salisbury/ Kerr, T.; Fireman, 7 Hanley St/ Ketchley, H.; Saloon Steward, 40 Northcote Rd/ Kieran, M.; Asst Kitchen Storekeeper, 7 Avenue Rd/ Kiernan, J.W.; Chief 3rd Class Steward, Inglewood, Bellmoor Rd/ Kielford, P.; Steward (Left by Consent April 10th, 1912), New Rd/ King, A.; Lift Attendant, 132 Mile St, Gateshead-on-Tyne/ King, E.W.; Clerk-Purser's Asst, Currin Rectory, Clones, Ireland/ King, G.; Scullion, 46 Threefield Lane/ King, T.; Master-At-Arms, 23 Middle Market Rd, Great Yarmouth/ Kingscote, W.P.; Saloon Steward, 24 Eglin Rd/ Kinsella, L.; Fireman, 7 Canal Walk/ Kirkham, J.; Greaser, 4 Chapel St/ Kitching, Saloon Steward, 170 Derby Rd/ Klein, H.; 2nd Class Barber, 56 Oakley Rd/ KNIGHT, G. (S); Saloon Steward, 45 Ludlow Rd/ Knight, L; Steward, 37 Spring Lane, Bishopstoke/ Knight, R.; Leading Hand Engineer, Employee of Harland & Wolff, Belfast/ KNOWLES, T. (S); Fireman's Messman, Fanners Lane, Lymington/ Krins, G.; Orchestra (viola), 10 Villa Rd, London

L

Lacey, B.W.; Asst Steward, 26 Southampton Rd, Salisbury/ Lahy, T.; Fireman, 19 Spullin Rd, East Dulwich/ Lake, W.; Saloon Steward, Florence Hotel/ Lane, A.E.; Saloon Steward, 207 Victoria Rd/ Latimer, A.; Chief Steward, 4 Glenwylin Row, Waterloo, Liverpool/ Lauder, A.; Asst Confectioner, Fenton Rd, Kelston, W. Southbourne/ LAVINGTON, B., Miss (S); Stewardess, Manor Farm, Headbourne Rd, Winchester/ Lawrence, H.; Saloon Steward, 66 Oxford St/ LEATHER, E.L.; Mrs. (S); Stewardess, 23 Park Rd, Port Sunlight/ Lee, H.; Trimmer, 94 Bevois St/ LEE, R.R. (S); Look-Out-Man, 62 Threefield Lane/ LeFevre, G.; Saloon Steward, 25 Orchard Pl./ Leonard, M.; Steward, 45 Charlesworth St, Belfast/ Levett, G.; Asst Pantryman, 5 Shirley Cottages/ LEWIS, A. (S); Steward, 99 Radcliffe Rd/ Light, C.; Fireman, 24 Lower Back of the Walls/ Light, C.; Platewasher, Thorney Hill, near Christchurch, Hants./ Light, W.; Fireman. 3 Marine Tce/ LIGHTOLLER, C.H. (S); 2nd Officer, Nikko Lodge, Netley Abbey, near Southampton/ LINDSAY, W. (S); Fireman, 3 Coleman St/ LITTLEJOHN, A.J. (S); Saloon Steward, 11 Western Tce/ Lloyd, H.; Saloon Steward, Chapel Rd, Oxford St/ Lloyd, W.; Fireman, 18 Orchard Pl./ Locke, A.; Scullion, 309 Portswood Rd/ Long, F.; Trimmer, 19 Sidford St/ Long, W.; Trimmer, 3 Maine Tce/ Longmuir, J.; Asst Bedroom Steward, 130 The Crescent, Eastleigh/ Lovell, J.; Grill Cook, 21 Highlands Rd/ LOWE, H.G. (S); 5th Officer, Penralet, Barmouth/ LUCAS, W. (S); Saloon Steward, 3 Cardigan Pl./ LUCAS, W. (S); Able Seaman, 2 Corporation Flats/ Lydiatt, C.; Saloon Steward, 12 Brunswick Sq./ Lyons, W.H.; Able Seaman (buried at sea from the Carpathia, 16 April 1912), 27 Orchard Pl

M

Mabey, J.; Steward, 190 Albany Rd/ MACKAY, C.D. (S); Saloon Steward, 18 Milton Rd/ Mackie, M.; Bedroom Steward, 31 Winchester Rd/ Mackie, W.D.; 2-B Margery Park Rd, Forest Gate, London/ MAJOR, A. (S); Fireman, 4 Oriental Tce/ Major, E.; Bath Steward, 9 Old Park Villas, London/ Mantle, R.; Steward, 60 Brintons Rd/ March, J.S.; Clerk (Post Office), Newark, N.J., U.S.A./ Marks, J.; Asst Pantryman, 93 Livingstone Rd/ Marrett, G.; Fireman, 32 Elm St/ Marriott, J.W.; Asst Pantryman, 7 Chilworth Rd/ MARSDEN, E. MISS (S).; Stewardess, 7 Westmorland Tce/ Marsh, F.; Fireman, 4 Back of the Walls/ MARTIN, A. MRS. (S); Stewardess, Postbrooke Rd, Portsmouth/ MARTIN, A. (S); Scullion, 13 High St, Fareham/ MARTIN, M.E., MISS (S); 2nd Cashier, 1 Apsley Villa, London/ Maskell, L.; Trimmer, 25 Albert Rd/ MASON, F. (S); Fireman, 30A Waverley Rd/ Mason, J.; Leading Fireman, 4 Wycombe Cottages/ Matherson, D.; Able Seaman, 20 Richmond St/ Mathias, M.; Mess Steward, Deck Dept, 2 western Esplanade/ Mattman, A; Iceman, 3 Orchard Pl./ MAUGE, P. (S); Chef's Asst, 53 Neal St, London/ Maxwell, J.; Carpenter, 27 Leighton Rd/ May, A.W.; Fireman's Messman, 75 York St/ MAYNARD, H. (S); Entrée Cook, 21 Highlands Rd/ Mayo, W.; Leading Fireman, 24 Cable St/ Maytum, A.; Chief Butcher, 12 Stafford Rd/ MAYZES, A. (S); Fireman, 8 Commercial St/ McAndrews, T.; Fireman, Sailor's Home/ McAndrews, W.; Fireman, 17 New Copley Rd/ McCarthy, F.; Bedroom Steward, Charlton Rd/ McCARTHY, W. (S); Able Seaman, 9 Gratton Hill Rd, Cork, Ireland/ McCastle, W.; Fireman, 53 French St/ McCawley, M.; Gym Instructor, 22 Camden Pl./ McElroy, H.W.; Chief Purser, Polygon House/ McGANN, J. (S); Trimmer, 18 George's Pl./ McGarvey, E.; Fireman, 54 College St/ McGaw, E.; Fireman, 6 Broadlands Rd/ McCOUGH, J. (S); Able Seaman, St George's St/ McGrady, J.; Saloon Steward, Platform Tavern/ McGregor, J.; Fireman, 7 Briton St/ McInerny, T.; Greaser, 38 Elston St, Liverpool/ McINTYRE, W. (S); Trimmer, 20 Floating Bridge St/ McLAREN, H. Mrs. (S); Stewardess, 9 Shirley Rd/ McMICKEN, A. (S); Saloon Steward, 43 Suffolk Ave/ McMULLEN, J.; Saloon Steward, 120 St Mary's Rd/ McMurray, W.; Bedroom Steward, 60 Empress Rd, Liverpool/ McQuillan, W.; Fireman, 79 Sea View St, Belfast/ McRay, W.; Fireman, 43 Threefield Lane/ McReynolds, W.M.E.; Jnr 6th Asst Engineer, 1 Laggan Villas, Belfast/ Mellor, A.; Saloon Steward, 6 Carlton Pl./ Middleton, A.; Asst Electrician, Ballisodare, Sligo, Ireland/ Middleton, M.V.; Saloon Steward, 84 Felsham Rd, London/ Milford, G.; Fireman, 3 Grahan St/ Millar, R.; Extra 5th Asst Enginr., 19 North St; Alloa, Belfast/ Millar, T.; Asst Deck Engineer, 19 Meadowbrook St, Belfast/ MILLS, C. (S); Asst Butcher, 94 Albert Rd/ Mintram, W.; Fireman, 15 Chapel Rd/ Mishellany, A.; Printer, 123 Ledbury Rd, London/ Mitchell, B.; Trimmer, 45 Bevois Valley/ Monoros, J.; Asst Waiter, 27 Tenison St, London/ Monteverdi, G.; Asst Entrée Cook, 4 Queen's Park Tce/ Moody, J.P.; 6th Officer, St James House, Grimsby/ Moore, A.E.; Saloon Steward, 142 St Mary's Rd/ MOORE, G. (S); Able Seaman, 51 Graham Rd/ MOORE, J.J. (S); Fireman, 64 Arthur Rd/ Moore, R.; Trimmer, Manor Cottage, Headbourne, St/ Moores, R.; Greaser, 174 Northumberland/ Morgan, A.; Trimmer, 18 Threefield Rd/ Morgan, C.F.; Asst Storekeeper Kitchen, 46 Bessborough Rd, Birkenhead/ Morgan, T.; Fireman, Sailor's Home/ Morrell, R.; Trimmer, 51 Malmesbury Rd/ Morris, A.; Greaser, 18 Short St/ MORRIS, F.H. (S); Bath Steward, 46 Deloune St, London/ Morris, W.; Trimmer, 5 Marine Parade/ Moss, W.; Saloon Steward, 37 Charlton Rd/ Moyes, W.Y.; Snr 6th Engineer, 11 Douglass Tce, Stirling, Scotland/ Muller, L.; Interpreter, 67 Oxford St/ Mullin, T.; Saloon Steward, 12 Onslow Rd/ Murdoch, W.M.; 1st Officer, 94 Belmont Rd/ MURDOCK, W. (S); Fireman, Sailor's Home

N

Nanineri, F.; Head Waiter, 34 Aubert Rd, Highbury Hill/ NEAL, H. (S); Asst Baker, 10 Cliff Rd/ Nettleton, G.; Fireman, 23 Empress Rd/ Newman, C.; Storekeeper, Engineering, 9 Latimer St/ Nichols, A.; Boatswain, Oak Tree Rd, St Cloud./ Nicholls, T.; Saloon Steward, 3 Brunswick Sq./ Nichols, A.D.; Steward, 43 Suffolk Ave/ NICHOLS, W.H. (S); Steward, 16 Kent Rd/ Noon, J.; Fireman, Sailor's Home/ Norris, J.; Fireman, 5 Spa Rd/ Noss, B.; Fireman, 8 St Peter's Rd/ NOSS, H. (S); Fireman, 12 Black Lane/ NUTBEAN, W. (S); Fireman, Sportsman's Arms, High St

O

O' CONNOR, J. (S); Trimmer, 9 Tower Pl./ O' Connor, T.; Bedroom Steward, 12 Linacre Lane, Liverpool/ Olive, C.; Greaser, 43 College St/ Olive, E.R.; Clothes Presser, 37 Hanley Rd/ OLIVER, H. (S); Fireman, 15 Nichols Rd/ OLLIVER, A. (S); Quartermaster, 38 Anderson Rd/ O' Loughlin, Dr. W.F.; Chief Surgeon, Polygon House/ Orpet, W.H.; Saloon Steward, 1 Vaundry St/ Orr, J.; Asst Vegetable Cook, 45 Coleman St/ Orovello, L.; c/o Gatti; Waiter/ Osborne, W.; Saloon Steward, 7 Hewetts Rd, Freemantle/ OSMAN, F. (S); Able Seaman, 43 High St, Itchen/ OTHEN, C. (S); Fireman, 6 Northumberland Rd/ Owen, L.; Asst Steward, 29 Earl's Rd

P

Pacey, R.J.; Lift Attendant, Cambridge Villa, Millbrook Rd/ Pacherd, J.; Asst Larder, 3 Orchard Pl./ Painter, C.; Fireman, 172 Mortimer Rd/ Painter, F.; Fireman, 10 Bridge St/ Painton, J.A.; Captain's Steward, 48 Stadford St, Oxford/ Palles, T.; Greaser, 25 Upper Palmer St/ Parker, T.; Butcher, Upper Boyle St/ Parks, F.; Plumber Apprentice, Employee of Harland & Wolff, Belfast/ Parr, W.; Asst Manager Electr. Dept, Employee of Harland & Wolff, Belfast/ Parsons, E.; Chief Kitchen Storekeeper, Robert's Rd/ Parsons, F.A.; Snr 5th Engineer, 38 Bugle St/ Parsons, R.; Saloon Steward, Ashbrittle, near Wellington, Somerset/ PASCOE, C.H. (S); Able Seaman, 68 High St/ Pearce, A.; Steward, 76A Holdenhurst Rd, Bournemouth/ PEARCE, J. (S); Fireman, 14 Drummond Rd/ PEARCEY, A.V. (S); 3rd Class Pantryman, 23 Kent Rd/ Pedrini, A.; Asst Waiter, Bowling Green House/ PELHAM, G.; Trimmer, Sailor's Home/ Penney, A.; Trimmer (Deserted on 10 April 1912), Chantry Rd/ Pennal, F.; Bath Steward, 16 West St/ Penny, W.; Asst Steward, 29 Lodge St/ Penrose, J. P.; Bedroom Steward, 30 Southview Rd/ Perkins, L.; Telephone Operator, New Inn, Soberton, Hants./ PERKINS, W.J. (S); Quartermaster, Victoria Rd/ Perotti; Asst Waiter, 2 Denmark Pl., London/ Perrin, W.; Boots., 24 Bellmore Rd/ Perracchio, S.; Asst Waiter, 4 Richmond Building, Dean St, London/ Perriton, H.; Saloon Steward, 11 St Andrew's Rd/ PERRY, E. (S); Trimmer, 3 Ryde Tce/ Perry, H.; Trimmer, 3 Ryde Tce/ PETERS, W.C. (S); Able Seaman, 114 Ludlow Rd/ Petty, E.H.; Bedroom Steward, 26 Orchard Pl./ Phillips, J.G.; Snr Marconi Operator, Farncombe, Godalming/ Phillips, G.; Greaser, 5 Grove St/ Phillips, J.; Storeman, 8 Jessie Tce/ PHILLIMORE, H. (S); Bath Steward, 72 Priory Rd/ Piatty, L.; Asst Waiter, 15 Princess St, London/ Piazza, P.; Waiter, 94 Newport Building, London/ PIGOTT, P. (S); Able Seaman, 2 Windsor Tce/ Pitfield, W.; Greaser, 13 Albert Rd/ PITMAN, H.J. (S); 3rd Officer, Castle Cary, Somerset/ Platt, W.; Scullion, 107 Belgrove Rd/ PODESTA, J.; (S); Fireman, 31 Chantry Rd/ Poggi, E.; Waiter, Bowling Green House/ POIGNDESTRE, J. (S); Able Seaman, 4 Elm Rd/ Poiravanti, B.; Asst Sculleryman, 52 St James Rd, London/ Pond, G.; Fireman, Sailor's Home/ Pook, R.; Asst Bedroom Steward, 102 Alexandra Rd/ PORT, F.; (S); Steward, Foundry Lane/ PREGNALL, G.; (S); Greaser, 3 Brew House Court/ PRENTICE, F.W. (S); Asst

Storekeeper Kitchen (according to Eva Hart – a passenger survivor – F.W. Prentice was the last surviving crew member of Titanic living in England. He died in 1982), Denzil Ave/ Preston, T.; Trimmer, 42 Millbank St/ Price, E.; Barman, 93 Grove Rd, London/ Price, R.; Fireman, 30 Houndwell Gardens/ Prideaux, J.A.; Steward, 23 Cotlands Rd/ PRIEST, J. (S); Fireman, 27 Lower Canal Walk/ PRIOR, H.J. (S); Steward, 48 Padwell Rd/ PRITCHARD, A. Mrs (S); Stewardess, 9 Rosslyn Rd, London/ Proctor, C.; Chef, 29 Southview Rd/ Proudfoot, R.; Trimmer, 2 Pear Tree Green/ Pryce, W.; Saloon Steward, Hatherdene, Newlands Rd/ PUGH, A. (S); Steward, 72 Orchard Lane/ Pugh, P. (S); Steward, 22 Fell St/ PUSEY, R.W. (S); Fireman, School Lane, Hythe/ Puzey, J.E.; Saloon Steward, 61 Manor Rd, Itchen

R
Randall, F.H.; Saloon Steward, 182 Empress Rd/ RANGER, T. (S); 81 Greaser, Middle Rd/ Ransom, J.; Saloon Steward, 72 Harrowdene Rd, Knowle, Bristol/ Ratti, E.; Waiter, 5 Lumber Court/ RAY, F.D. (S); Saloon Steward, Palmer Park Ave, Bristol/ Read, J.; Trimmer, 3 Nelson Pl./ Reed, C.; Bedroom Steward, 140 Derby Rd/ Reed, R.; Trimmer, 3 Wickham's Court/ Reeves, F.; Fireman, 22 Cable St/ Revell, W.; Saloon Steward, 102 Malmesbury Rd/ Ricadone, R.; Asst Waiter, 50 Greek St, London./ RICE, C. (S); Fireman, 12 Oriental Tce/ Rice. J.R.; Asst Purser, 37 Kimberly Drive, Great Crosby, Liverpool/ Rice. P.; Steward, 40 Tanqueray Rd/ Richards, J.; Fireman, 25 Summers St/ Ricks, C.G.; Asst Storekeeper Kitchen, 1 Hanley Rd/ Rickman, G.; Fireman, 40 Derby Rd/ Ridout, W.; Saloon Steward, 6 Queen Anne Buildings/ Rigozzi, A.; Waiter, 6 Titchfield St, London/ Rimmer, S.; Saloon Steward, 50 Cranbury Ave/ Roberts, F.; 3rd Butcher, 7 Dawson Cottages/ Roberts, G.; Fireman, 5 Withers Court/ Roberts, H.H.; Bedroom Steward, 39 Mary Rd, Liverpool/ ROBERTS, M.K., MRS. (S); Stewardess, 9 Chestnut Grove, Nottingham/ Robertson, W.G.; Asst Steward, 36 Mount St/ ROBINSON, A. MRS. (S); Stewardess, 128 Shirley Rd/ Robinson, J.M.; Saloon Steward, Vine Cottage, Carlisle Rd/ Rofers, E.J.W.; Asst Storekeeper Kitchen, 120 Oxford Ave/ Rogers, M.; Saloon Steward, 13 Greenhill Ave, Winchester/ ROSS, H. (S); Scullion, 70 Inkerman Rd/ Rotto, A.; Waiter, 10 West St, London/ Rous, A.; Plumber, 18 Ratcliffe Rd/ Rousseau, P ; Chef, 7 Kennerton Pl., London/ ROWE, G.T. (S); Quartermaster, 63 Henry St, Gosport/ Rowe, M.; Saloon Steward, 86 Bridge Rd/ Rudd, H.; Storekeeper, Engine Dept, 20 Peel St/ RULE, S.J. (S); Bath Steward, 81 Atherley Rd/ Rungem, T.; Greaser, Middle Rd/ Russell, R.; Saloon Steward, Anchor Hotel, Redbridge/ Ryan, T.; Steward, 87 Albert Rd/ RYERSON, W.E. (S); Saloon Steward, 18 Salop Rd, London

S
Saccaggi, G.; Asst Waiter, 22 Ponsonby Pl.; London/ Salussolia, G.; Glassman, 7 Colbath Sq., London/ Samuel, O.W.; Saloon Steward, 125 Osborne Rd/ Sangster, C.; Fireman, 83 Bevois St/ Sartori, L.; c/o Gatti; Employee (Failed to join)/ Saunders, D.E.; Saloon Steward, 29 Albert Rd/ Saunders, F.; Fireman, 17 Sussex Tce/ Saunders, W.; Fireman, 136 Edwards St/ Saunders, W.; Trimmer, 1 Southbrook Sq./ SAVAGE, C.J. (S); 3rd Class Steward, 8 Harold Rd/ Sawyer, R.J.; Window Cleaner, 55 Bevois St/ SCARROTT, J. (S); Able Seaman, 36 Albert Rd/ Scavino, C.; Carver, 231 Hamstead Rd, London/ Scott, A.; Fireman, 3 Lower Ditches/ SCOTT, F. (S); Greaser, 107 Clifford St/ Scovell, R.; Saloon Steward, 141 Foundry Lane/ Sedunary, S.P.; 2nd Third Class Steward, 34 Emsworth Rd/ Self, A.; Greaser, 75 Romsey Rd/ SELF, E. (S); Fireman, 3 Kingsley Rd/ SENIOR, H. (S); Fireman, 17 South Rd, London/ Sesea, G.; Waiter, 3 Little Putney Chambers,

London/ Sevier, W.; Steward, Westbourne St Mews, Paddington/ SEWARD, W. (S); Chief
Pantryman 2nd Class, 54 Stamford St, London & 5 Shirley Rd, Southampton/ Shaw,
H.; Scullion, 47 Towcester St, Liverpool/ Shaw, J.; Fireman (Deserted April 10th, 1912),
Northumberland Rd/Sheal, J.; Saloon Steward, 77 Portsmouth Rd/ Shea, T.; Fireman,
18 Briton St/ SHEATH, F. (S); Trimmer, 12 Bell St/ Shepherd, J.; Asst 2nd Engineer, 16
Bellevue Tce/ Shillaber, C.; Trimmer, 21 Nelson Rd/ SHIRES, A. (S); Fireman, 5 Peel
St/ Siebert, S.C.; Bedroom Steward (Buried at sea from the Carpathia, April 15th, 1912), 8
Harold Rd/ Simmonds, F.C.; Saloon Steward, 203 Middlebrook Rd/ SIMMONS, A. (S);
Scullion, 80 Bevois Valley Rd/ Simmons, W.; Passenger Cook, 2 Thackeray Rd/ Simson,
Dr. J.E.; Asst Surgeon, Packenham Rd, Belfast/ Sims, W.; Fireman (Left by consent
April 10th, 1912), Charlotte St/ Skeats, W.; Trimmer, 29 King St/ Skinner, E.; Saloon
Steward, Criterion Restaurant; Oxford St/ Slade, D.; Fireman (deserted 10 April 1912),
Chantry Rd/ Sla48 Be de, T.; Fireman (deserted 10 April 1912)/ Slight, H.J.; Steward,
48 Bellevue St/ Slight, W.; Larder Cook, Hillside, Broadland Rd/ SLOAN, M., MISS
(S); Stewardess, 1 Kersland Rd, Belfast/ Sloan, P.; Chief Electrician, 77A Clovelly Rd/
SLOCOMBE, M. (S); Masseuse (Turkish Bath), 8 Leopold Tce, Tottenham, London/
Small, W.; Leading Fireman, 14 Russell St, Liverpool/ Smillie, J.; Saloon Steward, 16
Malmesbury Rd/ Smith, C.; Scullion, 35 Itchen Ferry/ Smith, C.; Bedroom Steward,
Portsmouth Rd/ Smith, Captain Edward John; Commander Titanic, Woodhead, Winn
Rd/ Smith, F.; Asst Pantryman, 33 Ordnance Rd/ Smith, J.R.J.; Clerk (Post Office),
?, England/ Smith, J. ; Asst Baker, 5 Sir George's Rd, Freemantle/ Smith, J.N.; Jnr 4th
Engineer, Millars Rd, Itchen/ Smith. R.G.; Saloon Steward, 46 Stafford Rd/ SMITH,
T.E. MISS. (S); Stewardess, Balmoral, Cobbett Rd/ Smith, W.; Able Seaman, 42 Bridge
St/ Smither, H.; Fireman, 1 Ash Tree Rd/ Snape, Mrs.; Stewardess, Hill Lane, Sandown/
Snellgrove, G.; Fireman, 9 Cecil Ave/ Snooks, W.; Trimmer, Sailor's Home/ SNOW, E.
(S); Trimmer, 21 Lower Canal Walk/ SPARKMAN, H. (S); Fireman, Spring Rd, Sholing/
Stafford, M.; Greaser, 4 Southbrook Sq./ Stagg, J.H.; Saloon Steward, 66 Commercial
Rd/ Stanbrook, A.; Fireman, 36 York St/ STAP, S.A. MISS. (S); Stewardess, 41 Bidston
Ave, Birkenhead/ Stebbings, L.; Chief Boots., 25 Richfield Rd/ Steel, R.; Trimmer, No
Address/ STEWART, J. (S); Steward (Veranda Café), 77 Earles Rd/ Stocker, H., Trimmer,
Middle Rd, Sholing/ Stone, E.; Bedroom Steward, 91 Shirley Rd/ Stone, E.J.; Bedroom
Steward, 105 St Andrew's Rd/ STREET, A. (S); Fireman, 10 Crown St/ Stroud, A.; Saloon
Steward, 167 Shirley Rd/ Stroud, E.A.; Saloon Steward, 167 Shirley Rd/ Strugnell, J.;
Saloon Steward, Scullers Hotel/ Stubbings, H.; Cook & Steward's Mess, North Cottage,
Woodside, Lymington/ Stubbs, H.; Fireman, 11 Spa Rd/ Sullivan, S.; Fireman, 27 Marsh
Lane/ Swan, W.; Bedroom Steward, 62 Hale Rd, Walton, Liverpool/ Symonds, J.; Saloon
Steward, 61 Church St/ SYMONS, G. (S); Look-Out-Man, 55 Franchise St, Weymouth

T
Talbot, G.F.C.; Steward, 4 Alpha Villas, Lemon Rd/ Tamlyn, F.; Mess Steward, Deck Dept,
20 Southampton St/ Taylor, C.; Able Seaman, 85 High St/ Taylor, C.; Steward, 5 Oxford
St/ Taylor, F.; Fireman, 94 Manor Rd/ Taylor, J.; Fireman, 23 Queen's St/ TAYLOR, J. (S);
Fireman, 35 Russell St/ Taylor, L.; Turkish Bath Attendant, 6 Sherbourne Rd, Blackpool/
Taylor, P.C.; Orchestra (Cello), 9 Fentiman Rd, London/ Taylor, W.; Saloon Steward,
43 Morris Rd/ TAYLOR, W.H. (S); Fireman, 2 Broad St/ Terrell, B.; Able Seaman, 2
Trinity Cottages/ TERRELL, F. (S); Asst Steward, 5 Grove St/ Testoni, E.; Asst Glassman,
32-A St James Buildings, London/ Thaler, M.; Steward, 19 Station Rd, West Croydon/
THESSINGER, A. (S); Bedroom Steward, 102 French St/ THOMAS, A.C. (S); Saloon

Steward, 11 Brunswick Rd/ THOMAS, B. (S); Saloon Steward, 122 Avenue Rd/ Thomas, J.; Fireman, 20 Newman St/ Thompson, H.; 2nd Storekeeper Kitchen, Eastwood, Lumsden Ave/ THOMPSON, J. (S); Fireman, Primrose Hill, 2 House, Liverpool/ Thorley, W.; Asst Cook, 18 John St/ THRELLFALL, T. (S); Leading Fireman, 128 St Martin's Court/ THRESHER, G. (S); Fireman, 36 Mount Pleasant Rd/ Tietz, C.; Kitchen Porter, Richmond Tavern, Bridgewood/ Tizard, A.; Fireman, 23 Lower York St/ TOMS, F. (S); Saloon Steward, Bitterne Park/ Topp, T.; 2nd Butcher, 89 Millbrook Rd, Farnborough/ Tozer, J.; Greaser, 6 Chattis St/ TRIGGS, R. (S); Fireman, 3 Canal Walk/ Tucker, B.; 2nd Pantryman, 43 Suffolk Ave/ Turley, R.; Fireman, Sailor's Home/ Turner, G.F.; Stenographer, Bond Rd/ Turner, L.; Saloon Steward, 19 Terminus Tce/ Turvey, C.; Page Boy, 90 Cornwall Rd, London

U

Urbini, R.; Waiter, 16 Manette St, London

V

Valassori, E.; Waiter, 7 Great Russell St, London/ Veal, A.; Greaser, 15 Imperial Ave/ Veal, T.; Saloon Steward, 20 Forster Mount/ Vear, H.; Fireman, 2 Spa Gardens/ Vear, W.; Fireman, 2 Spa Gardens/ Vicat, J.; Fish Cook, 13 Howley St, London/ Villablange, P.; Asst Soup Cook, 8 Rue National, Albroise, France/ Vioni, R.; Waiter, 8 Lynton Mansions, London/ Vine, H.; Asst Controller, 55 Leith Mansions, London/ Vogelin, H.; Coffeeman, 3 Lumber Court, London

W

Wake, L.; Asst Baker, 2 Glouster Passage/ Wallis, Mrs.; Matron 3rd Class, 23 St Mary's St/ Walpole, J.; Chief Pantryman, 12 Stafford Rd/ Walsh, K., Miss; Stewardess, 57 Church St/ Ward, A.; Jnr Asst 4th Engineer, Manor House, Romsey/ Ward, E.; Bedroom Steward, 6 Blechynden Tce/ Ward, J.; Leading Fireman, 22 James St/ Ward, P.; Bedroom Steward, 36 Richmond Tce/ WARD, W. (S); Saloon Steward, 107 Millbrook Rd/ Wardner, F.; Fireman, 45 Endle St/ Wareham, R.A.; Bedroom Steward, 46 Park Rd/ Warwick, T.; Saloon Steward, Totton, Hants./ Wateridge, E.; Fireman, Millbrook Rd/ Watson, E.H.; Electrical Apprentice, Employee of Harland & Wolff, Belfast/ Watson, W.A.; Bell Boy, 23 Oakley Rd/ Watson, W.; Fireman, 13 York St/ Weatherstone, T.; Saloon Steward, 5 Kenilworth Rd/ Webb, B.; Smoke Room Steward, 34 Hanley Rd/ Webb, S.; Trimmer, Sailor's Home/ Webber, F.; Leading Fireman, 49 Avenue Rd/ WEIKMAN, A.H. (S); Barber, 9 Dyer Rd, Ivybank/ Welch, H.; Asst Cook, Bond St/ WELLER, W. (S); Able Seaman, Holyrood House/ WHEAT, J.T. (S); Asst 2nd Steward, 14 Cobden Gardens/ WHEELTON, E. (S); Saloon Steward, Norwood House/ White, A.; Asst Barber, 36 Purbrook Rd, Portsmouth/ WHITE, A.; Greaser, 3 Southampton Place/ White, F.; Trimmer, 14 Northbrook Rd/ White, J.; G.H. Steward, 41 Thackeray Rd/ White, L.; Saloon Steward, 248 Romsey Rd/ WHITE, W.G. (S); Trimmer, 9 Coblence St, Woking/ WHITELEY, T. (S); 1st Class Saloon Steward, 29 St John's Park, Highgate, London/ Whitford, A.; Saloon Steward, 33 Richmond St/ WIDGERY, J.G. (S); 2nd Class Steward, 25 Rokeby Ave, Bristol/ Wilde, H.T.; Chief Officer, 25 Grey Rd, Walton, Liverpool/ Willis, W.; Steward, 59 Derby Rd/ Williams, A.J.; Asst Storekeeper Kitchen, 52 Peter Rd; Walton, Liverpool/ Williams, E.; Fireman, 2 Canal Walk/ WILLIAMS, W. (S); Asst Steward, 52 Northumberland Rd/ Williamson, J.B.; Clerk (Post Office), ?, England/ Wilson, B.; Snr 2nd Engineer Asst, 40 Richmond Rd/ Wilton, W.; Trimmer, 5 Queen's St/ Wiltshire, W.; Asst Butcher, 8

Britannia Rd/ WINDEBANK, A. (S); Sauce Cook, Elmhurst/ Witcher, A.; Fireman,
9 Wilson Place/ Witt, F.; Trimmer, St Michael's House/ Witt, H.; Fireman, 28 Lower
Cottage St/ WITTER, J. (S); Smoke Room Steward, 56 Porchester Rd/ Wittman, H.;
Bedroom Steward, 12 Richville Rd/ Wood, J.T.; Asst Steward, 7 Norfolk Rd, London/
Woods, H.; Trimmer, St Michael's House/ Woodford, F.; Greaser, 14 Clovelly Rd/
Woodward, J.W.; Orchestra (Pianist), The Firs, Windmill Rd, Headington, Oxfordshire/
Woody, O.S.; Clerk (Post Office), Washington, D.C./ Wormald, F.; Saloon Steward, 5
Testwood Rd/ Wrapson, H.; Asst Pantryman, 33 Southampton St/ Wright, F.; Squash
Court Attendant, 12 Steur St, Shepherd's Bush, London/ Wright, W.; G.H. Steward, 9
Elmsworth Rd/ Wyeth, J.; Fireman, 14 Millbank St/ WYNN, W. (S); Quartermaster, 8
Church St

Y
YEARSLEY, H.; Saloon Steward, 6 Gloucester Passage/ Yoshack, J.; Saloon Steward,
Malmesbury Rd/ Young, F.; Fireman, 28 Russell St

Z
Zanetti, M.; Asst Waiter, Cairo Cafe, 3 Soho St, London/ Zarracchi, L.; Wine Butler, 9
Orchard Place

Titanic's Engineers

All were lost in the disaster. Although Tom Andrews was previously listed as a passenger, and the remainder as crew, I list them together again.

ALLSOP, ALFRED SAMUEL; Junior Electrician/ ANDREWS, THOMAS Jnr.; Chief Designer of Titanic/ BELL, W. JOSEPH; Chief Engineer/ CHISNALL, GEORGE ALEXANDER; Senior Boilermaker/ COY, FRANCIS ERNEST GEORGE; Junior Assistant Third Engineer/ CREESE, HENRY PHILIP; Deck Engineer/ DODD, EDWARD C.; Junior Third Engineer/ DODDS, RENNEY WATSON; Junior Assistant Fourth Engineer/ DUFFY, WILLIAM LUKE,; Chief Engineer's Clerk (writer)/ DYER, HENRY RYLAND; Senior Assistant Fourth Engineer/ ERVINE, ALBERT GEORGE; Assistant Electrician/ FARQUHARSON, W. E.; Senior Second Engineer/ FITZPATRICK, HUGH; Assistant Boilermaker/ FRASER, JAMES; Junior Assistant Third Engineer/ HARRISON, NORMAN; Junior Second Engineer/ HARVEY, HERBERT, GIFFORD; Junior Assistant Second Engineer/ HESKETH, J. H.; Junior Second Engineer/ HODGE, CHARLES; Senior Assistant Third Engineer/ HODGKINSON, LEONARD; Senior Fourth Engineer/ HOSKING, GEORGE FOX; Senior Third Engineer/ JUPE, HERBERT; Assistant Electrician/ KEMP, THOMAS HULMAN; Extra Assistant Fourth Engineer (refrigerator)/ MACKIE, W.D.; Junior Fifth Engineer/ McREYNOLDS, WILLIAM; Junior Sixth Engineer/ MIDDLETON, ALFRED PIRRIE; Assistant Electrician/ MILLAR, ROBERT; Extra Fifth Engineer/ MILLAR, THOMAS; Assistant Deck Engineer/ MOYES, WILLIAM YOUNG; Senior Sixth Engineer/ PARSONS, FRANK ALFRED; Senior Fifth Engineer/ ROUS, ARTHUR J.; Plumber/ SHEPHERD, JONATHAN; Junior Assistant Second Engineer/ SLOAN, PETER; Chief Electrician/ SMITH, JAMES M.; Junior Fourth Engineer/ WARD, ARTHUR; Junior Assistant Fourth Engineer/ WILSON, BERTIE; Senior Assistant Second Engineer.

From: Institute of Marine Engineers – vol. XXIV, Memorial to the Titanic Engineering Staff (reprint THS, April 1990)

Grateful thanks to Brian Ticehurst and to Don Lynch. The latter is historian of the Titanic Historical Society, Inc.

Titanic Passenger List

The White Star Line's final list of lost and saved, dated 9 May 1912. Those saved are in italics.

FIRST-CLASS PASSENGERS

A

Allen, Miss Elizabeth Walton/ Allison, Mr H.J./ Allison, Mrs H.J. *and maid*/ Allison, Miss L./ *Allison, Master T. and nurse Anderson, Mr Harry*/ *Andrews, Miss Cornelia I.*/ Andrews, Mr Thomas/ *Appleton, Mrs E.D.*/ Artagaveyta, Mr Ramon/ Astor, Colonel J.J. and Manservant/ *Astor, Mrs J.J. and Maid*/ *Aubert, Mrs N. and Maid*

B

Barkworth, Mr A.H/ Baumann, Mr J./ *Baxter, Mrs James*/ Baxter, Mr Quigg/ Beattie, Mr T.; *Beckwith, Mr R.L.*/ *Beckwith, Mrs R.L.*/ *Behr, Mr K.H.*/ *Bishop, Mr D.H.*/ *Bishop, Mrs. D.H.*/ Bjornstrom, Mr H./ Blackwell, Mr Stephen Weart/ *Blank, Mr Henry*/ *Bonnell, Miss Caroline*/ *Bonnell, Miss Lily*/ Borebank, Mr J.J./ *Bowen, Miss*/ *Bowerman, Miss Elsie*/ Brady, Mr John B./ Brandeis, Mr E./ *Brayton, Mr George*/ Brewe, Dr. Arthur Jackson/ *Brown, Mrs.J.J.*/ *Brown, Mrs J.M.*/ *Bucknell, Mrs W. and Maid*/ Butt, Major Archibald W.

C

Calderhead, Mr E.P./ *Candee, Mrs Churchill*/ *Cardoza, Mrs J.W.M.; and Maid*/ *Cardoza, Mr T.D.M.; and Manservant*/ Carran, Mr F.M./ Carran, Mr J. P./ *Carter, Mr William E.*/ *Carter, Mrs William E.and Maid*/ *Carter, Miss Lucile*/ *Carter, Master William T. and Manservant*/ Case, Mr Howard B./ *Cassebeer, Mrs H.A.*/ Cavendish, Mr T.W./ *Cavendish, Mrs T.W. and Maid*/ Chaffee, Mr Herbert F./ *Chaffee, Mrs Herbert F.*/ Chambers, Mr N.C./ *Chambers, Mrs N.C.*/ *Cherry, Miss Gladys*/ *Chevré, Mr Paul*/ *Chibnall, Mrs E.M. Bowerman*/ Chisholm, Mr Robert/ Clark, Mr Walter M./ *Clark, Mrs Walter M.*/ Clifford, Mr George Quincy/ Colley, Mr E.P./ *Compton, Mrs A.T.*/ *Compton Miss S.P.*/ Compton, Mr A.T., Jnr/*Cornell, Mrs R.G.*/ Crafton, Mr John B./ Crosby, Mr Edward G./ *Crosby, Mrs. Edward G.*/ *Crosby, Miss Harriet*/ Cummings, Mr John Bradley/ *Cummings, Mrs John Bradley*

LOST.		SAVED.
First Class Passengers.	118 Men.	57 Men.
	4 Women.	140 Women.
	0 Children.	6 Children.
Second Class Passengers.	154 Men.	14 Men.
	13 Women.	80 Women.
	0 Children.	24 Children.
Third Class Passengers.	387 Men.	75 Men.
	89 Women.	76 Women.
	52 Children.	27 Children.
Total Passengers.	659 Men.	146 Men.
	106 Women.	296 Wmn.
	52 Children.	57 Children.
Total Crew.	670 Men.	192 Men.
	3 Women.	20 Women.
Total Passengers and Crew.	1329 Men.	338 Mn.
	109 Women.	316 Wmn.
	52 Children.	57 Children.

Chart showing the proportion of those lost and saved. Report, British Inquiry.

D

Daly, Mr P.D./ Daniel, Mr Robert W./ Davidson, Mr Thornton/ *Davidson, Mrs Thornton/ de Villiers, Mrs B/ Dick, Mr A.A./ Dick, Mrs A.A./ Dodge, Dr Washington/ Dodge, Mrs Washington/ Dodge, Master Washington/ Douglas, Mrs F.C./ Douglas, Mrs F.C./* Douglas, Mr W.D./ *Douglas, Mrs W.D.* and Maid/ Dulles, Mr William C.

E

Earnshew, Mrs Boulton/ Endres, Miss Caroline/ Eustis, Miss E.M./ Evans, Miss E.

F

Flegenheim, Mrs A./ Flynn, Mr J.I./ Foreman, Mr B.L./ Fortune, Mr Mark/ *Fortune, Mrs Mark/ Fortune, Miss Ethel/ Fortune, Miss Alice/ Fortune, Miss Mabel/* Fortune, Mr Charles/ Franklin, Mr T.P./ *Frauenthal, Mr T.G./ Frauenthal, Dr Henry W./ Frauenthal, Mrs Henry W./ Frohlicher, Miss Marguerite/* Futrelle, Mr J./ *Futrelle, Mrs J.*

G

Gee, Mr Arthur/ *Gibson, Mrs L./ Gibson, Miss D./* Giglio, Mr Victor/ *Goldenberg, Mr S.L./ Goldenberg, Mrs S.L./* Goldschmidt, Mrs George B./ *Gordon, Sir Cosmo Duff/ Gordon, Lady Duff and Maid/* Gracie, Colonel Archibald/ Graham, Mr/ *Graham, Mrs William C./ Graham, Miss Margaret/ Greenfield, Mrs L.D./ Greenfield, Mr W.B./* Guggenheim, Mr Benjamin/ *Harder, Mr George A./ Harder, Mrs George A.*

H

Harper, Mr Henry Sleeper and Manservant/ Harper, Mrs Henry Sleeper/ Harris, Mr Henry B./ *Harris, Mrs Henry B./* Harrison. Mr W. H./ *Haven, Mr H./ Hawksford, Mr W.J./* Hays, Mr Charles M./ *Hays, Mrs Charles M.* and Maid/ *Hays, Miss Margaret/* Head, Mr Christopher/

Hilliard, Mr Herbert Henry/ Hipkins, Mr W.E./ *Hippach, Mrs Ida S./ Hippach, Miss Jean/ Hogeboom, Mrs John C./* Holverson, Mr A.O./ *Holverson, Mrs A. O./ Hoyt, Mr Frederick M./ Hoyt, Mrs Frederick M./* Hoyt, Mr W. F.

I

Isham, Miss A. E./ *Ismay, Mr J. Bruce* and Manservant

J

Jakob, Mr Birnbaum/ Jones, Mr C.C./ Julian, Mr H. F.

K

Kent, Mr Edward A./ Kenyon, Mr F. R./ *Kenyon, Mrs F. R./ Kimball, Mr E.N./ Kimball, Mrs E.N./* Klaber, Mr Herman

L

Lambert-Williams, Mr Fletcher Fellows/ *Leader, Mrs F.A./* Lewy, Mr E. G./ *Lindstroem, Mrs J./ Lines, Mrs Ernest H./ Lines, Miss Mary C./* Lingrey, Mr Edward/ Long, Mr Milton C./ *Longley, Miss Gretchen F./* Loring, Mr J.H.

M

Madill, Miss Georgette Alexandra/ Maguire, Mr J.E./ *Maréchal, Mr Pierre/* Marvin, Mr D.W./ *Marvin, Mrs D.W./* McCaffry, Mr T./ McCarthy, Mr Timothy/ *McGough, Mr J.R./* Meyer, Mr Edgar J./ *Meyer, Mrs Edgar J./* Millet, Mr Frank D./ Minahan, Dr W. E./ *Minahan, Mrs W. E./ Minahan, Miss Daisy/* Moch, Mr Philip E./ Molsom, Mr H. Markland/ Moore, Mr Clarence and Manservant

N

Natsch, Mr Charles/ Newell, Mr A.W./ *Newell, Miss Alice/ Newell, Miss Madeline/ Newsom, Miss Helen/* Nicholson, Mr A. S.

O

Omont, Mr F./ Ostby, Mr E.C./ *Ostby, Miss Helen R./* Ovies, Mr S.

P

Parr, Mr M.H.W./ Partner, Mr Austin/ Payne, Mr V./ Pears, Mr Thomas/ *Pears, Mrs Thomas/* Penasco, Mr Victor/ *Penasco, Mrs Victor* and Maid/ *Peuchen, Major Arthur/* Porter, Mr Walter Chamberlain/ *Potter, Mrs Thomas, Jr*

R

Reuchlin, Jonkheer J.G./ *Rheims, Mr George/ Robert, Mrs Edward S. and Maid/* Roebling, Mr Washington A., 2nd/ *Rolmane, Mr C./* Rood, Mr Hugh R./ *Rosenbaum, Miss/* Ross, Mr J. Hugo/ *Rothes, the Countess of and Maid/* Rothschild, Mr M./ *Rothschild, Mrs M./* Rowe, Mr Alfred/ Ryerson, Mr Arthur/ *Ryerson, Mrs Arthur/ Ryerson, Miss Emily/ Ryerson, Miss Susan/ Ryerson, Master Jack*

S

Sallfeld, Mr Adolphe/ Schabert, Mrs Paul/ Seward, Mr Frederick K./ Shutes, Miss E.W./ Silverthorne, Mr S.V./ Silvey, Mr William B./ *Silvey, Mrs William B./ Simonius, Oberst Alfons/ Sloper, Mr William T./* Smart, Mr John M./ Smith, Mr J. Clinch/ Smith, Mr. R.W./

Smith, Mr L.P./ *Smith, Mrs L.P./ Snyder, Mr John/ Snyder, Mrs John/ Soloman, Mr A.L./ Spedden, Mr Frederick O./ Spedden, Mrs Frderick O. and Maid/ Spedden, Master R. Douglas and Nurse/* Spencer, Mr W.A./ *Spencer, Mrs W.A. and Maid/* Stahelin, Dr Max/ Stead, Mr W.T./ *Steffanson, H.B./ Stehli, Mr Max Frolicher/ Stehli, Mrs Max Frolicher/* Stengel, Mr C.E.H./ *Stengel, Mrs C.E.H./ Stephenson, Mrs W.B./* Stewart, Mr A.A./ *Stone, Mrs George M. and Maid/* Straus, Mr Isidor and Manservant/ Straus, Mrs Isidor *and Maid/* Sutton, Mr Frederick/ *Swift, Mrs Frederick Joel*

T
Taussig, Mr Emil/ *Taussig, Mrs Emil/ Taussig, Miss Ruth/ Taylor, Mr E.Z./ Taylor, Mrs. E.Z./* Thayer, Mr John B./ *Thayer, Mrs J.B. and Maid/ Thayer, Mr J.B., Jnr/* Thorne, Mr G./ *Thorne, Mrs G./ Tucker, Mr G.M., Jnr.*

U
Uruchurtu, Mr. M.R.

V
Van der Hoef, Mr Wyckoff

W
Walker, Mr W. Anderson/ Warren, Mr F.M./ *Warren, Mrs. F.M./* Weir, Mr. J./ White, Mr Percival W./ White, Mr Richard F. and Manservant/ *White, Mrs J. Stuart and Maid/* Wick, Mrs George D./ *Wick, Mrs George D./ Wick, Miss Mary/* Widener, Mr George D. and Manservant/ *Widener, Mrs George D. and Maid/* Widener, Mr Harry/ *Willard, Miss Constance/* Williams, Mr Duane/ *Williams, Mr. R.N., Jnr/ Woolner, Mr Hugh/* Wright, Mr George/ *Young, Miss Marie and Maid*

SECOND-CLASS PASSENGERS

A
Abelson, Mr. Samson/ *Abelson, Mrs Hanna/* Aldworth, Mr C./ Andrew, Mr Edgar/ Andrew, Mr Frank/ Angle, Mr William/ *Angle, Mrs/* Ashby, Mr John

B
Baily, Mr Percy/ Baimbrigge, Mr Chas. R./ *Balls, Mrs Ada E./* Banfield, Mr Frederick, J./ Bateman, Mr Robert J./ *Beane, Mr Edward/ Beane, Mrs Ethel/* Beauchamp, Mr H.J./ *Becker, Mrs A.O. and three children/ Beesley, Mr Lawrence/ Bentham, Miss Lilian W./* Berriman, Mr William/ Botsford, Mr W. Hull/ Bowenur, Mr Solomon/ Bracken, Mr Jas. H./ Brito, Mr Jose de/ *Brown, Miss Mildred/* Brown, Mr S./ Brown, Mrs/ *Brown, Miss E./* Bryhl, Mr Curt/ *Bryhl, Miss Dagmar/Buss, Miss Kate/* Butler, Mr Reginald/ Byles, Rev. Thomas R. D./ *Bystrom, Miss Karolina*

C
Caldwell, Mr Albert F./ Caldwell, Mrs Sylvia/ Caldwell, Master Alden G./ Cameron, Miss Clear/ Carbines, Mr William/ Carter, Rev. Ernest C./ Carter, Mrs Lilian/ Chapman, Mr John H./ Chapman, Mrs Elizabeth/ Chapman, Mr Charles/ *Christy, Miss Alice/ Christy, Miss Juli/* Clarke, Mr Charles V./ *Clarke, Mrs Ada Maria/* Coleridge, Mr R. C./ Collander,

Mr Erik/ *Collett, Mr Stuart/ Collyer, Mrs Charlotte/ Collyer, Miss Marjorie/* Corbett, Mrs Irene/ Corey, Mrs C.P./ Cotterill, Mr Harry

D
Davies, Mr Charles/ *Davis, Mrs Agnes/ Davis, Master John M./ Davis, Miss Mary/* Deacon, Mr Percy/ del Carlo, Mr Sebastian/ del Carlo, Mrs/ Denbou, Mr Herbert/ Dibden, Mr William/ *Doling, Mrs Ada/ Doling, Miss Elsie/* Downton, Mr William J./ *Drachstedt, Baron von/* drew, Mr James V./ *Drew, Miss Lulu/ Drew, Master Marshall/ Duran, Miss Florentina/ Duran, Miss Asuncion*

E
Eitemiller, Mr G.F./ Enander, Mr Ingvar

F
Fahlstrom, Mr Arne J./ Faunthorpe, Mr Harry/ *Faunthorpe, Mrs Lizzie/* Fillbrook, Mr Charles/ Fox, Mr Stanley H./ Funk, Miss Annie/ Fynney, Mr Jos.

G
Gale, Mr Harry/ Gale, Mr Shadrach/ *Garside, Miss Ethel/* Gaskell, Mr Alfred/ Gavey, Mr Lawrence/ Gilbert, Mr William/ Giles, Mr Edgar/ Giles, Mr Fred/ Giles, Mr Ralph/ Gill, Mr John/ Gillespie, Mr William/ Givard, Mr Hans K./ Greenberg, Mr Samuel

H
Hale, Mr Reginald/ *Mr Hamalainer, Mrs Anna and Infant/* Harbeck, Mr Wm H./ Harper, Mr John/ *Harper, Miss Nina/ Harris, Mr John/* Harris, Mr Walter/ Hart, Mr Benjamin/ *Hart, Mrs Esther/ Hart, Miss Eva/ Herman, Miss Alice/ Herman, Miss Jane/ Herman, Miss Kate/* Herman, Mr Samuel/ *Hewlett, Mrs Mary D./* Hickman, Mr Leonard/ Hickman, Mr Lewis/ Hickman, Mr Stanley/ Hiltunen, Miss Martha/ Hocking, Mr George/ *Hocking, Miss Elizabeth/ Hocking, Miss Nellie/* Hocking, Mr Samuel J./ Hodges, Mr Henry P./ Hoffman, Mr *and two children (Lolo and Louis)/ Hold, Miss Annie/* Hold, Mr Stephen/ Hood, Mr Ambrose/ *Hosono, Mr Masaburni/* Howard, Mr Benjamin/ Howard, Mrs Ellen T./ Hunt, Mr George

I
Ilett, Miss Bertha

J
Jacobsohn, Miss Amy F./ Jacobsohn, Mr Sidney S./ Jarvis, Mr John D./ Jefferys, Mr Clifford/ Jefferys, Mr Ernest/ Jenkin, Mr Stephen/ *Jervan, Mrs A.T.*

K
Kantor, Mrs Miriam/ Kantor, Mr Sehua/ Keane, Mr Daniel/ *Keane, Miss Nora/ Kelly, Mrs F./* Kirkland, Rev. Charles L./ Kvillner, Mr John Henrik

L
Lathinen, Mrs Anna/ Lahtinen, Mr William/ Lamb, Mr J.J./ *Lamore, Miss Amelia/* Laroche, Mr Joseph/ *Laroche, Mrs Juliet/ Laroche, Miss Louise/ Laroche, Miss Simonne/ Lehman, Miss Bertha/ Leitch, Miss Jessie/* Levy, Mr R.J./ Leyson, Mr Robert W.N./ Lingan, Mr John/ Louch, Mr Charles/ *Louch, Mrs Alice Adela*

M

Mack, Mrs Mary/ Malachard, Mr Noel/ Mallet, Mr A/ *Mallet, Mrs/ Mallet, Master A./* Mangiavacchi, Mr Emilio/ Mantvila, Mr Joseph/ Marshall, Mr/ *Marshall, Mrs Kate/* Matthews, Mr W.J./ Maybery, Mr Frank H./ McCrae, Mr Arthur G./ McCrie, Mr James/ McKane, Mr Peter D./ *Mellenger, Miss Elizabeth/ Mellenger, Miss M./ Mellers, Mr William/* Meyer, Mr August/ Milling, Mr Jacob C./ Mitchell, Mr Henry/ Morawick, Dr Ernest/ Mudd, Mr Thomas C./ Myles, Mr Thomas F.

N

Nasser, Mr Nicolas/ *Nasser, Mrs/* Nesson, Mr Israel/ Nicholls, Mr Joseph C./ Norman, Mr Robert D./ *Nye, Mrs Elizabeth*

O

Otter, Mr Richard/ *Oxenham, Mr P. Thomas*

P

Padro, Mr Julian/ Pain, Dr Alfred/ *Pallas, Mr Emilio/* Parker, Mr Clifford R./ *Parrish, Mrs L. Davis/* Pengelly, Mr Frederick/ Pernot, Mr René/ Peruschitz, Rev. Jos. M./ Phillips, Mr Robert/ *Phillips, Miss Alice/ Pinsky, Miss Rosa/* Ponesel, Mr Martin/ *Portaluppi, Mr Emilio/* Pulbaun, Mr Frank

Q

Quick, Mrs Jane/ Quick, Miss Vera W./ Quick, Miss Phyllis

R

Reeves, Mr David/ Renouf, Mr Peter H./ *Renouf, Miss Lillie/* Richards, Mr Emile/ *Richards, Mrs Emile/ Richards, Master William/ Ridsdale, Miss Lucy/* Rogers, Mr Harry/ *Rogers, Miss Selina/ Rugg, Miss Emily*

S

Sedgwick, Mr C.W.F./ Sharp, Mr Percival/ *Shelley, Mrs Imanita/ Silven, Miss Lyyli/ Sincock, Miss Maude/ Sinkkenen, Miss Anna/* Sjostedt, Mr Ernest A./ *Slayter, Miss H.M./* Slemen, Mr Richard J./ Smith, Mr Augustus/ *Smith, Miss Marion/* Sobey, Mr Hayden/ Stanton, Mr S. Ward/ Stokes, Mr Philip J./ Swane, Mr George/ Sweet, Mr George

T

Toomey, Miss Ellen/ Trant, Miss Jessie/ Tronpiansky, Mr Moses A./ *Troutt, Miss E. Celia/* Turpin, Mrs Dorothy/ Turpin, Mr William J.

V

Veale, Mr James

W

Walcroft, Miss Nellie/ Ware, Mrs Florence L./ Ware, Mr John James/ Ware, Mr William J./ *Watt, Miss Bertha/ Watt, Mrs Bessy/ Webber, Miss Susie/* Weisz, Mr Leopold/ *Weisz, Mrs Matilda/ Wells, Mrs Addie/ Wells, Miss J./ Wells, Master Ralph/* West, Mr E. Arthur/ *West, Mrs Ada/ West, Miss Barbara/ West, Miss Constance/* Wheadon, Mr Edward/ Wheeler, Mr Edwin/ *Wilhelms, Mr Charles/ Williams, Mr C./ Wight, Miss Marion*

Y
Yrois, Miss H.

THIRD-CLASS PASSENGERS

British subjects embarked at Southampton

A

Abbing, Anthony/ Abbott, Eugene/ *Abbott, Rosa*/ Abbott, Rosmore/ Adams, J./ *Aks, Filly*/ *Aks, Leah*/ Alexander, William/ Allen, William/ Allum, Owen G.

B

Badman, Emily/ Barton, David/ Beavan, W.T./ Billiard, A.van/ Billiard, James (child)/ Billiard, Walter (child)/ *Bing, Lee*/ Bowen, David/ Braund, Lewis/ Braund, Owen/ Brocklebank, William

C

Cann, Ernest/ Carver, A./ Celotti, Francesco/ *Chip, Chang*/ Christmann, Emil/ *Cohen, Gurshon*/ Cook, Jacob/ Corn, Harry/ *Coutts, Winnie*/ *Coutts, William* (child)/ *Coutts, Leslie*/ (child)/ Coxon, Daniel/ Crease, Ernest James/ Cribb< John Hatfield/ *Cribb, Alice*

D

Dahl, Charles/ Davies, Evan/ Davies, Alfred/ Davies, John/ Davis, Joseph/ Davison, Thomas H./ *Davison, Mary*/ Dean, Mr Bertram F./ *Dean, Mrs Hetty*/ *Dean, Bertram* (child)/ *Dean, Vera* (infant)/ Dennis, Samuel/ Dennis, William/ *Derkings, Edward*/ *Dowdell, Elizabeth*/ *Drapkin, Jenie*/ *Dugemin, Joseph*

E

Elsbury, James/ *Emanuel, Ethel* (child)/ Everett, Thomas

F

Foo, Choong/ Ford, Arthur/ Ford, Margaret/ Ford, Miss D. M./ Ford, Mr E. W./ Ford, M. W. T. N./ Ford, Maggie, (child)/ Franklin, Charles

G

Garfirth, John/ Gilinski, Leslie/ *Godwin, Frederick*/ *Goldsmith, Emily, A./* Goldsmith, Frank J./ *Goldsmith, Frank J. W./* Goodwin, Augusta/ Goodwin, Lillian A./ Goodwin, Charles E./ Goodwin, William F. (child)/ Goodwin, Jessie (child)/ Goodwin, Harold (child)/ Goodwin, Sidney (child)/ Green, George/ Guest, Robert

H

Harknett, Alice/ Harmer, Abraham/ *Hee, Ling*/ *Howard, May*/ *Hyman, Abraham*

J

Johnson, Mr A./ Johnson, Mr W./ Johnston, A.G./ Johnston, Mrs/ Johnston, William (child)/ Johnston, Miss C.H. (child)

K
Keefe, Arthur/ Kelly, James

L
Lam, Ali/ Lam, Len/ *Lang, Fang*/ Leonard, Mr L./ Lester, James/ Ling, Lee/ Lithman, Simon/ Lobb, Cordelia/ Lobb, William A./ Lockyer, Edward/ Lovell, John

M
Mackay, George W./ Maisner, Simon/ McNamee, Neal/ Meanwell, Marian O./ Meek, Annie L./ Meo, Alfonso/ Miles, Frank/ *Moor, Beile*/ *Moor, Meier*/ Moore, Leonard C./ Morley, William/ Moutal, Rahamin/ Murdlin, Joseph

N
Nancarrow, W.H./ Niklasen, Sander/ Nosworthy, Richard C.

P
Peacock, Alfred (infant)/ Peacock, Treasteall (child)/ Pearce, Ernest/ Peduzzi, Joseph/ Perkin, John Henry/ Peterson, Mairus/ Potchett, George

R
Rath, Sarah/ Reed, James George/ Reynolds, Harold/ Risien, Emma/ Risien, Samuel/ Robins, Alexander/ Robins, Charity/ Rogers, William John/ Rouse, Richard H./ Rush, Alfred George J.

S
Sadowitz, Harry/ Sage, John/ Sage, Annie/ Sage, Stella/ Sage, George/ Sage, Douglas/ Sage, Frederick/ Sage, Dorothy/ Sage, William (child)/ Sage, Ada (child)/ Sage, Constance (child)/ Sage, Thomas (child)/ Sather, Simon/ Saundercock. W. H./ Sawyer, Frederick/ Scrota, Maurice/ Shellard, Frederick/ Shorney, Charles/ Simmons, John/ Slocovski, Selman/ Somerton, Francis W./ Spector, Woolf/ Spinner, Henry/ *Stanley, Amy*/ Stanley, Mr E. R./ Storey, Mr T./ *Sunderland, Victor*/ Sutehall, Henry

T
Theobald, Thomas/ Thomson, Alex/ *Thorneycroft, Florence*/ Thorneycroft, Percival/ Tomlin, Ernest P./ Torber, Ernest/ *Trembisky, Berk*/ *Tunquist, W.*

W
Ware, Frederick/ Warren, Charles W./ Webber, James/ *Wilkes, Ellen*/ Willey, Edward/ Williams, Harry/ Williams, Leslie/ Windelov, Elnar/ Wiseman, Philip

Non-British embarked at Southampton

A
Abelset, Karen/ *Abelseth, Olaus*/ *Abrahamson, August*/ Adahl, Mauritz/ *Adolf, Humblin*/ Ahlin, Johanna/ Ahmed, Ali/ Alhomaki, Ilmari/ Ali, William/ Anderson, Alfreda/ *Anderson, Erna*/ Anderson, Albert/ Anderson, Anders/ Anderson, Samuel/ Anderson, Sigrid (child)/ Anderson, Thor/ *Anderson, Carla*/ Anderson, Ingeborg (child)/ Anderson, Ebba (child)/ Anderson, Sigbard (child)/ Anderson, Ellis/ Anderson, Ida Augusta/ Andreason, Paul Edvin/ Angheloff, Minko/ Arnold, Joseph/ Arnold, Josephine/ Aronsson, Ernest Axel A./ Asim, Adola/ Asplund, Carl (child)/ *Asplund, Felix* (child)/ Asplund, Gustaf (child)/

Asplund, Johan/ Asplund Lilian (child)/ Asplund, Oscar (child)/ *Asplund, Selma/* Assam, Ali/ Augustsan, Albert

B

Backstrom, Karl/ *Backstrom, Marie/* Balkic, Cerin/ Benson, John Viktor/ Berglund, Ivar/ Berkeland, Hans/ Bjorklund, Ernst/ Bostandyeff, Guentcho/ Braf, Elin Ester/ Brobek, Carl R.

C

Cacic, Grego/ Cacic, Luka/ Cacic, Maria/ Cacic, Manda/ Calie, Peter/ Carlson, Carl R./ Carlson, Julius/ Carlsson, August Sigfrid/ Coelho, Domingos Fernardeo/ Coleff, Fotio/ Coleff, Peyo/ Cor, Bartol/ Cor, Ivan/ Cor, Ludovik

D

Dahl, Mauritz/ Dahlberg, Gerda/ Dakic, Branko/ Danbom, Ernest/ Danbom, Gillber (infant)/ Danbom, Sigrid/ Danoff, Yoto/ Dantchoff, Khristo/ Delalic, Regyo/ Denkoff, Mito/ Dimic, Jovan/ Dintcheff, Valtcho/ Dyker, Adolf/ *Dyker, Elizabeth*

E

Ecimovic, Joso/ Edwardsson, Gustaf/ Eklunz, Hans/ Ekstrom, Johan

F

Finote, Luigi/ Fischer, Eberhard

G

Goldsmith, Nathan/ Goncalves, Manoel E./ Gronnestad, Daniel D./ Gustafson, Alfred/ Gustafson, Anders/ Gustafson, Johan/ Gustafsson, Gideon

H

Haas, Aloisia/ *Hadman, Oscar/* Hagland, Angvald O./ Hagland, Konrad, R./ Hakkurainen, Pekko/ *Hakkurainen, Elin/* Hampe, Leon/ *Hankonen, Eluna/* Hansen, Claus/*Hansen, Janny/* Hansen, Henry Damgavd/ Heininen, Wendla/ Hendekovic, Ignaz/ Hendekovic, Jenny/ *Hervonen, Helga/ Hervonen, Hildwe* (child)/ *Hickkinen, Laina/* Holm, John, F.A./ Holten, Johan/ Humblin, Adolf.

I

Ilief, Ylio/ Ilmakangas, Pista/ Ivanoff, Konio

J

Jansen, Carl/ Jardin, Jose Netto/ *Jensen, Carl/* Jensen, Hans Peter/ Jensen, Svenst L./ Jensen, Nilho R./ *Johannessen, Bernt/ Johannessen, Elias/* Johansen, Nils/ *Johanson, Oscar/ Johanson, Oscar L./* Johansson, Erik/ Johansson, Gustaf/ Johnson, Jakob A./ *Johnson, Alice/ Johnson, Harold/ Johnson, Eleanor* (infant)/ Johnsson, Carl/ Johnsson, Malkolm/, Jonkoff, Lazor/ Jonsson, Nielo H./ Jusila, Katrina/ Jusila, Mari/ *Jusila, Erik/* Jutel, Henrik Hansen

K

Kallio, Nikolai/ Kalvig, Johannes H./ Karajic, Milan/ *Karlson, Einar/* Karson, Nils August/ Kekic, Tido/ *Kink, Anton/ Kink, Louise/ Kink, Louise* (child)/ Kink, Maria/ Kink, Vincenz/ Klasen, Klas A./ Klasen, Hilda/ Klasen, Gertrud (child)

L

Laitinen, Sofia/ Laleff, Kristo/ *Landegren, Aurora*/ Larson, Viktor/ Larsson, Bengt Edvin/ Larsson, Edvard/ Lefebre, Frances/ Lefebre, Henry (child)/ Lefebre, Ida (child)/ Lefebre, Jeannie (child)/ Lefebre, Mathilde (child)/ Leinonen, Antti/ Lindablom, August/ Lindahl, Agda/ Lindell, Edvard B./ Lindell, Elin/ *Lindqvist, Einar*/ *Lulic, Nicola*/ Lundahl, John/ *Lundin, Olga*/ *Lundstrom, Jan*

M

Madsen, Fridjof/ Maenpaa, Matti/ Maidenoff, Penko/ Makinen, Kalle/ *Mampe, Leon*/ Marinko, Dmitri/ Markoff, Marin/ Melkebuk., Philemon/ *Messemacker,* Guillaum/ *Messemacker,* Emma/ *Midtsjo, Carl*/ *Mikanen, John*/ Mineff, Ivan/ Minkoff, Lazar/ Mirko, Dika/ Mitkoff, Mito/ Moen, Sigurd H./ *Moss, Albert*/ *Mulder, Theo*/ Myhrman, Oliver

N

Nankoff, Minko/ Nedeco, Petroff/ Nenkoff, Christo/ Nieminen, Manta/ *Nilson, Berta*/ *Nilson, Helmina*/ Nilsson, August F./ *Nyoven, Johan*/ Nyston, Anna

O

Olsen, Arthur/ Olsen, Carl/ Olsen, Henry/ Olsen, Ole M./ Olsen, Elon/ Olsson, John/ Ollson, Elida/ Oreskovic, Luka/ Orescovic, Maria/ Orescovic, Jeko/ *Orman, Velin*/ *Osman, Mara*

P

Pacruic, Mate/ Pacruic, Tome/ Panula, Eino/ Panula Ernesti/ Panula, Juho/ Panula, Maria/ Panulo, Sanni/ Panula, Urhu (child)/ Panula, William (infant)/ Pasic, Jakob/ Paulsson, Alma C./ Paulsson, Gosta (child)/ Paulsson, Paul (child)/ Paulsson, Stina (child)/ Paulsson, Torborg (child)/ Pavlovic, Stefo/ *Pekonemi, E./* Pelsmaker, Alfons de/ Peltomaki, Nikolai/ Pentcho, Petroff/ *Person, Ernest*/ Peterson, Johan/ Petersson, Ellen/ Petranec, Mathilda/ Petterson, Olaf/ Plotcharsky, Vasil

R

Radeff, Alexandre/ Rintamaki, Matti/ Rosblom, Helene/ Rosblom, Salli (child)/ Rosblom, Viktor/ Rummstvedt, Kristian

S

Saljilsvik, Anna/ Salonen, Werner/ *Sandman, Johan*/ *Sandstrom, Agnes*/ *Sandstrom, Beatrice* (child)/ *Sandstrom, Margreta* (child)/ Sdycoff, Todor/ *Sheerlinck, Jean*/ Sihvola, Antti/ Sivic, Husen/ *Sjoblom, Anna*/ Skoog, Anna/ Skoog, Carl (child)/ Skoog, Harald (child)/ Skoog, Mabel (child)/ Skoog, Margaret (child)/ Skoog, William/ Slabenolf, Petco/ Srniljanic, Mile/ Sohole, Peter/ Solvang, Lena Jacobsen/ Sop, Jules/ Staneff, Ivan/ Stoyehoff, Ilia/ Stoytcho, Mihoff/ Strandberg, Ida/ *Stranden, Jules*/ Strilic, Ivan/ Strom, Selma (child)/ Svensen, Olaf/ Svensson, Johan/ *Svensson, Coverin*/ Syntakoff, Stanko

T

Tikkanen, Juho/ Todoroff, Lalio/ *Tonglin, Gunner*/ Turcin, Stefan/ *Turgo, Anna*/ *Twekula, Hedwig*

U

Uzelas, Jovo

V

Van Impe, Catharine (child)/ Van Impe, Jacob/ Van Impe, Rosalie/ Van der Planke, Augusta Vander/ Van der Planke, Emilie Vander/ Van der Planke, Jules Vander/ Van der Planke, Leon Vander/ Van der Steen, Leo/ Van de Velde, Joseph/ Van de Walle, Nestor/ Vereruysse, Victor/ Vook, Janko

W

Waelens, Achille/ Wende, Olof Edvin/ *Wennerstrom, August*/ Wenzel, Zinhart/ Westrom, Huld A. A./ Widegrin, Charles/ Wiklund, Karl F./ Wiklund, Jacob A./ Wirz, Albert/ Wittenrongel, Camille

Z

Zievens, René/ Zimmermann, Leo

Embarked at Cherbourg

A

Assaf, Marian/ Attala, Malake

B

Baclini, Latifa/ Baclini, Maria/ Baclini, Eugene/ Baclini, Helene/ Badt, Mohamed/ *Banoura, Ayout*/ Barbara, Catherine/ Barbara, Saude/ Betros, Tannous/ Boulos, Hanna/ Boulos, Sultani/ *Boulos, Nourelain*/ Boulos, Akar (child)

C

Caram, Joseph/ Caram, Maria/ Chehab, Emir Farres/ Chronopoulos, Apostelos/ Chronopoulos, Demetrios

D

Dibo, Elias/ Drazenovie, Josip

E

Elias, Joseph/ *Elias, Joseph*

F

Fabini, Leeni/ Fat-ma, Mustmani

G

Gerios, Assaf/ Gerios, Youssef/ Gheorgheff, Stanio

H

Hanna, Mansour

J

Jean Nassr, Saade/ Johann, Markim/ *Joseph, Mary*

K

Karun, Franz/ Karun, Anna (child)/ Kassan, M. Housseing/ *Kassein, Hassef*/ Kassem, Fared/ Khalil, Betros/ Khalil, Zahie/ Kraeff, Theodoor

L
Lemberopoulos, Peter

M
Malinoff, Nicola/ *Meme, Hanna/* Monbarek, Hanna/ *Moncarek, Omine/ Moncarek, Gonios* (child)/ Moussa, Mantoura

N
Naked, Said/ Naked, Waika/ Naked, Maria/ Nasr, Mustafa/ *Nichan, Krokorian/ Nicola, Jamila/ Nicola, Elias* (child)/ Novel, Mansouer

O
Orsen, Sirayanian/ Ortin, Zakarian

P
Peter, Catherine Josep/ Peter, Mike/ Peter, Anna

R
Rafoul, Baccos/ Raibid, Razi

S
Saad, Amin/ *Saad, Khalil/* Samaan, Elias/ Samaan, Elias/ *Samaan, Hanna/* Samaan, Youssef/ Sarkis, Mardirosian/ Sarkis, Lahowd/ Seman, Betros (child)/ Shabini, Georges/ Shedid, Daher/ Sleirnan, Attalla/ Stankovic, Jovan

T
Tannous, Thornas/ Tannous, Daler/ Tannous, Elias/ Thornas, Charles/ *Thomas, Tamin/ Thomas, Assad* (infant)/ Thornas, John/ Tonflk, Nahli/ Torfa, Assad

U
Useher, Baulner

V
Vagil, Adele Jane/ Vartunian, David/ Vassilios, Catavelas

W
Wazli, Yousif/ Weller, Abi

Y
Yalsevae, Ivan/ Yasbeck, Antoni/ *Yasbeck, Celiney/ Youssef, Brahim/* Youssef, Hanne/ *Youssef, Maria* (child)/ Youssef, Georges (child)

Z
Zabour, Tamini/ Zabour, Hileni/ Zarkarian, Maprieder

Embarked at Queenstown

B

Barry, Julia/ Bourke, Catherine/ Bourke, John/ *Bradley, Bridget/*, *Buckley, Daniel/* Buckley, Katherine/ Burke, Jeremiah/ Burke, Mary/ Burns, Mary

C

Canavan, Mary/ Cannavan, Pat/ *Carr, Ellen/* Carr, Jeannie/ Chartens, David/ Colbert, Patrick/ Conlin, Thos. H./ Connaghton, Michael/ Connors, Pat/ *Conolly, Kate*

D

Daly, Marcella/ Daly, Eugene/ Devanoy, Margaret/ Dewan, Frank/ Dooley, Patrick/ Doyle, Elin/ *Driscol, Bridget*

E

Emmeth, Thomas

F

Farrell, James/ Flynn, James/ Flynn, John/ Foley, William/ Fox, Patrick

G

Gallagher, Martin/ *Gilnagh, Kathy/ Glynn, Mary*

H

Hagardon, Kate/ Hagarty, Nora/ Hart, Henry/ *Healy, Nora/* Hemming, Norah/ Henery, Delia/ Horgan, John

J

Jenymin, Annie

K

Kelly, James/ *Kelly, Annie K./ Kelly, Mary/ Kennedy, John/* Kerane, Andy/ Kilgannon, Thomas/ Kiernan, John/ Kiernan, Phillip

L

Lane, Patrick/ Lemon, Denis/ Lemon, Mary/ Linehan, Michel

M

Madigan, Maggie/ Mahon, Delia/ Mangan, Mary/ *Mannion, Margareth/ McCarthy, Katie/* McCormack, Thomas/ *McCoy, Agnes/ McCoy, Alice/ McCoy, Bernard/* McDermott, Delia/ McElroy, Michel/ *McGovern, Mary/* McGowan, Katherine/ *McGowan/* McMahon, Martin/ McMahon/ Mechan, John/ Moran, James/ *Moran, Bertha/* Morgan, Daniel J./ Morrow, Thomas/ *Mullens, Katie/ Mulvihill, Bertha/* Murphy, Kate/ Murphy, Norah/ Murphy, Mary

N

Naughton, Hannah/ Nemagh, Robert

O
O'Brien, Denis/ O'Brien, Thomas/ *O'Brien, Hannah*/ O'Connell, Pat. D./ O'Connor, Maurice/ O'Connor, Pat/ O'Donaghue, Bert/ *O'Dwyer, Nellie*/ *O'Keefe, Pat.*/ *O'Leary, Norah*/ O'Neill, Bridget/ O'Sullivan, Bridget

P
Peters, Katie

R
Rice, Margaret/ Rice, Albert (child)/ Rice, George (child)/ Rice, Eric (child)/ Rice, Arthur (child)/ Rice, Eugene (child)/ *Riordan, Hannah*/ Ryan, Patrick/ *Ryan, Edw.*

S
Sadlier, Matt/ Scanlan, James/ Shaughnesay, Pat/ *Shine, Ellen*/ *Smyth, Julian*

T
Tobin, Roger

Crew List of the SS Californian

I APRIL – 10 MAY 1912

(Age in brackets)

	NAME	BIRTHPLACE	RANK/RATING
I	Stanley Lord (35)	Bolton	Master[1]
2	G.F. Stewart (34)	Liverpool	Chief Mate[2]
3	H. Stone (24)	Devon	2nd Mate[3]
4	C.V. Groves (24)	Cambridgeshire	3rd Mate[4]
5	H. McGregor (41)	Liverpool	Carpenter
6	E Dick (32)	Liverpool	Bosun
7	G. Brennan (40)	Liverpool	Bosun's Mate
8	R. Jones (60)	Conway	Lamptrimmer, A.B.
9	L.V. Carswell (45)	Greenock	Qtrmaster & A.B.
10	John Dalziel (35)	Shetland	Qtrmaster & A.B.
11	J. Clapham (45)	London	Qtrmaster & A.B.
12	C. Le Comes (43)	Jersey	Qtrmaster & A.B.
13	W. Ross (26)	Everton	A.B.
14	G. Jacob (19)	Liverpool	A.B.
15	J. Ashton (21)	Waterloo, Liverpool	A.B.[5]
16	M. Ballantyne (49)	Glasgow	A.B.
17	W. Hayden (38)	London	A.B.
18	J. Lushey (56)	West Ham.	A.B.
19	B. Kirk (22)	Liverpool	A.B.
20	J. Onsworth (18)	London	A.B.
21	H. Lawes (17)	Plaistow	Deck Boy
22	W.S.A. Mahan (37)	Greenock	Chief Engineer[6]
23	J.C. Evans (31)	Bangor	2nd Engineer[7]
24	J. Fyfe (33)	Birkenhead	3rd Engineer
25	F.R. Hooton (23)	Liverpool	4th Engineer
26	T. Sintich (57)	Austria	Donkeyman
27	A. Hoffman (32)	Germany	Ass.Donkeyman[8]
28	Ernest Gill (26)	Sheffield	Fireman[9]
29	J. Zorusten (23)	Germany	Fireman[10]
30	G. Glenn (23)	Liverpool	Fireman
31	W.H. Parry (30)	Greenwich	Fireman
32	W. Thomas (46)	Jersey	Fireman[11]

33	T. Button (31)	London	Fireman
34	W. Kennerdale (43)	Liverpool	Fireman[12]
35	D. Donovan (42)	London	Fireman
36	W. Brennan (52)	Woolwich	Fireman[13]
37	H. Gerworski (42)	Germany	Fireman[14]
38	T. White (20)	London	Trimmer[15]
39	B. Young (20)	Liverpool	Fireman
40	G. Melville (20)	London	Trimmer
41	C. Jessop (29)	London	Trimmer[16]
42	W. Hughes (35)	Liverpool	Chief Steward
43	Sidney Beal (29)	Brighton	2nd Steward[17]
44	J.J. Bostman (26)	Amsterdam	3rd Steward
45	C. Wilson (32)	London	Mess Rm Strd[18]
46	P.W. Janssen (42)	Holland	Ship's Cook
47	Hy.J. Burlingham (41)	Worcester	2nd Cook/Baker
48	C.F. Evans (20)	Croydon	Telegraphist

Substitutes

49	W. Ward (38)	London	Fireman
50	A. Homans (20)	London	Trimmer
51	W. Willis (20)	Poplar E.	Trimmer
52	W. Burke (43)	Liverpool	Fireman[19]
53	A. Roberts (26)	Swansea	Fireman[20]

References

1 Captain Stanley Lord. Held extra Master's Certificate. Number, 030740
2 G.F. Stewart. Held extra Master's Certificate. Number, 033667
3 H. Stone. Held First Mate's Certificate. Number, 003708
4 C.V. Groves. Held First Mate's Certificate. Number, 006474
5 J. Ashton. Member, Royal Naval Reserve
6 W.S.A. Mahan. Held Chief Engineer's Certificate. Number, 32690
7 J.C. Evans. Held Chief Engineer's Certificate. Number, 43979
8 A. Hoffman. Failed to join ship's crew
9 E. Gill. Deserted at Boston, Massachusetts, April 20th
10 J. Zorusten. Promoted to Storekeeper April 5th, 1912
11 W. Thomas. Promoted to Greaser April 5th, 1912
12 W. Kennerdale. Died on voyage to Boston
13 W. Brennan. Failed to join ship's crew
14 H. Gerworski. Promoted to Assist. Donkeyman April 25th, 1912
15 T. White. Failed to join ship's crew
16 C. Jessop. Promoted to Fireman April 25th, 1912
17 S. Beal. Previous ship: Mount Temple
18 C. Wilson. Failed to join ship's crew
19 W. Burke. Signed on at Boston, April 26th, 1912
20 A. Roberts. Signed on at Boston, April 27th, 1912

O.S. = Ordinary Seaman
A.B. = Able Seaman

Bibliography

BOOKS

Beesley, Lawrence, *The Loss of the SS Titanic* (William Heinemann, 1912. New edition, Star Books, 1979)

Booth, John and Coughlan, Sean, *Titanic – Signals of Disaster* (White Star Publications, 1993)

Bristow, Diana, *Titanic – Sinking the Myths* (Katco, 1995)

Brock, A.H. *A History of Fireworks* (Harrap, 1949)

Gentile, Gary, *The Lusitania Controversies. Book One: Atrocity of War and a Wreck-Diving History* (Gary Gentile Productions, 1998)

Harding O'Hara, Monica, *Hands off the Titanic (and the Californian)* (Countyvise Limited, 1989)

Harrison, Leslie, *A Titanic Myth – The Californian Incident* (William Kimber, 1986 and 2nd edition 1992 The Self-Publishing Association)

Harrison, Leslie, *Defending Captain Lord – A Titanic Myth*, Part 2 (Images Publishing, 1996)

Lightoller, Commander C.H., *Titanic and Other Ships* (Ivor, Nicholson and Watson, 1935)

Lord, Walter, *A Night to Remember* (Longmans Green, 1956)

Molony, Senan, *Titanic and the Mystery Ship* (Tempus Publishing, 2006)

Myers, L.T., *Sinking of the Titanic and Great Sea Disasters* (Logan Marshall, 1912)

O'Sullivan, Patrick, *The Lusitania – Unravelling the Mysteries* (The Collins Press, 1998)

Padfield, Peter, *The Titanic and the Californian* (Hodder and Stoughton, 1965)

Ruffman, Dr Alan, *Further Considerations on Californian Speculations* (an unpublished document, 1997-98)

NEWSPAPERS AND PERIODICALS

The Times; Daily Telegraph; Daily Mail; Daily Mirror; Liverpool Echo; Daily Express; Nautical Magazine; Cork Examiner; Evening Echo, Southampton; Sunday World; MMSA Reporter; The Commutator; Voyage; Titanic Melding; The White Star Journal.

OFFICIAL DOCUMENTS

MAIB Reappraisal of Evidence relating to the SS Californian (1992).

Proceedings on a Formal Investigation into the Loss of the SS Titanic.

Report of a Formal Investigation into the Foundering of the British Steamship Titanic (HM Stationary Office, 1912).

Maritime Records Office, National Museums and Galleries on Merseyside.

Titanic Disaster: Hearing before a Subcommittee on Commerce, United States Senate (Document No.726).

Mercantile Marine Service Association data (general).

Specifications of the Steel Screw Steamer Californian (Messrs F. Leyland (Files) & Co. Ltd, Liverpool.

Titanic and Olympic Technical Data File (Harland & Wolff, Belfast).

The editor also relied on detailed private information supplied by Leslie Harrison.

Index

If you are interested in purchasing other books published by Tempus,
or in case you have difficulty finding any Tempus books in your local bookshop,
you can also place orders directly through our website

www.tempus-publishing.com